SHATTERED

By Kathryn Casey

Non Fiction
SHATTERED
EVIL BESIDE HER
A DESCENT INTO HELL
DIE, MY LOVE
SHE WANTED IT ALL
A WARRANT TO KILL

Fiction
SINGULARITY
BLOOD LINES

**THE TRUE STORY OF A MOTHER'S LOVE,
A HUSBAND'S BETRAYAL,
AND A COLD-BLOODED TEXAS MURDER**

SHATTERED

KATHRYN CASEY

HARPER

An Imprint of HarperCollins*Publishers*

Shattered is a journalistic account of the actual murder investigation of David Temple for the 1999 murder of Belinda Temple in Katy, Texas. The events recounted in this book are true, although some names have been changed and identifying characteristics altered to safeguard the privacy of these individuals. The personalities, events, actions, and conversations portrayed in this book have been constructed using court documents, including trial transcripts, extensive interviews, letters, personal papers, research, and press accounts. Quoted testimony has been taken verbatim from trial and pre-trial transcripts and other sworn statements.

HARPER

An Imprint of HarperCollins*Publishers*
10 East 53rd Street
New York, New York 10022-5299

First Harper paperback printing: July 2010

HarperCollins ® and Harper ® are registered trademarks of Harper-Collins Publishers.

Printed in the United States of America

For my husband, with love

These things are an abomination unto God: A proud look, a lying tongue, and hands that shed innocent blood.

Proverbs 6:16-17

1

I t couldn't be true. At any moment the nightmare would end, and Belinda Lucas Temple would be alive.

As on any other day, Belinda's parents would answer their telephone and hear her say, "Mops and Pops, it's Number Five." Or Belinda and her twin sister, Brenda, would gab, just happy to hear each other's voice. They bantered regularly about their jobs and their lives. But mostly Brenda was content to listen as Belinda rattled happily on about her children. Evan was three, a burly, shy little boy, and the center of his mother's life. Although she wasn't scheduled to enter the world for another month, baby Erin, too, had already claimed a Texas-size chunk of her mother's heart. A pretty, energetic woman with lush golden-brown hair, Belinda often ran her hands over her round belly, undoubtedly anticipating the joy of the first time she'd hold her infant daughter in her arms. Was there anything more breathtaking than the softness and smell of a newborn? Any sound more heart melting than a cooing infant?

At the very mention of her children, Belinda's face, her entire demeanor, visibly glowed with the deepest of loves.

Monday, January 11, 1999, however, wouldn't be just another day in Creekstone, a quiet Houston suburb, and

Belinda's family and friends would never recover from the heartbreak of that warm winter day that started like any other only to end in unfathomable tragedy.

Late that afternoon, Belinda's high-wattage smile vanished, forever. No one would ever again hear the soft lilt of her East Texas accent or see the sparkle in her expressive green eyes. The nursery on the second floor of the Temples' house, the one Belinda painted a color she dubbed "Big Bird" yellow, would never be used. The crib with its blue-and-white-plaid linens would remain empty, and baby Erin would never draw a first breath.

Murdered? Executed. But what kind of monster would kill an expectant mother and her unborn child?

Yet, it was true. And the reality was horrifying beyond description.

At sunset the usually sedate, middle-class neighborhood roiled with tension, as patrol cars lined the streets and officers strung crime-scene tape across the front yard of 22502 Round Valley Drive, Belinda and David Temple's meticulously kept redbrick two-story home. TV news stations rushed reporters and cameramen to the scene, as helicopters hovered overhead in the early evening winter darkness.

No one could have imagined the misery that waited inside that house.

So full of energy and kindness that her fellow high-school teachers called her the "Sunshine Girl," Belinda's cold, motionless, heavily pregnant body lay sprawled on a carpeted closet floor. A contact wound from a shotgun at the back of her head had shattered her skull, and what remained of her face was frozen in a grotesque death mask that recalled Edvard Munch's disturbing expressionist masterpiece, *The Scream.*

Like that of the strange, distorted figure in the painting, Belinda Temple appeared destined to forever silently cry out in utter agony.

Outside on the street, Belinda's husband stood next to a squad car, surrounded by his parents. His mother wept. His father appeared shaken and crestfallen. But David, a thick-necked, massive man who'd been a high-school and college football star, stood stoic, not shedding a tear. His wife and baby daughter had been brutally murdered, but to many on the scene, the young father didn't even look upset.

Perhaps it wasn't surprising that before long, the investigators eyed David Temple with suspicion. Still, could a husband and father do something so vile?

On his frantic call to 911, David said he'd returned from an outing with Evan and found the back door open and his wife's bloody, lifeless body. Shards of glass from the door's window littered the den floor, and drawers gaped ajar in the dining room. The crime scene unit photographed a television off its stand and lying on its side. Could the detectives' instincts be misleading them about David Temple? A popular high-school football coach, the man was a local legend, a small-town hero. How could he be a suspect? Wasn't it more likely that a would-be thief discovered he wasn't alone in the house and panicked?

That awful night on Round Valley Drive dissolved, leaving behind a long list of unanswered questions. Then the first week after the murders faded into memory, trailed by the first month, and the first year. One after another the years that followed extinguished without an arrest, while Belinda's and baby Erin's bodies lay in a sealed coffin, buried six feet under a rose granite headstone that read: *We feel the touch of angel wings.*

Yet, although time passed, they were never forgotten.

Detectives grew to expect to hear Belinda's dad, Tom Lucas, on the telephone, prodding for news. "What's happening?" he asked, his gruff voice thick with the unimaginable pain of a parent of a murdered child. "What can you tell me about what you're doing to solve this case?"

They didn't fault Lucas for calling, but the detectives could offer little reassurance. The Temple murder case was stalled, and some feared it would remain that way. If pressed, those who'd worked the scene would have admitted the distinct possibility that those who loved Belinda might go to their own graves without closure.

Meanwhile, in his cubicle in a run-down county building on Houston's east side, one detective in particular, an avuncular man with a brown flattop named Mark Schmidt, couldn't let go of the Temple case. It haunted his waking hours and invaded his thoughts each night as he closed his eyes hoping for sleep. Over and over again, Schmidt relived the night Belinda and Erin died, wondering what should have been done, what could have been done to solve the murders. Every time he read about a new forensic breakthrough, Schmidt resubmitted the Temple evidence. But no matter what he tried, the murder books on the case, the loose-leaf binders that held everything from the shocking autopsy photos to witness statements, sat on his desk collecting dust.

As the world went on about its business, Belinda Temple and her baby waited for justice. Would it ever come?

2

Parents loom large in their children's lives. They take on mythical proportions, even as their offspring age. A father's hands may always be remembered as strong, even after they've withered from arthritis. A mother's words have the power to endure even after death, in the memories of her children. Their laughs and their smiles may haunt as much as warm their children into middle age and beyond. If in the end Tom and Carol Lucas devoted themselves to the memories of Belinda and their unborn granddaughter, theirs wasn't a family of Norman Rockwell images and Currier and Ives Christmases.

"I don't know why we're not closer," Carol would say. "The kids just don't come around."

"Our door is always open," Tom pondered glumly. "But we don't see them much."

Although it was where their story would take them, the family's beginnings weren't in Texas. Thomas Eaton Lucas was born in Dunbar, West Virginia, and his hoarse, crusty voice, even in the waning years of middle age, would still betray those influences. He met Carol Maxine Morrison, a plainspoken Midwesterner, in her hometown of Port Huron, Michigan, when Tom was an assistant manager at a dime store, two doors from the dress shop where she worked as the credit manager. "There were lots of ten-cent stores in those days," Tom remembers. "We had a counter, where folks came in for lunch."

Carol's boss, the dress store manager, introduced them, and before long Tom noticed Carol lingering outside the store. "Sometimes she'd watch me decorate the windows," says Tom, a big, tall, dark-haired man with heavy jowls and a booming voice. "I guess it was about a year after we met that we started dating."

"I liked to look at him," admits Carol, a soft-spoken, round woman with deep-set eyes and thick, curly blond hair. "Sometimes I'd smile, and he'd smile back at me."

At the time, Tom's parents lived in Cambridge, Ohio. When Tom moved to be closer to them, he convinced Carol to follow. They married on July 22, 1962, and traveled through Ohio, settling in Martins Ferry, where Tom worked in a steel mill. The children arrived in a pack, first Brian, followed by Barry, and then Brent. Carol was pregnant a fourth time in five years when they learned some startling news about their second son, Barry. The four-year-old followed a ball into the street and never heard the school bus screech to a stop. It almost hit him. "Barry hadn't talked much, but we didn't think much of it. Brian talked for him," Carol says. "We'd asked the doctor, but he said not to worry. When we had Barry tested, we found out he was deaf."

Not much later, on December 30, 1968, a cold winter day, Carol went into labor. Tom loaded her into the family's Volkswagen and bumped along the country roads to get to the hospital. "We were expecting another big old baby boy," Tom says with a shrug. "After three sons, we'd given up on the idea of a daughter."

They rushed into the emergency room, and Carol was ushered in quickly while Tom filled out the paperwork. Ten minutes later, before Carol had time to get out of her dress and into a hospital gown, their first baby girl was born, at eight pounds and one ounce. Through all three boys, Carol had the name Brenda picked out, just in case they had a daughter. Now she held Brenda Therese Lucas in her arms. Carol didn't pay a lot of attention to the fact that the doctor continued to push on her abdomen and that the nurses hadn't left the room.

In the days before routine ultrasounds, Carol didn't know another surprise was in the offing. She'd never been told she carried twins. But eight minutes later, a second perfect, pink daughter entered the world, a bit smaller than her older sister, at six pounds, one ounce. Both infants were healthy.

"Here's your number two," the doctor said, holding up the baby.

"I was shocked," Carol said. "Absolutely shocked."

When the doctor came out to talk to the nervous father, he asked Tom, "What was it you wanted?"

"Well, Carol wanted a girl, but if it's a boy, it's okay with me," he answered.

"Well, your wife got her wish," the doctor said, and before Tom could get excited, the physician added, "And she got two of them!"

"I got weak in the knees and thought I was going down," Tom says, with a laugh. "I threw my wide-brimmed hat in the air and I whooped and hollered."

Carol had named the other four children, and when she held her final child in her arms, the proud mother came up with yet another "B" name, this one Belinda Tracie Lucas.

From the moment his parents brought his twin sisters home, Brian, who was five at the time, would remember being enthralled with them. He held them, especially Belinda, the smallest, helping to soothe the girls when they cried. He couldn't say *Belinda* and struggled with *Tracie*, ending up calling the youngest sibling *Katie-do-do*. When she got older, Belinda would reference her position as the last born in the Lucas family lineup, and nickname herself Number Five.

With so many youngsters to care for, Carol became a stay-at-home mom. "She could have worked, but we put the emphasis on taking care of the kids," Tom says. "That meant we didn't have as much money as some families, but when our kids got home from school, their momma was always there."

Delighted to finally have the daughters she'd longed for, Carol sewed matching dresses for her little girls. But the twins were fraternal, not identical, and before long the differences became apparent. The smaller at birth, Belinda, with her curly light brown hair, a wide smile, mischievous green eyes, and athletic build, quickly grew into the larger of the two. Meanwhile Brenda became a slightly built child, with straight dark brown hair. When it came to personalities, Brenda hung back, while Belinda overflowed with energy, often running ahead to open the door. Belinda wanted to be the first in every line. "No matter what was going on, Belinda was in the middle," Brian says with a laugh. "She was a good kid, and she had spunk."

Neither were girly girls—more of the tomboy variety who'd rather spend days climbing trees with their brothers than playing with dolls. Of the sisters, Belinda was the first to ride a bike. Once she learned, she taught Brenda. And before long Belinda began calling her older sister—albeit by eight minutes—"Shrimpie," a nickname that has stayed with Brenda for life and always makes her smile. "Belinda taught Brenda how to tie her shoes," remembers Carol. "Belinda was always kind of motherly, and if something needed to be taken care of, she was the one who'd do it."

From those early years, Belinda was also protective. Of the Lucas children, it was Belinda who learned sign language, to communicate with Barry. While he read lips, he'd remember years later what that meant to him. If kids at school talked behind Barry's back, making fun of his deafness, Belinda took them to task, even if the offenders were bigger than she. "Usually, Belinda would scare them off. I always went to her when I had a problem," says Barry. "I always wanted Belinda's opinion."

It was the same when anyone gave Brenda a hard time;

Belinda immediately stepped in to defend her more diminutive sister. And when they were at softball games, it was Belinda who took Brenda by the hand to the concession stand and gave the clerk her order. "Belinda never let anyone pick on me," says Brenda. "She was always there for me. Always."

Christmas was Belinda's favorite holiday. That morning, she was habitually the first shaking the packages under the tree. Since the family opened gifts starting with the youngest, she was also the first to tear off the green and red wrapping paper to see what waited inside.

Those were good years, and looking back, Brian would say that "we were a regular family, your normal middle-class kind of family. And we had fun together."

Sadly, before long, Brian would say that changed.

In the mid-seventies, Tom had an accident at the mill and an injury that led to a year's rehabilitation. He and Carol thought about leaving Martins Ferry. The steel industry was hurting in response to imports, and many people were moving away. "I wanted a place where they'd have more opportunity," he says. "Carol and I wanted to make things easier for the kids to get ahead."

That year the family moved to Nacogdoches, the oldest town in Texas, a graceful place where the dogwoods and azaleas bloom in the early spring. Once the area was the hunting grounds of the Caddo Indians, and a local legend depicts a Caddo chief with twin sons. When they reached manhood, the wise old man sent his sons off to begin their own tribes. One went three days west, toward the setting sun, and founded Nacogdoches. The other traveled three days east, toward the rising sun, and founded its sister city, Natchitoches, the oldest settlement in Louisiana. The trade route connecting the two marked the eastern end of El Camino Real, also called the Old San Antonio Road.

On an undulating green landscape, Nacogdoches is a place where after a rain the air fills with the rich scent of the thick East Texas pine forests. People are friendly, brisket is slow-cooked over wood, and natives talk with a soft Texas drawl. For the Lucases, the city's lure was family. Tom had a brother in the area and a sister three hours south in Houston. Later, Tom's parents followed and settled nearby as well. In their new hometown, Tom opened a cultured marble business, selling sinks and countertops from a building on the outskirts of the city.

Later, Brian would say that the problems in the Lucas household kicked in about the time of the move to Texas. "When he got injured, our dad changed," says Brian. "From that point on, it seemed like he was more demanding and we kids felt like Mom was always under his thumb."

There was little doubt that Tom Lucas was a formidable figure, simply based on his physical size, booming voice, and his imposing manner. Belinda, too, would later tell friends that she saw her father as overwhelming and, at times, suffocating. She talked about the way he ruled the household.

Carol, however, would describe Tom as a good husband. And there's little doubt that he was an involved dad. Tom and Carol believed in keeping their kids busy. For the girls that meant that by the time they hit junior high school, Belinda and Brenda were both active in Future Farmers of America and sports, baseball and basketball.

Of the two, Brenda was devoted to her animals. She raised chickens in the backyard of the family's one-story home on a quiet street in town and worked with steers the Lucas kids kept outside Tom's shop in the country. For Belinda, caring for the animals wasn't fun but work. Still, she was conscientious, starting out every morning in the backyard chicken coop while still in her pajamas. At the Piney Woods Fair one year, Belinda's broiler won grand champion, earning her $2,100, which she put away for college. The more outgoing of the sisters, Belinda showed Brenda's steers. One year, while Brenda's steer didn't win, Belinda did, taking home the fair's showmanship award.

Sports were to Belinda what FFA was to Brenda. While both girls played baseball and basketball, Belinda excelled.

"Basketball was Belinda's thing," says Brenda. In junior high school Belinda was a cheerleader until her teacher told her she couldn't do that and play on the team as well. At that point, Tom would later say, "Belinda decided to let the others cheer for her, and she stayed on the basketball team."

Looking back, Belinda wasn't a natural athlete. She wasn't one who automatically jumped the highest or ran the fastest. For her, being able to perform took hard work. Summers were spent lifting weights, running and getting in shape for basketball season. "She was determined," Tom says. "On the court, she didn't hog the ball. She wanted to win, and she was part of the team. At times, if she couldn't find girls to play with, she shot hoops with the boys."

Because of her natural zeal, even after she left cheerleading, Belinda led the cheers at pep rallies. On the gym floor, she urged her fellow students to support the school's teams and attend the games. Her fervor was contagious and, in the stands, Brenda shouted support for her twin sister. "Belinda was super-charged," says a friend. "You couldn't help but join in."

"Everyone knew Belinda," says another friend. "She was so in love with life, she just radiated happiness."

At games, her chin-length dark blond hair flying, Belinda ran across the basketball court, as her parents and Brenda cheered. After practices, never one to fuss with her looks, while her mom drove, Belinda peeled off her basketball clothes and threw on her uniform to go to work at Burger King. At home, when she turned on the television, she more often than not put on a football or basketball game and sat at rapt attention, eyes focused on the game, diagnosing plays, until it was over.

At the same time, although she never lost that tomboyish bent, Belinda developed into a beautiful young woman. Nacogdoches is a college town, and Lynn Graves, the head football coach at Stephen F. Austin, the local university, lived just down the block from the Lucases. Belinda and

Graves's daughter were good friends, and the coach would remember watching Belinda mature. "She was the type of young lady who'd be shooting hoops with the boys one minute and walking down the street in high heels the next," he says. "She was smart and funny, and she pretty much had everything going for her."

Through high school, Belinda dated off and on. During one crush, she wrote "I Love" and the boy's name all over the inside of her locker in permanent marker. By then, the eldest Lucas boy, Brian, was dating his future wife, Jill, a bright, friendly woman with short blond hair and large brown eyes. From the beginning, Jill was impressed by Belinda's appetite for life, so startling compared to the usually reserved Lucas clan that Jill once asked Belinda, "Where did you come from?" Jill drove a Corvette, and at times, Belinda took over the driver's seat, laughing as she floored it. After getting to know the two sisters, it never struck Jill as odd when she walked into the backyard and found Brenda wearing jeans and a T-shirt, while Belinda worked on her tan in a bikini.

As high school came to an end, Belinda talked about going into nursing, but before graduation, she changed her mind. "It was just natural that she'd want to be a teacher. I think she always knew she'd do something involving kids," says Angie Luna, a girlhood friend. Luna had young twin sisters, and Belinda happily spent hours talking and playing with the girls. When Belinda babysat for her basketball coach, and he talked to her about what it was like to work with young athletes, Belinda's plans took on more detail. "I don't remember when, but at some point Belinda announced that she wanted to be a teacher and a coach," says Luna. "And, with Barry in her family, I wasn't surprised she'd decide to work with special-needs kids, the ones who needed the help the most."

Nacogdoches High School's class of 1987, the one that included Brenda and Belinda Lucas, had 345 members, and chose as their school song the ballad "Lean on Me." That year, Belinda Lucas was voted Most School Spirit, and the girls' basketball team she played on went all-district.

When she talked to a friend about what she eventually wanted, there was no doubt what Belinda saw as most important. While she groused about her father, describing him as domineering, she loved her parents and her brothers and sister. Family was paramount to Belinda, and she wanted one of her own. "For Belinda not having a family was not in the cards," says Luna. "She wanted the right guy and a team of little athletes to raise."

The day of their high-school graduation, Belinda, Brenda and a friend spent time talking about the future—all that lay ahead—while riding around Nacogdoches with all the windows down in a brown Chevy pickup belonging to the third Lucas brother, Brent. We "bebopped to the music with the radio turned up all the way," says the friend.

The next year, Brenda followed her interests to Stephen F. Austin University, working toward a major in animal science with a minor in biology. On a Houston Livestock Show and Rodeo scholarship, she moved into a room on the university farm, a 400-acre spread outside Nacogdoches. Meanwhile, Belinda stayed at home, living with Tom and Carol, while she picked up credits at Angelina College, a small junior college in nearby Lufkin. Before long, however, Belinda and Tom clashed. "Our dad was always laying down the law, things like early curfews. Belinda was tired of being under his supervision," says Brian. "Belinda wasn't a bad kid. She wasn't going to get in any trouble. She just wanted a little freedom, to enjoy her college years."

The sticking point seemed to Jill to have been Tom's mandates. "He'd say, 'If you're going to live under my roof,' then tell her what she had to do," says Jill. "Belinda wasn't going to do anything crazy. She just wanted to be a normal college student."

That fall, Belinda paid for school by working at a Brookshire Brothers grocery store. In a weight-lifting class, she met Staci Rios. From the beginning they hit it off. "Belinda was easy to be with and fun," says Staci in her thick East Texas drawl. "Belinda told jokes all the time and loved to go out dancing. She was just really full of life, someone people just naturally wanted to get to know."

Before long, Staci was working at the grocery store with Belinda, who'd picked up a second job as an aerobics instructor at Ultrafit, a small women's gym. With a third friend, Belinda and Staci moved into a modest two-bedroom apartment. At the time, Belinda dated a guy she'd gone to high school with and they talked of marriage. But then, something happened. After they became engaged, she found out that her fiancé had been unfaithful. Hurt, Belinda didn't hesitate to end the relationship. "Belinda didn't want him anymore," says Brenda. "He wanted her back, but she wasn't interested. Once he was unfaithful, she was done with him."

As her family and friends would remember her, Belinda wasn't the kind of girl to hold on to a dying relationship. Once the trust was broken, she didn't need any prodding to pick up her life and move on.

The following year, Belinda left junior college and enrolled at Stephen F. Austin, to work on her teaching degree. She continued to share the two-bedroom apartment with Rios, their roommate, and a yellow cat named Tigger. Belinda didn't have a lot of extra time. In addition to classes and studying, by then she was working three jobs, still at the grocery store, at Ultrafit teaching aerobics, and at the SFA farm, where Brenda lived, helping with the stock. That Halloween, Belinda dressed up in a black-and-white Holstein cow costume and wore it to work at the grocery store, udder and all.

Years later, Staci laughed recalling the fun they had together, sharing the apartment, living on macaroni and cheese and beanie weenies. No matter what happened, it seemed that Belinda always saw the good side of the situation, and rarely got angry. She had a small blue Toyota Cressida she drove with the gas gauge habitually hovering near empty.

Belinda loved flea markets, and one Sunday when she and Staci were driving to one outside the city, the Toyota ran out of gas. Furious, Staci wondered how her friend could be so careless, but Belinda smiled as they walked down the highway with the gas can. "What a pretty day," she said. "I'm glad we're outside and we're not missing this!"

Sometimes, they stayed up late in the apartment, talking. As she had with Angie Luna, Belinda left no doubt in Staci's mind where she wanted her life to take her. Belinda's dreams were solid, the kind lives are built on. She wasn't dreaming of becoming a celebrity or living in a mansion. Instead, she wanted to teach, to help special-needs kids, and to have a husband and children to love.

Yet there were years ahead to get serious, and Belinda enjoyed being in college, having the freedom of being single and young. After they finished for the night at Brookshire Brothers, she and Staci drove to one of the local clubs where the college kids congregated. "We talked and danced and just had a great time," says Rios. "We laughed and had fun."

Some nights, after the clubs closed, they drove to Ultrafit, where Belinda, still not tired, worked out her aerobics routines for the coming week, setting exercise moves to music. As Belinda demonstrated the moves, Rios was in charge of writing down the exercises. The problems popped up the next day. "I'd have them all messed up," Rios would say with a laugh. "Belinda would get so mad. She'd done a turn and a kick, and I'd written down a kick and a turn."

The long days and nights working out, both at Ultrafit and her daily workouts at SFA, where she was a physical education and special education major, had toned her body perfectly. At nineteen, Belinda was beautiful. She'd curled her long, golden-brown hair, her skin had a rich, suntanned sheen, and her green eyes sparkled. When she walked into a room, Rios says, "No one missed her. She truly stood out in a crowd."

Still, there was something else special about Belinda

that many would later say drew them to her. "She had so much love and happiness inside," says Rios. "You couldn't be around Belinda and not feel good. If you weren't happy when you met up with her, pretty soon, you'd be grinning, ear-to-ear."

It was at Stephen F. Austin that Belinda Tracie Lucas would meet David Mark Temple. In hindsight, it would have been remarkable if Belinda attended SFA during those years and wasn't at least aware of him. Posters displaying his picture in his Lumberjack football uniform hung in stores, restaurants and businesses throughout Nacogdoches, promoting the SFA team. In this East Texas town, where, like much of the Lone Star State, football rules, David Temple was a star.

"I guess you'd say that back then David was kind of a hero in town. Everybody knew who he was," says Tom sadly. "I have to admit that I was impressed with him, at least at first. He seemed like a fine young man."

3

Railroad tracks run through the center of Katy, Texas, the town half an hour west of Houston, where David Temple grew up. Off and on through the day, traffic bunched at intersections, gates came down, and the quiet was pierced by a locomotive's shrill horn. The majority of the town's nearly 12,000 residents were middle income and white, and for more than a century, the fields surrounding Katy had been regularly flooded by rice farmers, who shipped their crops via those same railroad tracks. The terrain in this part of Texas is coastal prairie, and many of the street names in Katy are as monotonous as the landscape, numbers and letters: Avenues A, B, C and D, First, Second, Third, Fourth, and Fifth Streets. But Katy was a good place to live. The locals were friendly and hardworking, and there was a palpable sense of pride in family, faith and football.

"Football is king in Katy, Texas," says one local resident. "In the fall, folks live by the record of the high-school football team."

Where Katy got its name was something of a controversy. Some say it came from the Missouri-Kansas-Texas (M*KT*) railroad, others that the city was named after Katy Mares, a popular pre-Prohibition saloonkeeper. Along with rice, other crops have been harvested in the area, including cotton and citrus. And in 1934, Humble Oil drilled west of town and struck black gold, to help supply Allied forces during WWII.

At the rice industry's height, there were more than 300 rice farmers in the Katy area, with fields stretching out as far as the eye could see. By the late nineties, there would be less than twenty, as the developers gobbled up the rice fields and built subdivisions. Yet the city never shed its image. The rice silos remained in downtown, and after the fall harvest, the city celebrated the Rice Festival, with music, cook-offs and craft shows, symbolized by Riceman, a caricature of a rice kernel riding a tractor and holding an American flag.

Follow Interstate 10 east thirty miles from Katy and the road slices into the heart of Houston, Texas's largest city, and its glittery skyscrapers. Many of those who have moved to the Katy area commute to work in Houston's high-rise offices. Yet, the link between the two cities, at least in the minds of those who live in Katy, is tenuous. "Houston is Houston, and Katy is Katy," says one longtime resident. "Folks need to keep that straight, because there's not much except I-10 that really connects us."

Over the decades, expansive subdivisions have sprung up, fanning out from I-10 toward Houston, and many of the residents commute to the big city to work. While considered part of the Katy area, the new developments are thought of by those who grew up in Katy as suburbs of Houston, not really part and parcel of their town. Katy proper, or Old Katy, is strictly the 15.5 square miles north of the freeway that make up the incorporated city. For natives, driving that half hour into Houston for even an afternoon is akin to taking a trip.

Such folks, those from families who've settled for generations in Katy, view the new high schools the district built to educate the children of the recently arrived suburbanites as pretenders. For them, *the* local football team that counts is the original one, the team that plays for Katy High, with its mascot, the Bengal Tiger.

It's not just the high school that backs the team, but also the entire town. During the season, signs in the windows of local businesses urge, *Go Tigers!* On Friday game days, businesses close early and there's an air of excitement as cars arrive at Jack Rhodes Memorial Stadium, capable of seating 9,600 fans, more than three quarters of Katy's residents. During a winning season, open seats are scarce on the home team's side, and tickets are at a premium.

"This is *Friday Night Lights* taken to the nth degree," says a former player. "This is small-town Texas football at its best."

David Temple's mother, the former Maureen Evans, was part and parcel of this world. "Her family is interwoven in the fabric of Katy," says a longtime resident.

Maureen Temple's family lineage extended back generations in Katy, to her maternal grandfather, who settled in the area in the late 1800s, and her Uncle Albert, who spent his life farming rice north of the town. Although Maureen, a woman with an erect bearing, was born in Houston, the daughter of a police officer, her roots ran deep in Katy, and when her parents retired, they bought land, carved from Uncle Albert's rice fields, to build a home. In 1961, Maureen married Ken Temple, who was born in Kentwood, Louisiana. His family had moved to Houston when he was ten, and Ken or "Kenny Temple," as Maureen called him, worked in computers, for companies like British Petroleum. He was also an ordained Baptist minister. They lived in Houston, and Ken and Maureen, who did office work, had three sons, born three years apart: Darren in 1965, David Mark Temple born on July 19, 1968, and Kevin in 1971.

Four years after David's birth, Maureen and Ken purchased land down the road from her parents. Before long, her brother, Bill, and sister, Nancy, and their families did the same, and by the seventies the entire extended family lived on lots cut out of Uncle Albert's rice fields along Katy-Hockley Road. Some who met them saw Ken and Maureen as rather aloof, conservative, "old timey," says one neighbor.

But others who knew the family described them as salt of the earth, and more than one would liken Maureen to Aunt Bee from television's sixties classic *The Andy Griffith Show*. "She was the kind of woman who had a slice of pie to go with the cup of coffee she offered," says a friend. "A good Christian woman."

Of the two, friends describe Maureen, a heavyset woman with dark arched eyebrows and a cap of short hair, as the more gregarious, and Ken Temple as a tall, thin, quiet man who enjoyed throwing a ball around with his brood of boys. They weren't wealthy people, but the Temples were well known, not just in the community but also at the First Baptist Church of Katy. "They were the kind of family that kept up appearances," says a friend. "They weren't the kind to air their dirty laundry."

On Sundays the entire extended family congregated at one house or another. On such days, Maureen often set up lunch starting after church, about three most afternoons. She called it "coming for coffee," and her parents, her brother, her sister and their spouses and children would join them. Over the years, as the children had children, the crowd grew, and the Temples' home buzzed with the conversation of a close-knit family.

"Family was it," says Cindi Thompson, a distant cousin. "The gatherings were large, boisterous, fun."

A single-story unpretentious house set back off the road, Maureen and Kenny's home sat on an acre-and-a-half that backed up to the rice fields. It was a tranquil place to live, one surrounded by nature. Since much of Katy is on a central flyway, a main migratory route for waterfowl, throughout the year flocks of birds flew overhead. Not surprisingly, Katy was known for its bird hunting. Ken Temple wasn't a hunter, and it was Maureen's father, the Houston policeman, who taught her three boys to shoot.

"The Temple brothers went dove hunting all the time, most of the kids in the area did," says Mike Fleener, a close friend of David's, who'd estimate that 75 percent of boys who grew up in Katy had a shotgun. "It was a blast out behind the Temples' house, hunting in the rice fields."

"Shotguns and bird hunting were synonymous with growing up male in Katy, Texas," says another of David's friends. "Every boy got a shotgun for a birthday or Christmas, and everyone learned how to shoot them."

In September, snows, blues, and Canada geese flew overhead. November to March, it was pheasant, and in mid-December, the prey became long-necked sandhill cranes. Many times over the years, David would brag to friends about how he hunted as a boy. His parents, he said, bought him and his two brothers shotguns for Christmases. "Dove hunting was a big deal for the whole family," remembers Thompson. "Some of the family had leases outside town, farther in the country."

While all three of the Temple sons were hunters, it was the youngest, Kevin, who seemed to enjoy it the most. Meanwhile, friends describe Darren, the oldest, as the most business-minded and ambitious of the three. All the Temple sons were active in athletics, playing Little League. Their parents went in different directions on weekends, to cover all three of their games. While David, the middle son, enjoyed baseball, from the beginning he was better suited to another game, the one that held a special place in Katy's heart. Football would make David Temple a local star and shape his life. In fact, his exploits between the goalposts would make his entire family feel even more special. Not only were the Temples a founding family in Katy, they spawned a local celebrity.

"It was a lot of fun to be a parent of a star athlete," Maureen would say. "To be able to say, 'That's my son out there on the football field, making all the tackles.'"

Physically, David Temple was born to play football. From a young age, he was a thickly built boy, one with a powerful body and a keen enthusiasm for the game. His brow was heavy and his eyes deep set and intense. At the age of eight, David played with Katy Youth Football, a league that trains boys from age four and up. "He loved it from the beginning," his mother would say. Yet, it wasn't practicing out in the open air, getting in some exercise, that he found appealing. Instead David liked the rough-and-tumble action that took place on the field. "He wanted to play the game every day," his mother says. "He didn't want to go to practice, he wanted to play a game."

Opposing a competing team, David was fast and agile, and, perhaps most impressive, he showed no fear. Even in those early years, friends would remember how tough David played and his command of the game. "The rest of us were just having fun, but it was different with David," says a teammate and friend. "He was out there to win."

When it came to personality, David was the entertainer. Husky and good-looking, with a wide smile and a wicked sense of humor, he loved to tell jokes and seemed to find pleasure in making others laugh. All three of the Temple sons were "charmers," says a family friend, but David went out of his way, even as a child, to win people over. Perhaps that was another reason why his parents treated him as if he was special.

"From an early age on, Kenny and Maureen were different with David. Someone would come to them and say David did something bad, and they'd ask David about it. Then they'd go to the person and say, 'David said he didn't do that.' As far as Maureen and Kenny were concerned, the issue was closed," says Thompson. "It was as if David was untouchable. I don't ever remember him being held accountable."

In grade school, David was held back a year, which only helped when it came to football, making him older, bigger and stronger than the other kids on the field. Although few believed that he needed any more advantages. "He was just so much better than the other kids," says the father of one teammate. "David, from the beginning, was a standout."

By junior high, David was one of the starters on the team. He'd continued to bulk up and grow stronger every year. "We used to make fun of how big David's head was," says a friend. Off the field, he continued to be a contradiction. He had the ability to be funny and even charismatic. One afternoon, at the home of a friend whose dad was a deputy sheriff, David donned the man's uniform and paraded through the house, mimicking a tough cop, and eliciting squeals of laughter from his amused friends, who turned to him when they wanted someone to fight their battles. "When we needed someone taken care of, we told David," says a friend. "He'd wait for the kid when school let out. Most of the time, the kid took one look at David and ran."

Another friend puts it this way: "David had a gentle side about him, but there was absolutely a dark side. There was this egotistical side, the part of him that thinks the world revolves around him."

In Katy, there was no reason for David Temple to think anything other than that he was exceptional. As junior high passed and his exploits on the football field were bantered about in town, many viewed him as a hope for the future, one of those who might help turn around the fortune of the Katy High School football team. Despite the town's support and the impressive stadium on a hill off Katyland Drive with the U.S. and Texas flags flying overhead, the Tigers had gone through a long dry spell. And many were hopeful that David Temple would help lead the local kids to victory.

When it came to girls, David had the advantage every star athlete enjoys, of being considered special and therefore wanted. By junior high, he'd found himself attracted to girls much like him, young athletes. Yet part of David didn't appear to believe that cute and athletic was enough. "He always fit better with the tomboys," says Thompson. "But he always thought he was supposed to be with a bombshell."

In junior high and early in high school, David dated a perky, energetic young woman with dark hair whose father worked for the Katy School District. Hillary Brooks was enthusiastic and fun, she played basketball, and she appeared to adore him. But as much as, at times, he seemed dedicated to her, David often pushed her to the side in favor of another girl, a pretty blond named Jimi Barlow. Friends would recall how, going into ninth grade, David fluctuated between the two girls, getting serious with Hillary only to suddenly disappear from her life and return to Jimi. "I remember this going on for years," says a friend.

Finally, Hillary had had enough, planting her feet and holding her ground. She refused to take David back when he asked. No matter how he pleaded, Hillary was finished, even though her own father idolized David. It was one of the few times David's friends would remember when he became openly emotional. "I saw him cry when she broke up with him," says a friend. "I was so amazed. I actually saw David Temple cry."

Although he'd professed his affection, that wouldn't protect Hillary from Temple's temper. Once she rebuffed him, he attacked, jeering at her and calling her names, including "horse head," because she had a slightly long face. David urged his friends to join in and do the same, and before long, Hillary was greeted with catcalls as she walked across the school grounds. Throughout high school, David confronted any young man who asked Hillary on a date. "Guys were scared of David, so they backed off. It was pretty brutal," says one of David's friends. "A counselor told David to stop, but he never did."

In fact, at one point David's revenge apparently became even harsher. One night Hillary's family discovered her pet rabbits were missing. Later, a classmate told her that David Temple had wrung their necks.

The Katy High School football team was known as the army of red, for Katy's red and white school colors. In the stands, fans painted their faces red and white, some checked or with stripes, and they held out fingers, claiming they were number one. "There's so much tradition there, but before the mid-eighties the team was really dormant," says Dexter Clay, who wrote *KatyNation*, a book on the history of the team. "The program started in 1939, with six-man football, by recruiting kids off tractors. Their first winning season was in 1959, and then they were dormant again until the mid-eighties, when Mike Johnston took over as coach." One of the players who'd lead Johnston's charge was David Temple.

"People don't understand how intense football is and how violent it is. And David was brutal on the field. You got scared when you had to go up against David, even in practice," says Fleener, who describes David at the time as like a big brother to him. "David was so tough, he'd go through two or three helmets a year. He literally wore them out."

By high school, David approached his adult height of five feet, eleven inches, and weighed nearly 210 pounds. Before games, he and his teammates got "into the zone," concentrating on the task ahead. Some called it "skull time," because it meant clearing their minds of everything but the game. Among the most intense players, some would remember how David paid attention to strategy, coaching the others on how to win. At times, he put on his pads and rammed into the lockers, building a formidable bravado. When the team walked out on the field, "David was ready," says Fleener.

As the middle linebacker, David wore a red jersey with his number, 83, in white. He led the defense, and it was his job to shut down the other team's attack, to call the plays and do whatever possible to stop the opposing players from advancing the football. "Middle linebackers have to be aggressive," says Mike Johnston, Katy High School's head football coach during those years. "David was one of the most intense players I ever coached. On the field, he was one of the meanest. The other team's offense didn't like to see David bearing down on them."

One of the girls on Katy's sidelines during those years would grow up to have more than a little notoriety of her own. Slightly built, with long blond hair, a pretty face and a scratchy voice, Renée Zellweger worked her pom-poms and led the cheers for David and his teammates. Considered something of a "nerd" in high school, Zellweger would later become an Academy Award-winning actress, performing in movies such as *Cinderella Man, Bridget Jones's Diary, Cold Mountain,* and the musical *Chicago.* But at the time, fewer students were aware of Zellweger than of David Temple. Another of David's coaches, Ken Bruno, would say what he saw in the young football player was someone who was "determined and calculating. One strong son-of-a-gun."

In many ways, David was the same off the field. Always tight with his teammates, he had close friends. He could be charismatic and caring. When Mike Fleener broke his arm playing football, David went with him to the hospital and stayed throughout the surgery, late into the night. "David was the last person I saw before they put me out, and the first one there when I woke up," Fleener says.

Yet the words *rude, mean* and *intimidating* were used more often in connection with David, not by those in his inner circle, the upper echelon of the school's jocks, but by the average kids, the ones not held in high enough athletic esteem to earn his respect. "David Temple was always ready for a fight, and he acted like he thought he was better than the other kids. He was a bully," says one classmate. "He treated ninety percent of us like we were a step down from him, ignoring us unless he singled us out for some kind of abuse."

"Kids walked on pins and needles around David because he had a bad temper, and they were never sure what would set him off," says a high-school friend. "Everyone, even his friends, knew they didn't want to be on the receiving side when David got pissed."

Always meticulous about planning events, the way he dressed and setting strategy on the football field, when it came to pickup games or any activity, David pulled the particulars together, setting up the teams and making all the arrangements. Even as a teenager, he seemed obsessed with being in control. Sometimes, when his friends didn't go along, David became peeved. "He'd call us momma's boys when we didn't do what he wanted," says a friend. "David ridiculed us. We didn't say anything. Most of the time, we just let it go, hoping he'd stop."

Still, when he was playing so well on the football field, others were willing to cut David a considerable amount of slack. "Katy is all about football. It's all Katy is," says one resident. "Players like to talk about winning with heart and seeing through the eye of the Tiger."

There was little doubt that David had more than his share of courage. Once, while running the bleachers, he slipped and sliced his leg open, cutting it nearly to the bone. One teammate looked at the wound and felt like throwing up, it was so bloody and angry-looking. To his astonishment, David laughed. Although taken aback, his friend wasn't completely surprised; he'd once seen David fall on a piece of plywood with nails hammered through it. That day David suffered puncture wounds but never shed a tear.

In the stands on Friday nights, David's family cheered him on. Despite their deep roots, "the Temples were just another family in the rice fields of Katy, Texas," says one resident. "What they had going for them was a son who was a star football player."

Off the field, David talked confidently of the future. He speculated about college at a big-name university, followed by a career in the pros. "David was very physical, built for the game," says the team's defensive coach, Don Clayton. "And he was aggressive. That's what you want to see. He understood that getting hit was part of the game."

"Getting hit by David, even at practice, was like getting hit by a freight train," says Tommy Raglin, one of David's close friends and a teammate. "On the field, we sometimes used David as a kicker. He was good, and it faked the other team out. They didn't guess that a kicker would be able to tackle and run the ball."

Then disaster. In his sophomore year during the first scrimmage, David, who'd been elevated to the varsity team, hurt his knee, so badly he required not one surgery but two. It could have been a football-ending injury. David was out the entire season. But he was determined not to end his career on the field. "I've never seen anybody work harder at rehab than David," says Clayton. "He was in the gym constantly, working that knee. He worked his upper body and developed incredible strength."

Once the knee heeled, David came back tougher than ever. Friends say that he could bench-press 430 pounds, and stories circulated on the high-school campus. The gossip suggested that David wasn't just working in the gym to build those muscles. Some said he'd begun taking anabolic steroids.

During the eighties, the drugs spread from professional sports onto high school and college campuses. The word *anabolic* is from the Greek, translating as "to build up," and the drugs increase the production of proteins and thwart the breakdown of muscle. Although outlawed in all major sports, they can give athletes a competitive edge. At times, they also have psychological or emotional side effects, including angry outbursts, called roid rage. By increasing testosterone levels in the body, it's thought that aggression is accentuated and, in extreme cases, paranoia and anger.

Coach Clayton maintains that he saw no evidence that David was on steroids, and that he viewed the muscle building David did his senior year as simply the well-earned product of hard work. "We'd see the players walk around after showers, and I never saw David's back break out or any of the other telltale signs of steroid use."

Yet one of David's fellow players who admitted using the drugs during his junior and senior year at Katy High School was told by his supplier the names of others who were customers. "David was huge. He bulked way up and could out weight-lift everybody else on the team. The guy who sold me steroids said he was selling to David," says the Katy player. "I never asked David about it, but I also never questioned that it was true."

When David made his return, he dominated on the field and became even more feared on the campus. "The football team had a sense of owning the school," says Fleener. "We had our own table at lunch, and it always seemed like we could get away with things. The football players and the cheerleaders were on the A-list. David was cocky, but so was the whole team. Since David was a star, he was cockier than the rest of us."

Players would remember seeing David get into heated arguments with the coaches, especially Mike Johnston. When David thought he or any of his fellow defensive players was being unfairly treated, he became insistent and his size made him frightening. One player recalled how David screamed at the coach, his face inches from Johnston's. Both of them were furious. "David crossed a line and possibly I did, too," Johnston would say years later. "When I'd see him get out of control, I'd intervene. Sometimes I talked to him about keeping the aggression on the field, where it belonged. David could be explosive, and he didn't always know how to turn it off."

By then, David Temple had a bad reputation at Katy High School. "It was common knowledge among the teachers that David was a problem at school," says one of his teachers. "He tried to intimidate the teachers, and sometimes he succeeded. He was a big kid, and a lot of people were afraid of him."

A close friend would say that Maureen and Kenny Temple weren't heard to raise their voices to David, and that they were perpetually patient and soft-spoken with him. But then David was a different kind of kid than his brothers. "Wound tighter," the friend maintains. "He needed constant stimulation."

One Katy High teacher would say, "We got really tired of David Temple's mother coming up to school to get him out of trouble."

It was sometime about then that an incident was whispered about, one some of David's classmates gossiped about but never knew if it was true. Years later, it would take on a frightening forbearing.

At the time, Cindi Thompson dated David's older brother, Darren. They'd been together for a year or more, and their relationship would take her through high school. She always enjoyed the entire Temple family, and found David to be fun. But she'd heard rumors in school that he was getting into trouble. That fall, Cindi says there'd been turmoil in the Temple family. Ken Temple was out of work, and David worsened the situation by getting into trouble at school.

One night, Darren showed up at Thompson's house, shaking and upset. He said that David and their mother had been arguing about David's behavior. "Darren said David got disrespectful to Maureen, and then Darren said that he stepped in between them, ordering David to stop talking to his mother that way," Cindi says. From that point on, Darren said David turned his anger on him. The argument between the brothers escalated, and David grabbed a shotgun and held it in Darren's face, backing him into a corner. Darren told Cindi that he'd had to beg his brother for his life, and their mother begged, too, pleading with David to put the shotgun down.

"Darren said David's whole demeanor changed," Cindi says. "His eyes got big and he stared at them with a blank look. Finally, David put the shotgun down and left the room."

As Darren told her about what had just transpired, Cindi said she was shocked. "I'd never seen Darren like this before. He was angry and hurt," she says. "He'd cry, then he'd be angry again."

That evening, Cindi's father flashed the porch lights, signaling her to come inside. When she did, she told her dad what Darren had just described. "And I never forgot," Cindi said. Yet, looking back, she didn't find the episode completely shocking. "It was David being David."

By his junior year, David Temple was garnering interest from colleges watching his performance on the football field. "He had a collection of letters from all the big-name schools," says a friend. "Oklahoma, Nebraska, the University of Texas. David had so many, he made a collage and pasted them onto his bedroom wall."

On the Katy High campus, as well, David Temple's legend grew. The Rebels were born that year as part of an intramural volleyball game. David and his friends decided they needed a name for their team. They chose the Rebels because of a popular song at the time, British rocker Billy Idol's "Rebel Yell," with lyrics that depict an insatiable girl who screams, "More, more, more." In the song, the lyrics say the man would "sell his soul" to have the girl he calls his "little angel."

"One of the guys had a rebel flag, and we liked the lyrics," says one of the group. The cheerleaders and the boys' girlfriends became known as the Rebel Women.

"There were a lot of people jealous. We were the athletes," says Tommy Raglin, one of David's close friends. "That was just the way it was. A lot of people in high school said David was crazy and fearless. It was just boys being boys."

Teenage years are a time when many feel indestructible, but David, as he did with so much in life, took his boldness to the extreme. Once he dove from a high dive trying to hit the shallow end of a pool. Another time, when the team was staying at a hotel, David jumped into a swimming pool from a second-floor balcony. And whenever the possibility of a fight opened up, David appeared ready. "Everyone wanted to fight David because he was huge," says Raglin. David's celebrity grew, based, at times, on no more than gossip, like the time rumors circulated that he'd beaten up three guys at a mall. "It never happened," says Raglin. "When David heard the story, he laughed."

It was a heady coming of age, one in which David and the other players felt on top of the world, singled out for greatness. On Fridays the teachers at Katy High School and most of the student body wore red, in support of the football team. At the afternoon pep rallies, the football team was called out to the gym floor by the principal and coaches, where they were lauded for their accomplishments. There was reason to celebrate. The Tigers did well David's final two years at Katy High School. "As David progressed, so did the team," says Coach Clayton. "By senior year, we were winning, and David was outstanding."

Throughout the football season, as the team won game after game, David's renown grew in the small town. Before long, he walked into local restaurants with his parents and townsfolk got up out of their chairs and stood to congratulate him. On Friday nights, nearly 10,000 filled Rhodes Stadium; news vans filled the parking lot, while TV helicopters circled overhead, and for much of the game all eyes were on the star linebacker, David Temple.

That year, the fall of 1986, the Katy Tigers won every game and took home a district championship for the first time in twenty-two years. David was the defensive captain, and one of the stars of the team. "He was a hometown hero, and it didn't matter what David pulled," says Thompson. "Because everyone just adored him. The little kids wanted to be like him. And the adults wanted to shake his hand."

After the games, parents threw parties, or the team went to victory dances where DJs played rock and roll and country and western. David dated a girl from another school, but his prominence was such that many of the Katy High girls wanted to be his girlfriend. At least on the surface, David Temple had it all. He was handsome, powerfully built, had a devil-may-care charisma, and he was high up on the school's hierarchy, on the tier reserved for the most popular students.

The season ended when the Tigers lost, 24 to 13, to the Madison Marlins in Houston's Astrodome on November 15, 1986, but that final loss never diminished the year's importance. It would seem in the decades to follow that the team had begun a tradition of winning, one Katy High would carry forward. And the members of the team, especially David, would be forever viewed as the players that started it all.

In early 1987, just weeks after his team's most impressive season on the field of combat, however, all wouldn't be well for David Temple. He'd talked confidently to friends throughout his football career of being picked up by a big-name school, the University of Texas, Arkansas, or any of the others in the big conferences that went to bowl games and whose star players signed multimillion-dollar NFL contracts. But by that winter, it was evident that wouldn't be David's fate.

Early on, there had been interest in David, especially from the University of Oklahoma. "On film, David looked good. He was a fine player," says Clayton. "Before Oklahoma came out to see him in person, they were saying all the right things, calling David a full-tilt guy, that he could play in their program. But the big schools wanted linebackers to be six feet and up. David was just five eleven, and too short."

The night the previous fall when an Oklahoma coach came to watch David play football, Clayton had heard the man say, "Temple's not as big as we thought he was."

From that point on, Oklahoma pulled back. They showed no interest in David Temple, and none of the other top-tier schools recruited him. As 1987 began, it became evident that an offer from a big-ticket school wasn't in David's future. Although he must have been disappointed, David brushed off the situation with friends, saying it didn't matter. But to one friend he labeled the height requirement "B.S.," and groused about the unfairness of it all, pointing out that he was just an inch shorter than Mike Singletary, a Hall of Fame linebacker who played for the Chicago Bears. How much difference that one inch in height made. Ironically, if David took steroids in high school, in the long run the drugs may have hurt more than helped. One potential side effect is bone shortening, and both of David's brothers were taller than he was. Without steroids would David Temple have grown that all-important inch? There was no way to predict what might have been, but the frustration at being left behind must have stung.

"We were all disappointed for David," says a friend. "He'd worked hard. He deserved to be able to grab the golden ring."

Crime wasn't much of a concern in Katy, Texas. Yet a rash of car burglaries had begun the previous summer, and continued through fall and into that winter. Someone was stealing what was then the latest hot technology, radar detectors. Euphemistically called fuzz busters, they were used to warn when police were near with radar guns, monitoring speed and writing tickets. The burglaries were sporadic, taking place in unlocked cars. In early 1987, the frequency intensified, and the thieves began breaking car windows.

In early February 1987, a little more than a month after football season ended, a detective from the Katy Police Department went to the high school to talk to the group of boys he'd heard about, the ones who called themselves the Rebels. "They were known to have caused some trouble," says then Katy police captain Robert Frazier.

Afterward, David and his friends laughed about the detective's questions. "It was like the police showed up and made threats, and after the detective left, the car thefts increased," says one of the Rebels. "It was like the guys involved were showing the police they could do it. There was this mentality that this was our school. This was our town. We could do what we wanted. Most of us, but especially David, felt invincible."

With complaints piling up from the victims, a source led the investigating detective to the fence buying the stolen goods. The man cooperated, saying he bought the radar detectors from two Katy football players. One was David Temple.

Captain Frazier had already heard plenty of gossip about the high school's star middle linebacker. Although Frazier had never been able to confirm them, rumors circulated that Temple had once hit a man with his car and then beat the guy up. Another report recounted an afternoon David was supposed to have been driving with a girlfriend, when he spotted an elderly couple walking along the road. That day, as the story went, David swerved toward the couple, who had to jump into a ditch to avoid being mowed down. The girl in the car with him told friends that David stared straight ahead, as if in a trance, eerily reminiscent of the way Darren described his brother to Cindi Thompson, on the evening he told her that David threatened him with the shotgun.

"There were a lot of folks in Katy afraid of David Temple," says Frazier.

For a family like the Temples, one with such a pristine image, it must have been more than embarrassing when their middle son's name appeared in an article in the *Katy Times* on February 22, 1987. This time instead of lauding David's football accomplishments, the headline read, TWO KHS ATHLETES ARRESTED, and the article detailed burglary charges pending against David and another Katy High player. Next to their son's name, Maureen and Kenny's home address was listed, all on the front page in plain view, for the entire town, all of the Temples' family and friends, to read.

Yet not everything had been revealed in the newspaper. One thing that didn't make the article was that the other player arrested told police the radar detectors were being stolen to make money for steroids.

"We were a small town and the arrest of the star football player was big news," says David's friend, Mike Fleener.

After his arrest, David gave a voluntary statement. At first he only admitted being involved in one burglary, but his fingerprints matched those taken in another smash-and-grab theft. Before long others came forward who tied David to at least six and perhaps as many as eight car burglaries. Although David was legally an adult, police consulted his father. The investigating officer wrote in his report that this was done because Ken Temple was "known to be a reputable man and a long-term resident of Katy."

In the end, David and his friend were given deals; although police had a confession and witnesses, his charges were plea-bargained down to a single charge. That February, David pleaded to a single Class A misdemeanor, attempted burglary of a vehicle. He was sentenced to three days in jail and a $100 fine.

Two months later, David Temple graduated from Katy High. Nowhere in 1987's *Tiger Echo* was there a mention of the February arrest. But as befitting his football accomplishments, David was featured prominently on the glossy pages of the school yearbook. On one page, against a blue background like the other seniors, he was spit-and-polish groomed and wearing a tuxedo. A handsome nineteen-year-old, David had dimples, a strong chin, and a broad smile, and his brown hair was high off his forehead and combed carefully back.

Renée Zellweger had been voted the school's "Dream Date," but David was singled out as well. In his letterman's jacket, surrounded by friends, in one photo David had his right index finger held up, indicating the Tigers were number one. He had a tousled-hair bad-boy look about him, and a disarmingly appealing smile. On other pages, there were photos of David in his uniform on the football field and coaching a powder-puff game. In another, he collected a plaque for being an outstanding member of the "Fighting Tigers." With a girl on his lap, David slumped back in a chair wearing a blue sweater with jeans. They'd both been voted "Most Athletic."

The 1987 Katy High graduation ceremony was held at the city's equestrian center. By then, David's future had been planned. Although the top-tier universities with their multimillion-dollar football programs had passed him by, David's exploits on the football field had earned him an offer. He'd accepted a five-year scholarship from Stephen F. Austin University, in Nacogdoches, Texas, the same college Belinda Lucas would attend. It was a 1-AA athletic program, a good-sized school in a town that worshipped football and the players who represented it on the field.

The world waited for David Temple. But before he left

Katy for Nacogdoches, Coach Johnston pulled his star line-backer to the side. The head coach worried about David's inability to separate football-field aggression from what was permissible in the real world. "I told him that if I heard he got in any trouble, I'd be calling Coach Graves at SFA and letting him know," says Johnston.

Another of David's teachers, too, had misgivings about him as the Katy seniors collected their diplomas. "I remember thinking that there would be problems down the road with David," she'd say years later. "It wasn't anything solid. I just had a bad feeling that we hadn't heard the last of him."

4

At the time Belinda Lucas and David Temple enrolled at Stephen F. Austin University the fall of 1987, the enrollment hovered around 12,000 students. The campus covered 401 rolling, heavily wooded acres, originally private property, the bucolic homestead of Senator Thomas J. Rusk. Perhaps not surprisingly, since the university's roots traced back to a 1923 teachers college, the campus was rich in history along with reports of ghostly apparitions. Mays Hall dormitory, once a hospital with a morgue in the basement, had an unexplained coldness, while a ghost named Chester was said to appear at times in the university fine arts auditorium, his face once seen by students on the theater's curtain. Legend has it that Chester was either the building's architect, who died before its completion, or the prowling spirit of a drama student who'd committed suicide.

One of the oldest buildings on campus was the Stone Fort, the site of an old trading post. Campus folklore warned that any SFA student who dared enter the Fort before finishing was destined to never graduate. Most students saw little reason to visit, since the structure housed a museum. The more popular destinations were campus bars, including Monday Night Football at the Sports Shack, happy hours with live music at the Crossroads, and weekend evenings at Speak-EZ.

SFA's school colors were purple and white, and the football team, befitting the school's heavily forested setting, was dubbed the Lumberjacks. As SFA was an NCAA Division 1-AA school, the "Jacks" were part of the Southland Conference, made up of twelve universities in Texas, Arkansas, and Louisiana. On game days, students posted homemade signs outside Homer Bryce Stadium, on the north edge of the campus, urging their team to victory. And in the stands the student body, wearing shirts in their school colors, became a mass of screaming bodies dubbed the Purple Haze.

As a 1-AA team, the Lumberjacks traveled by plane, and the stadiums they played accommodated from 10,000 to 15,000 fans. On the football field, as ever, David ranked high on the list of players. Wearing number 42, he'd gained a little weight since high school, coming in at 220 pounds, and his strength was formidable. As in Katy, players dreaded coming up against him, even his friends. "David had a great sense of humor. He joked around all the time. But you didn't want to be on his bad side," says Jeremy Rakes, a teammate. "He had a temper."

At night, when the players went out, David got in fights in the bars, more often than not with the frat boys he loved to ridicule. One night when he talked to a girl, another student said hello. David picked the guy up and threw him against the wall. David even became incensed with teammates if he felt they weren't being respectful to one of his dates. "He'd yell and scream and threaten," says Jeremy, who one night caught the brunt of David's anger just for talking to his date. "He said I was being disrespectful to the girl, but I wasn't. When he dated someone, he put them on a pedestal, and if any of the guys got close, David went ballistic."

Anything could set him off. One night he showed up at a bowling alley late, and the worker who answered the door said the place was closing. According to the rumors that circulated afterward, David expressed his disappointment by pummeling the alley's attendant. "We didn't know if the guy didn't know who David was or if it was all covered up," says a teammate. "But nothing ever happened to David."

As at Katy High School, the SFA team was a tight unit. Many ate together and lived in the same coed dorm, a low-rise building that resembled a motel, with doorways to the outside. The first two floors housed football players, with women students on the top two floors. During those years, the late eighties, when steroids were a topic across the nation, Jeremy and others heard a lot of talk about SFA players injecting the drugs, but not from David. If he used them, he kept it quiet. While some of the players filled syringes and injected in front of others, if he used them, David didn't. "I don't know if David was on them or not," says Jeremy. "All I know is that on the field, he was tough, and that he had a hair-trigger temper. The rest of us were careful around him, not to set him off."

So tough that although he played little during his first year, something both awful and remarkable happened. One night, when the Jacks were playing Nicholls State, from Thibodaux, Louisiana, David tackled a player who didn't see him coming. It was a legal hit, and a hard one. David struck the other player with so much force that he dislocated two of his opponent's vertebrae. "David nearly broke the guy's back," says Jeremy.

Maybe Coach Graves shouldn't have been surprised by his new linebacker's power and fierceness. When Graves recruited David, a Katy coach told him that David was the "meanest" player he'd ever worked with. That fall, Graves learned something else about David Temple: the defensive player displayed a consuming need to be in charge. "David was a lot about control," says Graves. "On the football field, even when he was furious, he never totally lost control. What I saw in David Temple was a heavy-minded person. Focused."

What players noticed about their new teammate was that the kid from Katy also had a few quirks. When it came to appearances, David left nothing to chance. Obsessive about his clothes, he wore only name brands, like Tommy Hilfiger shirts and jeans and Nike warm-up suits. Everything had to be precisely clean and pressed, and it all had to match, down to his socks and tennis shoes. Perhaps most remarkable, his personal hygiene was more than fastidious. David Temple was so meticulous, he sometimes showered three or four times a day.

At the beginning of his second year, David was put on the Lumberjacks' roster as a starter, and the coaches groomed him for special teams and middle linebacker, a position Graves called "the hub of the defense." Few doubted that he deserved the slot. On the football field, David was always 100 percent, fighting tough. And beginning on Sunday mornings, David studied the coming week's opponents, committing to memory new plays tailored to thwart them. "He read them over and over," says a friend. "David was obsessive about planning. He had to have everything lined up, everything ready. He didn't leave anything to chance."

As they had since he'd first played football as a youngster, Maureen and Kenny Temple attended nearly every game. At times that meant beginning the three-hour drive from Katy to Nacogdoches early in the morning and returning late at night. For evening games, they sometimes pulled into their driveway at two in the morning. Instead of Tiger red, the Temples now wore SFA Lumberjack purple-and-white sweatshirts. They weren't disappointed during the games. Playing special teams and defense, David got a lot of time on the field. His parents had always been David's biggest supporters, and to those Maureen and Kenny Temple met at SFA, that didn't appear to have changed.

The team played well in the fall of 1988, David's first season as an SFA starter. They won their homecoming game against Nicholls State, 30 to 7, the first win against that Louisiana team since 1983. David was a big part of the Jacks' improving fortunes. "He loved playing, and he carried that mental attitude to the game," says Graves. "David had good speed and strength. He prepared, and on the field, he was a leader."

Still, Graves would later wonder if he should have seen more, something dangerous in David Temple. "You don't look back and see signs about what someone can do, because on the football field, you're looking for that aggression. It's a good thing," says Graves. "But there's another side to that equation. Because of the degree of violence in football, it's not far-fetched for a player to go too far off the field."

In August of his second year at SFA, David met Pam Engelkirk, an elementary education major. Slim and pretty, with cascading blond curls, Pam had a wide, engaging smile. She was smart and fun loving. David, as he often did with women, poured on the charm.

At the time, Pam wore a pink shirt with a black bow tie and shorts as her uniform at Nacogdoches's nicest restaurant, the Californian. Her parents had recently divorced, and Pam was feeling a little lost, a little less connected to family. David was affectionate and thoughtful. He sent her flowers, most often red roses, even when there wasn't an occasion. There were those times he got in fights in bars, but Pam wrote them off. "Everybody on the football team liked David. His friends were his friends and everyone else stayed clear of David," she says, with a shrug. "That's just the way it was."

It never seemed like a burden to stand close to him in the clubs, never venturing away from him. She would say later that she instinctively understood that he wanted her there, and that she wasn't to leave his side. "It was like we were joined at the hip," she says. "David required that. And I never minded."

Besides, it was exciting dating one of the Lumberjacks' star players. In the stands, she sat with the other players' girlfriends, cheering their boyfriends on. After the games, the girls were allowed on the field with their boyfriends. Even outside the university, with the team winning, David was something of a celebrity in Nacogdoches. "It was a big deal on campus and around town," says Jeremy. "Everyone knew who we were."

A lot of the girls envied Pam. There were the after-the-game parties and all the excitement of watching David's powerful performances on the football field. "I knew the quarterback and the cheerleaders," says Pam. "It was fun, and I felt important to be his girlfriend. I was happy."

That fall, when Maureen and Ken Temple drove in for a game, Pam waited to meet them at David's apartment. She had balloons, and they all laughed and seemed to get along well. Since her own family was going through a tough time, Pam found herself drawn to David's parents. Maureen was matronly but fun, and David's father was fatherly and kind. She began spending all the holidays at the Temples', even Christmas. At Easter, Pam brought her sister, and they slept in the family room and colored eggs. The following July, she went along to New Braunfels, in the Texas Hill Country, for the Temples' annual vacation. "David's parents took me in, and I felt close to them," she says. "His whole family really put David on a pedestal, but they were good people."

Looking back, it was as if David took over Pam's life. He held her hand, looked into her eyes, and whispered in her ear. He was serious and solid, magnetic with a good sense of humor. "David was my first real relationship," she says. "He was a football star, a really cool guy, and he was my first love."

Later, others would talk of the way they saw David control Pam, but she didn't see it that way at the time. "I just felt loved," she says.

Pam sat with the Temple family at games, and no one ever mentioned David's tumultuous high school career or the 1987 burglary arrest. While she saw some of the other football players giving each other shots, she never saw anyone giving one to David, and she never suspected that he was on steroids. To Pam, David Temple was an All-American boy, a small-town football hero. And he loved her.

He didn't have a car, and Pam often drove. When she

wasn't working, she and the other girlfriends traveled with the team, following the bus in their cars. By then, David appeared to have come to terms with his future. He didn't talk of playing with the pros but of being a coach. "At a 1-AA school, you needed to get your degree," says one of the other players. "There wasn't an NFL contract waiting out there for you, so everyone knew if we stayed in the game, we'd be coaching."

On Thursdays, the Californian restaurant, where Pam worked, booked bands and served quarter beers in the lounge. Afterward, David and Pam went out. It was at those times, when he'd been drinking, that David's other side emerged. Usually it wasn't aimed at Pam, but anyone else who crossed him, and often the excuse was that he was protecting her. On one such night, Pam and her sister walked to the car a short distance ahead of David and a friend. Two college students approached them, and after Pam slipped into the driver's seat, one of the guys kept her from closing the door, flirting with her. For his own protection, Pam knew he had to leave, fast. "I'm not kidding you. You need to back off, because my boyfriend's coming," she warned.

It was too late. By the time she'd finished talking, David had picked up the young man and body-slammed him onto the hood of a parked car. Without comment, David and his friend got in Pam's car. As Pam's sister sobbed, Pam pulled away and drove off. "I knew better than to argue with David," she says. "I was upset, but I didn't say a word."

Remarkably, David immediately returned to his usual demeanor. "He was fine," Pam says. "It was like he had taken care of business, and it was over."

At other times, usually when they'd both been drinking, they argued. "He'd become so angry, he'd punch walls. He once kicked my car door, and once he hit a mirror in a men's room at a bar and shattered it," says Pam. "Usually it was over jealousy issues. Most of the time, I wasn't sure what started it."

By the next morning, David was back to normal, charming and kind, bringing flowers and going out of his way to let her know that he loved her. "I'd forget about it," she says. "I just thought that he really loved me. That when you have a real boyfriend who cares about you, this is what it's like."

The following fall, 1989, was a big year for the Lumberjacks, and on the field, David was outstanding. "He brought his fighting face to every game," says Graves. "He was on special teams and defense and he got a lot of recognition." Soon, the Jacks were racking up wins. They played North Texas, Lamar, Eastern Washington, Boise State, and Jackson State, and piled up wins. The night of homecoming, the cheerleaders led the traditional torchlight parade to the bonfire, and the next day the Jacks crushed Sam Houston State's Bearkats, 45 to 7.

After one game, getting on the bus, a squabble broke out between a defensive and offensive player. David jumped in the middle of it, and Coach Graves ended up pulling David off one player. The player David fought dwarfed even him, but David didn't back off. He didn't appear to even care. By then, David Temple's fierceness had earned him a nickname: the "Temple of Doom."

Throughout that season, David's reputation spread, so much so that it attracted the attention of the big city newspaper. That November 22, 1989, in a *Houston Chronicle* article on Nacogdoches' star linebacker, one Lumberjack coach called David "as tough a linebacker as you'd ever want. . . . When it gets tough, the better [David] gets."

When David was interviewed, he told the reporter: "I think I'm more aggressive than the normal player. I try to hit a player with a helmet, T-bar to T-bar. I just try to run through him. . . . My parents probably feel that way, too," David said about his intensity. "I've got a temper, a pretty short fuse."

Yet on the field, David's forcefulness paid off. By the time the article ran, David had racked up 114 tackles, including 64 unassisted stops and 5 sacks. In the article, Coach Graves said the SFA defense was young but maturing, and gave credit to David. "If we have a guy in that position who didn't do the job, then we don't have a very good defense."

That winter, SFA won the Southland Conference title for the first time in their sixty-three-year history. When the Jacks beat the Indians of Northeast Louisiana 66 to 45, the energized fans counted off the final seconds in unison. At the end of that winning season, the NCAA ranked the Stephen F. Austin Lumberjacks third in the 1-AA, the highest ranking in SFA history. A few months later, David and his fellow teammates collected heavy gold-domed Southland Conference Championship rings with their initials.

That year, David shared his dorm room with Reno Moore, one of his fellow players. They hung out together, grilling on the patio, with Pam and Reno's girlfriend, Stephanie. Sometimes, at night, David and Reno snuck out on the golf course to retrieve balls from the pond, then sold them for extra money. The two players became good friends, and with their girlfriends they formed a family of sorts, at college, away from their homes.

As always, Pam was proud of David. They spent all their available time together, going to Sea World in San Antonio, and out with friends. By then, the outcome of their relationship seemed so predictable that their friends called Pam "Mrs. Temple." She wore a promise ring he'd bought her, and they'd often get waylaid walking through malls and detour to the jewelry stores, where they considered engagement rings. "David hadn't proposed, but it was more that it was understood," Pam says. "He talked all the time about what it would be like when we were married."

Despite their plans for the future, there continued to be that other side to David and to their relationship. On nights they went out and partied, their arguments spiraled, but Pam chalked it off to college days, when people studied hard, worked hard, and drank hard. Still, she wasn't prepared for what happened the following January 1990, when they were in Dallas for the wedding of a friend. That night David went out with the groomsmen, while Pam, who was standing up in the wedding, stayed in a hotel room with her friends. "We were doing girl stuff," she says. "Doing our nails, talking, and fixing each other's hair."

Late that night, David called, and said, "I want to come see you."

Unusual for her, perhaps the first time she'd done so, Pam refused.

"It was a night with the girls, and I said I'd see him the next day at the wedding." Pam would later hear that before David called her he'd gotten in a bar fight.

Despite her rebuff, soon after, David pounded on the hotel-room door. When Pam opened it, he burst through, shadowed by two friends. Furious, David screamed at her. They argued, and he came at her, confronting and pursuing her into the bathroom. "He was on fire," she says. "I'd never seen him like that before."

Years later, Pam would look back with the wisdom brought by age and marvel that she'd let anyone treat her as David did that night. But caught up in the relationship, at that moment, she didn't understand how dangerous their relationship had become. "As strange as it sounds, I guess I thought it was normal for a boyfriend to be like that," she says. "I didn't know better."

In the bathroom, David came at her, screaming and cursing. He backed her into the bathtub and then, as she cried out, pushed her against the wall, his face a mask of rage.

The other girls begged David's friends to force him to leave, and one finally wrestled David away from Pam. Sobbing, she tore at the gold necklace she wore, the one he'd given her just weeks earlier at Christmas. The clasp broke, and she threw it in the toilet, as David's friends pushed him out of the room and out the hotel-room door.

"It was ugly," says Pam. "Terrifying." This time she was angry enough to refuse to talk to him when he tried to apologize at the wedding the next day, and David drove back to Nacogdoches not with her but with other friends.

Still, Pam soon forgave him. "He promised it would never happen again, and I loved him," she says. "I believed him."

The following fall, 1990, was an even headier time for David Temple. Due to his outstanding performance the year before, his picture in his full uniform was on the cover of the Lumberjacks' football guide. Posters were made of the same photo, and they were displayed all over Nacogdoches with the team's schedule and ticket information.

Despite the blowup the January before, David appeared devoted to Pam. She went to the Temples' over the summer and for holidays, and she and David talked often of marriage. But then, one Friday night in November, she called in sick at the Californian to see out-of-town friends. Late that night, a friend called Pam, telling her that David was in the Californian's lounge slow dancing with another woman, a pretty young education major named Belinda Lucas.

Since she'd called in sick, Pam couldn't go to the restaurant. She'd seen Belinda on campus, around the kinesiology building, handing out towels to the football players and going to classes, but Pam had never considered that David was interested in the other girl. The next day Pam went to David's apartment and confronted him.

"It was nothing," David told her.

Hurt and angry, Pam said that the fact that David had danced with someone else hurt her, and she asked, "Are we breaking up?"

Immediately, David became remorseful. Crying, he got down on his knees. "No. I love you. We're going to be together forever," he told her, tears running down his cheeks. "That dance didn't mean anything."

They talked, and David held her and promised he was hers. Finally, she believed him.

A little while later, the doorbell rang. When David answered, Belinda stood outside. She looked at David, looked at Pam, and asked for one of David's roommates. David got him, and Belinda went to talk to David's friend.

Wondering what it all meant but believing in David, Pam

asked, and David repeated that Belinda meant nothing to him, that he was in love with Pam. She stayed awhile, but then had to leave. Although she traveled with him to almost every football game, Pam couldn't go that night. She hadn't been able to get off work. Instead, David said they'd spend the next day, Sunday, together. Pam offered to make a picnic lunch, they kissed, and she left David's apartment believing he loved her and that all was well.

Sunday morning, Pam made the picnic lunch she'd promised and waited to hear from David. He didn't call. Finally, at nine that evening, the phone rang. "I need a break from the relationship," David said. "We can get together later, but I need some time off."

Stunned, Pam didn't know how to respond. Twenty-four hours earlier, David Temple had been on his knees, crying, and professing undying love. Instead of reminding him of what he'd said only hours earlier, she simply said, "Okay."

The days passed, and Pam waited for David to call, believing he'd come back to her. Then, two nights after the phone call, a friend told Pam that she'd seen David out dancing with Belinda. Distraught, Pam stayed home that night and cried. In the weeks that followed, she became so depressed that she sought out a college counselor, needing someone to tell her story to. She had truly believed David Temple loved her, that they would marry, and she couldn't envision life without him. She thought about the Temples, about how close she'd become to the entire family. It was as if she'd lost them all. Grieving, Pam wrote to Maureen Temple. The way Pam would reconstruct that letter years later, it was on the order of: "I'm so sad. David's decision has me absolutely devastated."

David's mother replied, and as Pam would remember it, Maureen answered: "We know that your and David's decision was mutual. We wish you the best."

When she read the letter, Pam was deeply hurt that Maureen didn't believe her when she said that David had ended it.

Looking back, Pam would say, "It was like, when David was done with me, he was done, and he wanted me gone," she says. "One minute he was in love with me, and the next he was ready to move on, and he didn't give a thought to the person he was leaving behind."

5

In her third year at SFA, Belinda was thriving. She studied and worked hard, intent on becoming a coach and a special education teacher. She dated one of her fellow workers at Brookshire Brothers for a while, but it never got serious. Mostly, Belinda was looking toward the future and enjoying her life along the way. When she and Staci Rios went to Galveston for spring break one year, they met sailors who gave them a tour of the USS *Lexington*. "We were having so much fun," says Staci. "No matter what we did, Belinda was just great to be with."

When she'd pledged a sorority, then decided it wasn't for her, Belinda became a Pi Kappa Alpha little sister, acting as a hostess at their get-togethers. It was all lighthearted and easy. Belinda had plans, and she didn't seem particularly eager to complicate her life with a boyfriend. Besides, she still looked at her parents' relationship and worried. "Belinda felt that her mom took a backseat to her dad," says Rios. "And Belinda really wanted to be her own person."

Yet, from the moment David Temple came into her life, Belinda never appeared to pause long enough to wonder, *Am I doing the right thing?*

"Belinda wanted David, too," says Moore, his roommate. "I noticed her flirting with him, and, not too long after that, she was coming around. Once they got together, he broke up with Pam, and from that point on, I rarely saw David without Belinda."

To another teammate, Belinda and David seemed a good fit. "They both loved sports, and they were such good athletes," he says. "Belinda and David just matched."

Of course, Belinda must have wondered, *Why not?* David was a catch, a star football player with his photo all over her hometown. At least at first, it wasn't the contentious David that Belinda came to know. Instead, with her, David was, as he had initially been with Pam, affectionate and gentle. "He treated her like a princess," says Staci. "I didn't like David, right off. He made fun of my East Texas accent, and he could be cruel, calling me a redneck. But he was different with Belinda. With her, he was a gentleman."

While she was initially angry with Belinda, over the years Pam Engelkirk decided she understood what happened the day Belinda showed up at David's apartment. "I don't think she would have been there, not while I was there, if she'd realized David and I were still together," says Pam. "I think that David told her he was breaking it off with me."

Whatever she knew, at least in the beginning, Belinda didn't understand the real David Temple any better than Pam had.

That fall, Ken and Maureen drove in as they always did to watch David play. The team wasn't faring as well as the previous year. A group of the starters had graduated, and the others were foundering. David played well, but he couldn't do it alone. While his son's team wasn't winning, Ken would later say he and Maureen were excited about the trip, especially when they heard that David had a new girlfriend.

At the game, Ken looked out into the stands, wondering which girl it was. He'd later say he saw "hair and green eyes dancing in the sun, and I said, beneath my breath, 'Let this be her.' " Belinda looked up, winked at him, and later Ken Temple would insist, "I was hers, hook, line, and sinker."

When they were introduced after the game, Ken asked, "Your name is Melinda?"

"No, Belinda with a B," she corrected.

"From that point on, we called her 'B,'" Maureen would say.

While they'd appeared to care for Pam, it would seem that Maureen and Ken had little if any regret about their son's decision. Perhaps they did, as Ken said, simply fall in love with Belinda on that first day. Those who knew her would have agreed that she was an exceptional young woman, pretty and high energy, low-maintenance but a force to be reckoned with. Giving them perhaps a special kinship, Belinda shared their passion for flea markets and antiques.

When angry with Pam, David resorted to screaming and physical intimidation. In the beginning, he treated Belinda gently, and as much time as Reno Moore spent with them, he never heard David and Belinda even argue. Yet there may have been more going on behind closed doors, because David was having an effect on Belinda. Over the first months Belinda and David were together, Staci saw a transformation in her friend. Around David, Belinda wasn't the same opinionated and self-assured girl.

"He was very protective of her, treated her like she was made of glass," says Rios. "He would get angry. But he was always really in control. When he was mad, he'd get really quiet and just look at her, and Belinda would back down. Whatever David wanted, she'd say, 'Okay,' and do it. This was unusual for Belinda. Before, she'd never just backed off and did what someone else wanted her to. Belinda was a strong woman, until she met David Temple."

David's parents thought that Belinda was transforming him as well.

There was a lot of excitement in the Temple family over Belinda, as Thompson would later remember it. One weekend, David called his parents talking about Belinda, saying they were getting serious. What Cindi heard from Maureen and Ken was that the new girl in David's life was good for him. Where David had difficulty keeping track of his funds before, suddenly he monitored his checkbook. He seemed easier to get along with, and his wild side was tamed. David, it appeared, was finally growing up.

"They attributed that to Belinda, that David was becoming a man," says Cindi. "She brought out the good in him. David loved Belinda, and from the start, Kenny and Maureen loved her, too."

Perhaps David's parents saw in Belinda what others would remark on later, believing she was someone strong enough to hold her own with David. When they played Monopoly with her during one visit, Belinda and David fought for properties so hard that Ken and Maureen later said they wouldn't play with them again.

That fall, at a baseball game, a friend brought a litter of dogs for sale, chows. Belinda and David played with the puppies, and Belinda picked one out, a ball of fur they named Shaka. The dog would eventually grow to look like a small bear, with long brown fur that stood at attention. Chows are a protective breed, and Shaka was especially so. From puppyhood on, he bared his teeth and growled at anyone who came near David or Belinda. "That dog scared the fire out of me," says Rios.

Although the dog lived in their apartment, David's roommate didn't trust Shaka. "Even if you knew him, it could be iffy," Moore would say. He felt more certain of that assessment after his girlfriend once crawled in through a window to retrieve something after being locked out. Although she knew the dog well, Shaka snarled at the girl, warily watching her. "She had to talk the dog down to get inside," says Moore.

That fall, Maureen and Ken met Tom and Carol for the first time. Tom was impressed with the young man his daughter was dating. "It was hard not to be, with the boy's picture all over Nacogdoches advertising the football team," he said, with a glum expression. "We'd go places, and people would get up to greet him, like he was a big shot."

The meeting between the two families seemed to go well, but when Belinda's roommate met David's family, Rios felt even more distrustful of Belinda's new boyfriend. Like their son, Maureen and Ken ribbed Rios about her accent, but she didn't take it as if they were kidding. It felt more like ridicule. At one point, Rios admitted her doubts to Belinda, telling her that the Temple family, especially David, had overblown egos. "You know, being a redneck isn't the worst thing in the world. There are worse things than talking like you're from the country," Rios said. "That boyfriend of yours is a horse's ass."

"David's just teasing you," Belinda insisted. "He really likes you."

At that point, Staci reasoned that she'd had her say and dropped it. Plus, she kept reminding herself that David and his family didn't treat Belinda the way they acted toward her. The Temples appeared to adore Belinda, and David, as contentious as Rios found him, at least on the surface was good to Belinda. "I thought maybe I was wrong," Rios would say years later. "I wanted Belinda to be happy, and she was."

Coach Graves had known the Lucas family for years and watched Belinda grow up. Although he knew how violent the middle linebacker could be on the field, when Graves saw David with her, he, too, reasoned that all was well. "They looked like they were very much in love," says the coach.

Yet Belinda's twin, like Staci Rios, questioned the wisdom of her sister's choice in a boyfriend. When Brenda met David, she was struck by the way he turned every conversation around to football. "It was all he wanted to talk about," she says. "Football was everything."

Then Brenda noticed what Staci had, the way Belinda acted around David. For the first time Brenda saw her feisty sister take a backseat to a boyfriend. If David disagreed with her, Belinda went silent. Brenda thought about how odd it was that Belinda was willing to abandon her usual confidence for a man. Yet Brenda sensed that for her sister to be with David Temple, Belinda had no other choice. "It seemed like everything had to be his way," says Brenda. "But I couldn't say anything. Belinda was in love."

When he met David at family get-togethers, Tom's brother Chuck also had misgivings. "The boy didn't talk much to us," he says. "He never seemed to fit into the family. He just never showed very much affection for anyone."

It would seem later that Chuck Lucas had sensed a problem. As the holidays passed, Staci heard David referring to the Lucas family as rednecks and white trash. Then Belinda opened up just a little about the way the relationship was developing, statements like, "Well, David flew off the handle again today." Rios spoke up, telling Belinda that all wasn't well with David Temple. But as his parents had before her, Belinda made excuses for David, saying it was near finals and he was under a lot of pressure.

"We were so young," says Rios, who years later would lament that Belinda hadn't recognized the signs. "Neither of us really understood that there was anything to be really worried about. But I just didn't like David Temple."

That Easter, Belinda made her first trip to Katy, replacing Pam at the Temple family celebration. At the annual egg throw, Belinda winged one at Ken Temple. It cracked and he had egg all over, but he was left rolling in laughter. In his flamboyant manner of speech, Ken would later say Belinda "exploded into our lives," and that "the Temples must have had a void and she fell into it, and immediately everyone was drawn to her and it seemed to be reciprocal with our family and Belinda."

Ken Temple, Brian and Jill would later say, told the truth. Belinda did move easily and eagerly into her place as a member of the Temple family. By then, there were rifts in the Lucas family, and the children weren't gathering on holidays. "They just weren't coming around that much," says Carol. "Tom and me, we didn't understand why."

Her own family was important to Belinda, but there was

a distance between them, more than physical, emotional. In contrast, at least on the surface, David's family appeared close and loving, the embodiment of the traditional Norman Rockwell family, the type of homespun happiness Belinda had grown up longing for.

"David looked like the All-American football hero, and his family seemed like they had a lot to offer Belinda," says Jill. "She talked a lot about the Temples, how they were such a close family, and that there wasn't the strain her own family felt. At first, Brian and I were happy for her, grateful that she felt so loved."

Describing those early days, Ken Temple would say, "Belinda was there for keeps. We did everything for Belinda that we would have done for a naturally born daughter, and we loved her unconditionally and without hesitation."

By then, the youngest of the trio of Temple sons was also in Nacogdoches. Kevin and his girlfriend, Rebecca, a petite woman with long dark hair, moved into SFA dorms. They'd been dating since high school. Taller than David and with a mop of dark hair, Kevin circulated over to David's apartment often. Before long, Belinda was doing Kevin's laundry along with David's, and making them all quesadillas for dinners. They went to happy hours at the La Hacienda restaurant, laughed and talked. The daughter of an engineer and a schoolteacher, Becky and Belinda grew close. As her months with David passed, Belinda spent less time with her family and friends. Instead Belinda, as Pam had before her, devoted her free time to David. She was at his apartment often, where they grilled outside on the patio with Moore and his girlfriend. Or they went out dancing. "They both really enjoyed that," says Moore. "Two-stepping at country western bars."

Coming off their most successful season, the Lumberjacks only won one game that year. Months after their games ended, in March of 1991, Belinda and David were on a basketball court together, playing in a coed intramural game. David later told Moore that a player on the opposing team,

Erick Buck, had cursed in front of Belinda. Buck would describe it differently.

It began, he says, when a referee called a foul against David.

"Good call," Buck said to the ref, as he walked toward the foul line. Seconds later, from out of nowhere, someone clubbed him on the head, knocking Buck out. At 160 pounds, Buck was 60 pounds lighter than the man who hit him, David Temple.

An ambulance was called to transport Buck to the emergency room. After he woke up, a university policeman dropped in to see him, to ask if he wanted to press charges. It was then that Buck learned his assailant was one of the university's top football players. The officer suggested that if Buck let it slide, David would pay all Buck's medical expenses.

More worried about finances than getting even, Buck, who had a cut under one eye from the attack, agreed, and no charges were ever filed.

That summer, David circulated to some of the pro camps to try out for an NFL team. He wasn't chosen. Again, his coach, Lynn Graves, would say, "David just wasn't tall enough for the NFL."

The following fall, 1991, David was featured in the Lumberjack television commercials, touting ticket sales. The team again would not have a good year, but David won an honorable mention as an All-American linebacker.

Meanwhile, the more Tom and Carol saw David, the better they felt about him. He was polite with them, saying, "Yes, sir," and, "Yes, ma'am." Brenda was still less certain. When she saw the Temples, "they always acted as if everyone else was below them. And Belinda was spending more time with them, so I had to see them to see my sister."

Her family and friends had no doubt that Belinda was taken with David and the whole Temple family. "Belinda always did everything one hundred percent, and she loved the same way," says Rios. Of course, she had to admit that

David couldn't have been more engaging with Belinda, or sweeter. He'd call her late at night, sometimes just to hang on the phone for hours and talk. That he was a celebrity on campus must have made Belinda feel special. "People would say, 'Oh, you're dating *that* football player?' They were impressed. In Nacogdoches, people fawned over David, and David was good-looking. He could have had almost any girl, and he chose Belinda."

Rios continued to express concern when Belinda mentioned David's temper. Yet Belinda shrugged it off. "I can handle him," she said. "I know when to back off."

That's what Belinda did with Tony Luna, when they happened upon each other at a shopping mall. Three years younger than she, Tony, the kid brother of Belinda's good friend Angie, had a crush on Belinda. Yet the closest they'd ever come to a date was Belinda's senior year at Nacogdoches High, when she needed an escort for homecoming. Angie asked Tony to escort Belinda. He agreed and on that night brought Belinda a white flower corsage. "I only got to dance with her twice, and then she danced the rest of the night with a football player," he'd say. "She looked beautiful."

That day, years later, their paths crossed at the Beall's Department Store in the mall, when Tony was home on leave from the navy. Belinda ran up to him, giving him a big hug. She seemed delighted to see him, but they talked for only a few minutes before she became fidgety. "I need to go," she said. "My boyfriend is here somewhere, and he's the jealous type."

Saying nothing more, Belinda hurriedly turned and walked away.

If David was already attempting to control Belinda, she didn't reveal any concerns to her parents or Brenda, or confide in her friends. That November, David went to the hardware store where Carol worked, now that her children were grown, and said he had something he wanted to talk to her and Tom about at their home.

"It's a good thing," he said.

That evening, David Temple, spit and polished, looking every bit the All-American he was, sat down with Carol and Tom and announced, "I'd like your permission to ask Belinda to marry me."

Both Belinda's parents were impressed. How many young men took that formal, even old-fashioned, step before proposing? It seemed from all outward appearances that Belinda had found herself an exceptional young man.

"I thought he must be all right," said Carol.

"I figured Belinda was a smart gal, college educated and all," says Tom, looking dejectedly at his hands. Shaking his head with the painful wisdom of hindsight, he says, "Belinda was a grown woman, and I didn't think she'd pick the wrong man."

In David Temple's grand style of courtship, the proposal would be memorable. He seemed to have a penchant for showmanship, especially with the women in his life.

That October, after a game, David walked Belinda out onto the football field to the fifty-yard line. His friends were stationed in a ring around the perimeter, and on his command, they turned on their car headlights, sending funnels of bright light through the darkness. In the convergence of the headlights, David Temple dropped to one knee on the site of his greatest accomplishments and asked for her hand in marriage. On her left ring finger, he slipped an impressive diamond engagement ring. "I told her how much I loved her and asked her to marry me," David would later recount.

Crying, Belinda said, "Yes."

When she called to tell her twin, Brenda was excited for Belinda. Although Brenda had misgivings about David, Belinda couldn't have sounded happier, going into details about the romantic evening and David's chivalrous proposal. And not too long after, Belinda called an old high-school friend and suggested lunch. That afternoon, Belinda showed off her diamond and cooed about the excitement of David's romantic proposal.

The notice ran in the Nacogdoches newspaper on November 3, 1991. "Mr. and Mrs. Tom Lucas announce the engagement and approaching marriage of their daughter, Belinda Tracie Lucas to Mr. David Mark Temple."

That winter, David Temple's SFA football career ended on a grand note, leaving with three all-time Lumberjack records: most tackles, at 492; most unassisted tackles, at 309; and most assisted tackles, at 183. David had worked hard, played hard, and he left behind accomplishments that would remain unsurpassed at the university for decades to come.

The first view of what the Temple family was really like, perhaps, came during the wedding preparations. The Lucases booked their church, the North Street Church of Christ, and the date was set for the coming winter break, since David and Belinda both had one more semester ahead before graduation. Although the church didn't have music during services, Kevin, the best man, made a CD and brought equipment to play it on, and the Temples arranged the flowers, even helped pick out Belinda's dress. Carol did make Belinda's veil, a crown of flowers she wore on the back of her head, and a throwaway bouquet of silk flowers.

"The Temples descended on Nacogdoches in force and took over," says Rios, one of the bridesmaids. "From the beginning, they overpowered the Lucases and ran the show."

At Tom and Carol's church, the wedding party and guests gathered. It wasn't a large crowd, but the seats filled. As maid of honor, Brenda wore a dress covered with blue roses, a light blue ribbon cinched around her waist, and had her dark hair styled high and falling around her shoulders, as she carried two pink roses. In the photos taken that day, she stands beside her sister, smiling and happy, looking content that the life that waited ahead for both of them would fulfill their dreams.

Yet Brenda was overshadowed, as she should have been, by the bride.

In her white satin dress with a tight bodice and puffy, ribbon-capped sleeves, Belinda was breathtaking. She let her golden brown curls fall around her shoulders, as her veil fanned out from a ring of flowers set back on her head. As Tom walked her down the aisle, Belinda carried a large bouquet of pink and white roses.

Dressed in a black tux with a white rose boutonnière, David waited for her. Beside him stood Ken Temple in his role as the minister, ready to preside over the union and bring Belinda officially into his family. At the time, there seemed no doubt that Belinda was getting all she wanted. She looked radiant. On that day she married a man who professed to deeply love her, a hero on the football field who'd do anything to protect her. They planned a family that would complete her life. Even her in-laws loved her. Belinda would become part of the Temple clan, a big, boisterous, seemingly happy family. On that day, when David and Belinda took their vows, she looked confident and prepared for all life could bring.

As he watched the wedding, Brian, Belinda's oldest brother, held his wife, Jill's hand, and wondered if Belinda was making a good decision. He still had nagging doubts about David Temple. To him, his new brother-in-law had a football star's aloofness and a jock's mentality, where everything was centered on him. "Belinda was so sheltered, so innocent," says Brian. "I thought David Temple might overpower her."

6

All of us knew that Belinda loved David with all of her heart," says Staci Rios. "Belinda never did anything halfway."

At first it appeared, at least from the outside, that marriage didn't substantially change Belinda and David's lives. They graduated from SFA that May with degrees in physical education. Belinda had a second major in special education.

Another graduate that spring was David's old girlfriend, Pam. The night before the ceremony that marked the completion of their degrees, she went out with friends and ended up at a club where David had a part-time job as a bouncer, a good fit for his football-player physique. Spotting him in the crowd, she walked up and said hello, asking if he was well.

"I'm fine," he said.

Pam asked about his parents and family, and then, because she truly believed she had to know: "Are you happy?"

David had been married to Belinda for five months, and he didn't hesitate. He smiled at her and said, "Yes, I am."

The next day, after the graduation ceremony, Pam left SFA and Nacogdoches behind. She cried for the entire three hours in the car, but when she arrived home in Houston, she dried her tears and never cried over David Temple again. "He was my first love," she says. "But I was starting over."

Their diplomas in hand, David and Belinda were also making decisions about the future. Although he told friends he felt eager to get a job, Belinda wanted to continue on for one more year, to get a master's degree in education. He agreed, decided to work on one as well, and they spent a year living in SFA's married student housing. In the same town with the Lucases, they saw them infrequently. When the entire family gathered, Belinda's Uncle Chuck still felt uncomfortable around David. "I thought he had a hard time relaxing around us," he says. "Belinda seemed happy, but David looked uptight."

Brian, too, continued to have doubts. When he went deer hunting with his dad, his brother Brent, and David, Brian listened to his new brother-in-law talk. David boasted about dove hunting in Katy, claiming that he'd once bagged his limit with one box of shotgun shells. "That was fifteen birds with twenty-five shells," says Brian. "Good shooting. But it felt like he was just bragging, having to be the big shot who was showing the rest of us up."

That year during grad school, Belinda and David worked for the university's intramural sports program. Their studies were harder than they'd been for their undergrad degrees, and more than once Belinda confided in Brenda that David was having trouble. "Belinda said she had to help him with his papers so he'd get through," says Brenda. "She said he was out coaching, and she was the one doing most of his work."

When Reno Moore stopped in at his old roommate's apartment, Belinda and David looked happy. And the Lucases never questioned that Belinda had made a good decision. "David had really charmed Belinda," said Carol. "You could tell that she was just all excited about being married."

That New Year's Eve, Belinda and David went to the Lucases house for a small party. As far as Tom and Carol were concerned, everything went well that night, and David appeared to have fun. Belinda's parents would later say that they never thought it would be the last time their son-in-law would enter their house. "From that point on, he just never came," said Carol. "When we saw her, which wasn't often, Belinda came alone."

Yet, Belinda had her eyes firmly focused on the future, a future that included David and starting a family. That spring break, she went to visit her brother Barry when his son was born in Amarillo. She held the infant in her arms and talked wistfully about how she wanted a baby of her own. But it wasn't yet time for Belinda and David, their lives still unsettled, torn between work and school.

The following year, Belinda finished her master's and David was well on his way, when a call came in from one of his old Katy High School football coaches. Don Clayton was moving to the town of Livingston, Texas, to take over the head coach's slot at the high school, and he needed assistant coaches to flesh out his staff. "I felt his intensity as a player, he'd bring to coaching," says Clayton.

David took the job, and he and Belinda moved to Goodrich, just south of Livingston, where they rented a home she furnished with flea-market antiques. Belinda called Brian's wife, Jill, excited about the treasures, recounting how she refinished the furniture to a glossy shine.

For the most part, David was the same as always, meticulously groomed and carefully attired in his Tommy Hilfiger and Nike jogging suits, everything matching, down to his shoes and socks. At home, if football or any sport was on, David was into the game, analyzing every play. If not, he surfed the channels, often settling on a crime show, especially anything with a forensics angle. "He watched those shows all the time," says Brenda. "He loved them."

That fall, Belinda took a special-education teaching slot at a nearby middle school, and David went to work at the high school with Clayton, coaching the inside linebackers on the football team and working with the kids on the track team.

A little more than a year after their marriage, at least from the outside, David and Belinda looked happy.

Although David didn't see Tom and Carol often, he spent time with Brian and Jill. On occasion, they drove down from their home outside Dallas, and David grilled steaks in the backyard. Belinda, at such times, appeared excited and happy to have family close.

Brenda, too, came to visit off and on. Belinda had begun buying Coca Cola memorabilia, and soon Brenda was scouting for miniature trucks and buildings, and plaques with the Coca Cola logo. As they built their collections, this, too, would be something the sisters shared, kibitzing about their latest finds and helping each other track down special pieces. Although they saw each other infrequently, the sisters still had "the twin thing," as they called it, a special connection they credited with having shared their mother's womb. More often than not, when one called, the other said, "I was just going to call you." Sometimes they'd both get busy signals only to determine that they'd been calling each other at the exact same time. "It was strange," says Brenda. "We laughed about it a lot."

Despite their special connection, Brenda didn't sense what was actually going on in Belinda's life. Later, she would judge that a pattern was already forming, one where Belinda didn't confide in her family. Brenda, who Belinda still called "Shrimpie," had health problems, suffering from a stomach problem that stress worsened. There was something else, Jill and Brian would later suspect. They wondered if Belinda's pride kept her from admitting to her family that the marriage to David, although barely past the honeymoon phase, wasn't going well. "Belinda so wanted the whole thing, the happy home with the loving husband and kids. She was determined to have that," says Jill. "Maybe that's why Belinda didn't want us to know that they weren't getting along."

As they approached their second anniversary, Belinda did complain to friends that David was rarely home. He left early in the morning for work, and during football season, she rarely saw him. Even when the season ended, she told her old roommate Staci Rios, David didn't make it home many nights until well after dark. "I think David, after the marriage, became more himself around Belinda," says Rios.

When Staci visited, Belinda admitted that she wondered if David was having an affair. Belinda had no evidence, but he'd become progressively distant and came home less often. Then, almost immediately after she said it, Belinda contradicted herself. "Oh, I'm sure I'm just imagining things," she said. "He's just busy. That's all that's going on."

"Right or wrong, she loved him," Rios said years later. "Belinda knew David had his faults, but she loved him enough that she wasn't going to admit them, even to herself."

One year after they moved to Livingston, Belinda and David packed up all they'd acquired and moved again. A new high school was opening in Katy, and Don Clayton was leaving Livingston to take a job as an assistant coach. He didn't have a slot in Katy for David, but Clayton didn't want to leave him behind in Livingston. So he made a few phone calls and found an assistant coaching position opening at Hastings High School in the Alief Independent School District, between Houston and Katy. The head coach there was looking for an assistant to work with the football team's defensive players, David's expertise. With Clayton's recommendation, David got the slot.

Alief was interested in both David and Belinda, and that fall David began at Hastings, coaching football and track and teaching physical education, while Belinda signed on with the district's Albright Middle School as a special-education teacher and a girls' volleyball and basketball coach. They rented a house west of the school, south of I-10 on the outskirts of Katy, in one of the newer subdivisions that line I-10. One story, beige brick, with an attached garage, the house on Comstock Springs Drive was in the Cimarron Parkway area, just a fifteen-minute drive from the house David grew up in. Maureen and Ken were undoubtedly delighted that their middle son was moving nearby. By then, their oldest, Darren, was living outside Dallas, and Kevin, the youngest of the Temple boys, was graduating from SFA. Before long he'd move to Houston and marry Becky, his longtime girl-friend. In Houston, Kevin took a slot as an investigator for an insurance company.

The Alief Independent School District, with its student body of 45,000, covers a 36.6-square-mile section of the Houston suburbs and part of unincorporated Harris County. With more than 4,000 students, Hastings High School, where David began that fall as a coach, is part of a sprawling com-plex of facilities that include the Alief ISD headquarters, two elementary schools and even a second high school. On any given day, nearly 10,000 students attend classes within the immediate area. The district stadium, Crump, is a massive facility, one all the district's high schools call home field. Hasting's school colors are black and gold, and the stadium is a short walk from the campus, the pathway marked by painted gold bear paw prints.

Now that they were living in Katy, David and Belinda attended the First Baptist Church with his parents. David and Belinda weren't regulars, but went on holidays and off and on throughout the year. And they joined in the Temple family's Sunday tradition, afternoon gatherings with the family. Afterward, Maureen packed up leftovers for David and Belinda, making sure they had enough so that Belinda wouldn't have to cook on Monday night. "When they came, they still looked so happy," a family member would say later. "In the beginning, they were, I think, but over time, that changed."

As coaches, the days were long for both Belinda and David, sometimes well into the evenings. Still, David wasn't the type to let any disarray in his life. His hair, everything, looked precise. The coaches shared a bathroom with a shower, and David stocked it with not just the usual sham-poo and soap, but also powders, colognes, a razor and gels. At home, Belinda ironed even his T-shirts, and he brought extras to school to change into after his frequent showers, along with extra warm-up suits and jeans.

To the student body at Hastings, their new football coach appeared to keep to himself. "He wasn't friendly at all," says one. "He was a really intense guy. And when he didn't like something one of us did, he got right up to us, got into our space."

Coach Bill Norwood, one of David's colleagues at Hastings, would remember how the young football coach sometimes "lost it" with the kids. "He'd get too far out of line, and we'd have to reel him back in," says Norwood. "He never understood that his team was made up of high-school kids who made mistakes."

At times, Norwood wondered about Belinda. He noticed how she acted differently without David around—outgoing—but when the coaches and their wives went out as couples, Belinda seemed quiet. "I rarely saw her smile," he remembers. "She looked unhappy."

Yet, to most people, at least from the outside, the Temple marriage continued to look idyllic. The house on Comstock Springs Drive was neatly kept. "Everything was in its place. David insisted on it," says a friend. David and Belinda worked together on the yard, and it was precisely trimmed and always freshly mowed. At first they knew no one in the area, but, before long, Belinda met her new neighbors. It was a friendly place, one where people waved as they drove by in their cars and where neighbors stopped to talk. Belinda was like that, too. At times, they stood outside talking, in one of the yards. Some dropped over to sit in lawn chairs with Belinda in the driveway. She was friendly, talking about coaching and teaching. Gradually, she opened up with a few in the neighborhood, voicing her disappointment at David's long hours. One noticed that Belinda kept an eye on her watch, hurrying to go inside before David got home, saying, "I need to make dinner."

In contrast, David ignored the neighbors, barely acknowledging them, which led the neighborhood men to see David as distant. The only ones he talked to were the family who lived directly next door, the Fournerats. A little older than Belinda and David, Sheree Fournerat worked full time in an office, and her husband, who'd played football in high school, traveled. They had two youngsters, Evan and Shelby.

"I think maybe David talked to me because of the way I am," Sheree would say, with a hearty laugh. From the beginning, she went out of her way to approach David, almost forcing him to acknowledge her. Before long, Sheree, her two youngsters, and David and Belinda were going to James Coney Island, a hot dog restaurant, on Wednesday nights, when children ate free. When Belinda discovered she was pregnant in late 1994, she knocked on Sheree's door. Belinda and David had discussed names for the little boy she was carrying and wanted to name him Evan, after David's maternal grandfather, William Elvis Evans. Since Sheree's son was already named Evan, Belinda was concerned. "David and I wanted to ask if it would bother you," Belinda said.

Sheree insisted it wouldn't, that they'd be delighted to have another Evan in the neighborhood, and the two women laughed, talking about how they'd call one boy "Big Evan" and the other "Little Evan."

As the months passed, it was easy for Sheree to see how delighted Belinda and David were about the coming baby. They debated the wisdom of buying new furniture for the nursery or getting it secondhand. When they found furniture at a flea market, Belinda and David worked in the garage, sanding it down and refinishing it for their son, who was expected in April of the coming year.

By then, Brenda was living in Kansas, but she sent gifts for the nephew Belinda carried, and waited for news as the date neared. Preparing, Belinda and David bought a small football uniform with a cover for his diaper. The nursery was ready when, on the evening of April 13, 1995, Belinda went into labor. David wasn't home yet, and she called his parents to take her to the hospital. David arrived an hour later, and Evan Brett Temple was born at 2 A.M. He weighed seven pounds, fourteen ounces, and was 20½ inches long. The announcement the proud parents sent to friends and family had a train pictured on it and read: "It's a boy!" Evan, it said, was their first draft pick and "their little linebacker." When Belinda called to tell Brenda about the baby's birth, their twin connection kicked in again, Brenda immediately guessing the time and saying she'd woken up the night before at that precise moment and felt something important had happened. When Brenda visited not long after, she saw how happy Belinda was, holding her baby son, talking to him, kissing his soft head. "Evan was so important to her," says Brenda. "I've never seen Belinda more excited about anything than she was about him."

David appeared happy, too, but Brenda thought he acted oddly. He'd never been overly friendly, but now he kept her at arm's length. "I had the feeling he didn't want me around," she says. "I made a point to visit because of Belinda, but I didn't feel like David wanted me there. We kind of tolerated each other."

Two weeks after Evan's birth, Belinda sent Jill and Brian photos of the new baby along with a note: "We would love for y'all to come visit anytime. We could get some shrimp and do them on the grill. David has a student whose dad is a shrimper. Love, David, Belinda, and Evan."

Despite the invitation, it seemed to Jill that once Belinda moved to Katy, all she talked about was the Temple family. David and Belinda spent every holiday with his family, and nearly every Sunday afternoon. When David and Belinda traveled to Dallas for a birthday party for Jill and Brian's son, David wanted to leave an hour after they had arrived. Later, a friend mentioned David and said, "There's something odd about that guy."

That spring and summer, Belinda spent more time outside. She whipped through the streets on in-line skates behind Evan's stroller, trying to get back in shape after the pregnancy. When Sheree saw her skating, she shook her head at Belinda, laughed and said, "You've got to be nuts!"

"Well, I put on a little weight while I was pregnant," Belinda confided.

"Doesn't every woman?" Sheree asked.

"David doesn't like heavy women," Belinda said.

Sheree looked at her young neighbor. At twenty-six, even so soon after the birth, Belinda had a firm, athletic body, and she was pretty and full of life. "He doesn't have one," Sheree said. But Belinda didn't appear to believe her as she skated away.

At other times, Belinda sat in a lawn chair in the driveway. She chained Shaka up in the front yard or to the backboard that held the basketball hoop, and had Evan in the stroller beside her. Jackie Cerame, who lived across the street, had a child just a little older than Evan. Some afternoons, Jackie passed time with Belinda as they watched the children play. David was rarely around, and gradually, Belinda began confiding in Jackie, talking about the problems in her marriage. "David doesn't want me to see my family," she told her. "I feel as if I need to, but he doesn't like them, and he doesn't want Evan around them."

Jackie wasn't sure what to respond, other than to say that Belinda had the right to see her own parents. "I think it's good for Evan to have both families," Jackie said. Belinda agreed, but then said again that David didn't like it when she visited. At such times, Belinda talked wistfully of her family, missing them.

Jackie wasn't the only one who heard about the troubles in the Temple marriage. Not long after they became friends, Belinda revealed her disappointment to Sheree as well. "David says he's not comfortable around my family," Belinda told her one afternoon. Sheree and Belinda talked, and over time the older woman noticed changes in the young mother. When they first met, Belinda cleaved willingly to the Temples, talking of them often and saying how much she admired them. But as time passed and their lives continued to be centered on David's family, Belinda sounded less enamored, calling Maureen "Mother Temple."

"It wasn't always said with affection," says Sheree. "I think Belinda grew tired of spending every holiday and vacation with them."

If David kept Belinda and Evan away from the Lucases, their daughter made a point of not losing contact. Nearly every Sunday, she called. "Mops and Pops, it's Number Five," she'd say happily. Then she rambled on about what was new in her life, especially Evan's latest accomplishment, his first words and the funny things children do that bring smiles to their grandparents. What Belinda rarely talked about was David. "She didn't mention him, and when we asked, she just said, 'David's fine,'" remembers Carol.

That fall, Evan was in day care and Belinda was back at work. At school, she told stories about her infant son, putting his picture up in her classroom. But there was no doubt that Belinda also loved teaching. She joked with her students, urging them to study, ribbing them when they didn't bring in their work. She was the teacher with the most elaborate Halloween costumes and the one who shouted the loudest at pep rallies. Loving music, Belinda broke into song at any moment. When OMC's "How Bizarre" played on the radio, her fellow teachers laughed as Belinda sang along with her East Texas drawl, pronouncing the refrain, "How bizine."

While they didn't see each other often, David's Katy High School teammate and friend Mike Fleener and his wife came to the house a couple of times. Fleener took an immediate liking to Belinda. Although others noticed that Belinda was quieter around David, she still had that spark about her, a joy for life. While they were there, David locked Shaka in the bedroom, but the entire time, the dog snarled, making Fleener eager to leave. "I was afraid of that dog," says Fleener. "We didn't stay long."

On Comstock Springs, Shaka was well known among the neighbors. The children loved Belinda and congregated around her in the driveway when she was outside, wanting to talk and play with Evan, but they gave the dog a wide berth, and their parents watched the chow carefully, wary of it.

That fall, David worked outside one afternoon with Shaka chained in the front yard. A friendly lab mix from down the block roamed free, walking the street, and as a group of neighbors watched, the lab, tail wagging, ran up to Shaka as if wanting to play. Immediately, the dark brown chow lunged at the other dog, Shaka latching his powerful jaws onto the lab's neck and shaking it.

Remarkably, David just watched. He didn't shout or try to separate the dogs, and Jackie Cerame even thought that David looked amused.

"Call your dog off," one neighbor shouted as they ran toward David. At that, David appeared to snap out of a trance. He moved forward and pulled Shaka off the other dog as a neighbor helped the lab escape. The lab wasn't badly hurt, but talk of the incident filtered through the neighborhood, fueling even more rumors that the Temple's dog was dangerous and not to be trusted.

In most ways, Sheree Fournerat saw David as a good neighbor. When her son, Evan, was eleven or so, he made a game out of breaking the spotlights on the eaves of David and Belinda's house with a BB gun. Although he could have, David didn't get angry. Instead he talked to the boy, explaining how dangerous the shattered glass was, especially to little Evan when he played outside. Sheree thought at the time that David must have been like that with his students, kind and patient. She found it difficult to reconcile what she saw in David with what she heard from a niece who attended David's school, Hastings. "Coach Temple is mean," the girl said.

Jackie Cerame came to the same conclusion as Sheree's niece, but for a different reason. She hadn't seen David with his students, but she heard him yelling at Belinda. Out on the street talking to a neighbor or working in her yard, she saw Belinda drive up in her Toyota, open the garage door, and pull inside. Before Belinda got Evan out of his car seat, David was at the door leading from the house to the garage, furious, shouting at her to get inside.

Cerame couldn't see Belinda's face as she walked into the house, but from the tone of David Temple's voice she knew he was in a rage.

At other times, when Cerame talked to Belinda out on the driveway, David stuck his head out the door and ordered her inside. Belinda immediately said good-bye, and turned and left. "He seemed quick to anger, and she'd do what he said," Cerame says. "She didn't argue with him. Not ever that I saw."

At times, Sheree knew Belinda had to have been furious with David, and once or twice she heard the frustration in her neighbor's voice. "Well, duh," David said, mocking Belinda about something or other, Sheree never quite sure what.

"Sure, David. You're always right," Belinda replied, venturing no further. Sheree never thought of Belinda as a pushover, but she saw the cold, stern look in David's eyes.

"I could practically see steam coming out of Belinda's ears," Sheree would say years later. "It wasn't my husband, but if it had been, I'd have been furious."

That December, David and Belinda decorated the house and put deer outlined in white lights in the yard. A handful of David's football players came to help, as they did off and on with the yard in the summer and fall with the mowing and trimming. Sheree had always assumed that the boys did it because they wanted to, maybe to curry favor with their coach, but that December, she heard one boy grumble and refer to working at Coach Temple's house as punishment. The holidays came and Belinda convinced her brothers and sister to buy Carol a mother's ring with all their birthstones. Yet, she saw her parents less and less often. She told no one in the family that David was arguing with her about visiting Tom and Carol, but no one doubted that Belinda wanted to see them. By then, Brian and Jill were spending little time with the Lucases, and Belinda told Jill in no uncertain terms that she thought that was wrong. "She really came down hard on me for not going to Brian's parents' house," says

Jill. "Belinda wanted us all to be one big happy family, and we weren't. And that disappointed her greatly."

When David was at a coaching camp over the holiday break, Belinda took advantage of his absence to drive to Nacogdoches to spend one night with her parents. Carol and Tom played with Evan, getting to know their little grandson, but the next afternoon, Belinda and the baby were in the car and on their way back to Katy.

Perhaps not surprising, with an infant son to care for, Belinda's priorities had changed. Winter faded into spring, and she tired of the long hours coaching after classes ended for the day. That spring, Belinda called Coach Clayton in Katy, who'd helped her and David find the Livingston and Alief jobs, and told him that she was shopping for a position without coaching responsibilities. Clayton asked around, then called Belinda and suggested she apply at Katy High, where the district had an opening for a content mastery teacher, to tutor students in math and science.

Thin, with short dark blond hair, Debbie Berger was one of the Katy High staff members who interviewed Belinda that spring. "She absolutely blew us away," says Debbie, who worked in the department with the job opening. "Belinda was so full of life, she radiated it. We knew the kids would love her."

There was only one concern. Debbie had taught at Katy High a decade earlier, when David Temple had been a student. So had many of the other teachers at the high school, and they hadn't forgotten him. "When she told us whom she was married to, I thought that couldn't be right. People grow up and change, but I thought, *Oh, my gosh, no*," says Debbie, who'd known the football team's star linebacker to be a bully. "He had such a bad reputation, it really took me back. But Belinda acted so proud to be his wife, and she was so strong, so great. She was perfect for the job, and I thought maybe he'd changed."

In the spring of 1996, Belinda gave her notice at Alief and prepared to start the next fall at David's alma mater,

Katy High School. A few months later, two people entered the Temples' lives who'd play roles in the drama to come: Quinton Harlan, a tall, handsome high-school coach with a laid-back manner, and his wife, Tammey, a pretty, petite, dark-haired spitfire. The Harlans would become David and Belinda's best friends, but in the end Tammey would feel compelled to pull away to try to save her marriage, and Quinton would find himself entrapped in the vortex of a sensational and brutal murder.

7

I liked Belinda right off. We just automatically clicked, and we got close," says Tammey Harlan, fidgeting ever so slightly in a chair in her cozy kitchen. "It was tough not to like Belinda. Everyone did. She was just great to be around, more fun than it seemed possible. We were both coaches' wives, alone a lot while our husbands worked, and we became like family."

Quinton and Tammey met during high school at Wharton, a small city with a quaint downtown on the Colorado River, southwest of Houston. Tammey moved to Wharton from Tennessee but integrated quickly, becoming a cheerleader and homecoming queen. They'd married in 1990, two years earlier than David and Belinda, and both went on to be teachers. When they moved to Katy, the Harlans had a toddler named Sydnee, a year older than Evan, and Tammey was pregnant with their second daughter. A few years older than Tammey, Quinton towered over his diminutive wife. Tammey, with dark hair and eyes, was just four feet eleven and, when not pregnant, weighed a little more than a hundred pounds, but like Belinda, Tammey was vivacious and strong willed.

The first time they met Belinda and David was that summer, in 1996, days after moving to Katy, when the Harlans dropped in at Pappasitos, a cavernous, loud, brightly decorated Mexican restaurant that serves platter-size portions of highly seasoned chicken, beef, and shrimp, to wrap in warm flour tortillas, alongside pico de gallo and bowls of pinto beans. That day, David and Belinda were at the restaurant with other Hastings coaches and their spouses, including the head coach, Bobby Stuart, and his wife, Kay. The Harlans recognized Stuart and stopped over to say hello. Quinton hadn't yet started at the school, and Stuart walked him and Tammey around the table, making introductions.

The following week, Quinton and David worked with the new crop of football players at the high school, and Belinda invited Tammey and Sydnee over so the little ones could play. From that point on, the two women and their children bonded, sharing dinners on evenings their husbands worked late, taking the kids to Discovery Zone and the park, to the movies and McDonald's. Before long, the Harlans joined David, Belinda, Evan, and their next door neighbors, the Fournerats, for Wednesday-night, kids-eat-free hot dogs at James Coney Island.

When the Harlans, who'd bought a house just five minutes away, came over to Belinda and David's on the weekends, David had everything planned, from the time they were to arrive to when he put the hamburgers on the grill, to the exact time they were expected to play games. Belinda seemed to take her husband's need to be in control in stride, never complaining. At times, when the men shot hoops on the driveway, she left Evan with Tammey and Sydnee and played ball, as competitive as any of the men under the net.

Afterward, the deck of cards came out. The children fast asleep, the four adults gathered around the kitchen table, and they played teams, the women against the men. Off and on, David talked about Katy, referring to it as "my town," and acting as if he had an exceptional claim to celebrity within the city limits. Belinda, too, sounded proud to be a Temple in a place where the name made her feel special. Most nights, Tammey and Belinda won the card game, celebrating loudly with high fives and catcalls. Afterward, on the way home, Quinton and Tammey joked about the Temples' *Leave it to Beaver* lifestyle, the way David insisted the house had to be spotless, all of his clothes immaculate, and Evan dressed just so, like his father, in name brands only, with everything matching.

While David had quirks, initially they both liked him. Tammey found him charismatic, a strong personality with a dry sense of humor. "There was something about David," she'd say years later, as if still trying to understand. "He was this big, broad-shouldered guy, with a quiet, kind of a soft manner, but this incredible intensity. He was able to persuade people to do things they wouldn't normally do, especially women, and he was all about appearances."

As she got to know them better, Tammey discovered that David had his rules, edicts he passed down to Belinda, to uphold the proper image. One was that Belinda was only allowed to shop at certain stores, the more upscale ones. Like his ironed T-shirts and immaculate yard, being seen in the right stores cultivated a prosperous image. David hated his truck, the 1991 blue Chevy Silverado pickup he'd had since graduating from SFA. When they traded Belinda's old Corolla late that summer for a new red Isuzu Rodeo, David drove it whenever he could, only taking the truck to work. He kept the old Chevy immaculate inside and out, but he complained often and loudly, saying he wanted a new truck. That was one of the only subjects Tammey heard her friend argue back about. Whenever David brought the subject up, Belinda reminded him that they were saving to buy a house, and they couldn't afford a home of their own and two car payments.

If Tammey sometimes felt something wasn't entirely right about David, she couldn't put her finger on what. At least on the surface, he was charming and amusing. He was a great father, devoted to Evan. When they went out as a family, Tammey marveled at the way David had Belinda drive so that he could sit in the backseat next to Evan's car seat. Protective of the boy, David didn't want his son sitting alone. It seemed odd behavior to Tammey, but she shrugged it off when she realized that Belinda didn't seem to be bothered by David's actions. In fact, to Tammey it appeared that Belinda adored her husband. "She had him on a pedestal," says Tammey. "It was David this and David that. She told him everything. It was like they had this perfect home life, only later did I realize it was all a façade."

Looking back, Tammey would grow angry recounting what she saw in the Temples' marriage. "David needed everything to be perfect," she says, her dark eyes passionate. "The perfect little house, perfect yard, perfect family. And Belinda bought totally into it."

At school, Quinton and David worked closely, both training the team's defensive players, Quinton the secondary and David the defensive backs. From the beginning, David was a puzzle. When they worked on strategy for the games, Quinton quickly learned that David was highly competitive, insisting that every idea be his own. Before long, to make the process easier, Quinton planted ideas and let David believe he'd come up with them.

That fall, Belinda burst into Katy High School and quickly became part of the fabric of the faculty and the student body. "After Belinda was there for a month, it was hard to imagine the school without her," says Debbie Berger.

Along with Berger, Belinda worked in a suite of rooms with Cindy O'Brien, a petite, motherly woman with a high voice and a soft manner. All of them were in the content mastery department, where Belinda tutored thirty-five students over the course of the day, those who needed help with math and science. Debbie did the same in social studies, while Cindy tutored English. With Belinda's perkiness, bright green eyes and wide smile, along with her soft drawl, Debbie and Cindy started calling Belinda their East Texas Beauty Queen. They laughed and joked, and before long Debbie and Cindy, who were older than Belinda, were treating her like an unofficial daughter.

It would seem that many found it easy to want to be with Belinda.

When the faculty needed a volunteer to head up the Sunshine Club, the ad hoc organization that sent flowers when one of the staff had a baby or suffered an illness or a loss, Belinda volunteered, jumping in with both feet, taking the job over with her characteristic enthusiasm. She kept up with the faculty, sending flowers and cards, but also made it a point to e-mail daily pep talks and silly jokes, often humorous takes on children and teaching. Some came to rely on the morning e-mails to brighten their days.

To many it seemed that Belinda had boundless zest. Another teacher worked with the hall monitors, making sure students moved quickly on to their classrooms. Without being asked, Belinda pitched in. Soon Belinda became known as the Four Corners Lady, since she stood where two of the main hallways intersected, calling out to the teens and prodding them to hurry to class. When students walked by with cans of soda they weren't supposed to have, Belinda confiscated them, but always with a smile, and none of the teenagers seemed particularly upset. That year, the faculty gave Belinda a "rookie sheriff's award," as a bit of fun and to acknowledge her services.

Yet, as they had been during her own high-school years, Friday-afternoon pep rallies were Belinda's favorite times. She dressed in the school colors, red and white, sometimes with red heart sunglasses and a homemade hat, and cheered as loudly as the students. But at night, at game time, Belinda wasn't in the Katy stands. Instead she sat in Crump Stadium, cheering on David's football team, the Hastings Fighting Bears. As they had throughout their son's football career, Maureen and Ken Temple came, too, eager to support David's team. Yet, on this one night of the week, Belinda splintered off from David's family and spent the evening with the other coaches' wives, going out to dinner and cheering with them from special seats in the stands. Of all of the fans in the bleachers, Quinton would remember hearing Tammey and Belinda's voices above the crowd. "They were wild," he says with a laugh. "Tammey always really gets into the games, and Belinda was as loud or louder."

Remembering those happy evenings, Tammey would smile and recall, "I'd take my cue from her and shout at the officials, but most of the time, I wasn't sure why. Then I'd ask Belinda, 'Was that right?' and Belinda, who'd be all worked up, would say, 'Yes, it's right! That was a bad call!' "

On nights the team wasn't faring well, fans around them mumbled complaints, but if anyone criticized the coaches within Tammey and Belinda's hearing, the two women took them on. "We really put them in their places," Tammey remembers, with a chuckle. "When our side scored, there were touchdown hugs."

Hastings was large, with a good crop of athletes, and Quinton would later say it was a rewarding place to coach. "The kids were motivated," he says. "And David was a good coach. The players liked him, and they worked hard for him. In fact, everybody loved David, all the coaches, including me. In the beginning, I thought he was just a great guy."

"There was something about David," Tammey would say. "It was like he could put people under a spell. He could be mesmerizing. He knew how to play people, to get them to do what he wanted."

With women, David had a way of focusing on them, making it appear he was interested only in them, and complimenting them. "David knew how to make a woman feel awesome," Tammey says, and with men, "He wore his big gold championship ring, talked about football and growing up duck hunting in Katy. He was a guy's guy."

After the games, Tammey and Belinda went home and put the children to bed, while Quinton and David cleaned up in the coaches' showers. But David's intention, even though it was ten or eleven at night, wasn't to end the evening. Instead, groomed and dressed in fresh clothes, he cajoled Quinton into joining him at a bar, even supplying an alibi to use with Tammey. If Quinton balked, David pushed harder, calling him "a pussy," and telling him to run his home, not kowtow to his wife.

Sometimes Quinton gave in, but other times he held his ground. He knew it bothered David that he couldn't always get his way. "David was all about control," says Quinton. "He'd get mad because I wouldn't let him order me around."

At the bars, David, not wearing a wedding ring, flirted and sometimes left with women. The next day at the field house, when the coaches and players gathered to do a post-mortem on the prior night's game, Quinton asked David how the night had ended. David made a fist and smiled, indicating that he'd scored a touchdown.

Did Belinda know? Later, it would be difficult to tell. Certainly she had periods of concern about David's behavior, as in Livingston when she'd confided in Rios that she thought David might be having an affair. If she suspected, she wasn't ready to acknowledge her fears.

Each morning, Belinda took Evan to Tiger Land day care, in a one-story building not far from Katy High School. She pranced into the day care with Evan on her shoulders, making a game of their arrival. She kissed him good-bye, nuzzling him happily and telling him to be a good boy. Afternoons, on her way out the door at Katy, she told Debbie and Cindy, "I'm going to get my little man." Acting as if she couldn't get there soon enough, Belinda hurried to the day care with juice and cookies. From those first days when he learned to walk, Evan rushed to his mother, laughing and excited, throwing his arms around her and rewarding her with kisses. As they left Tiger Land, often on their way to playtime at the park, Evan jabbered happily about his day.

David rarely came to pick up Evan at day care, but when he did, the staff noticed that Evan didn't run to his father as he did to Belinda. There just didn't seem to be the joy Evan had for his mother. "David treated Evan like the male child, like a mini-David," says one of the teachers. "We didn't see the kisses and the smiles."

"David was into other things, so Belinda poured herself into the child, and they did everything together," says Debbie. "Evan was her first priority, always."

But then, Belinda was like that with everyone she loved. Throughout Tammey's pregnancy, Belinda catered to her, picking up Sydnee and taking her places, trying to ease the stress of caring for a child while pregnant. The Harlans' baby came, and Quinton and Tammey named her Avery. A year later, while Tammey was pregnant with their third daughter, Reese, she'd take a respite from her teaching career and open a little girls' party place called the Storybook Cottage in a quaint old house on First Street, in Katy proper. She worked part time, throwing birthday and tea parties for little girls in fancy dresses and their favorite dolls and teddy bears.

At times, Belinda talked about her plans, that she and David were thinking of expanding their family, hoping that she'd get pregnant and this time, that they'd have a little girl. First, they were shopping for a home of their own. Late in 1996, David and Belinda tried to convince their landlord to sell them the Comstock Springs Drive house. They liked the neighborhood, had friends nearby, and it was convenient to David's parents and both of their jobs. For the $900 they paid in rent, Belinda had figured out they could pay a mortgage. But the landlord wouldn't sell, and in November, David and Belinda put money down on a house at 22502 Round Valley Drive, a five-minute drive away in the neighboring Creekstone subdivision. The Round Valley house was larger, more impressive. A two-story redbrick colonial with cream trim, it had a center entrance, a treed corner lot, and a good-size fenced backyard for Shaka and Evan. Bubbling with excitement, Belinda knocked on Sheree's door. The two women put the kids on their bikes, Belinda with Evan in a seat behind her, and pedaled to the new house.

It was easy to see that the Temples' new neighborhood was a step up, more affluent, with larger houses than Comstock Springs Drive, and Belinda appeared proud. "I didn't think we could afford anything this big," she told her mother when she called. "Wait until you and Pops see it. It's just beautiful."

David seemed happy as well. The Harlans saw it as just another of David's attempts to hone his image when they realized that he made a point of telling guests to take a certain route to the new house. "It was longer, but it went past bigger houses," says Tammey. "It made the neighborhood look more expensive."

Still, as the deal came together, Belinda and David hit a roadblock, coming up short on money for the down payment. If there was anyone Belinda could count on, it was Brenda, and that was whom she called, asking for a loan. Dedicated to her sister, Brenda didn't have cash, but she pulled out money from a credit card and sent Belinda a check.

When Brenda came as she always did for their birthday a few weeks later, she helped Belinda unpack. Downstairs the house had a living room, kitchen, den and dining room, with a half bath and a center staircase to the second floor. All the bedrooms were upstairs, and Belinda had decorated Evan's room with a colorful bedspread of a fanciful city with a plane flying overhead, and a rug with a railroad track for his Thomas the Tank Engine cars. Over his desk she had painted a fire engine and squad car at a stoplight, and she stenciled a truck that read "Evan's Room." Belinda had decorated Evan's bathroom with jungle animals and put a futon in the extra bedroom. Down the hall was the master bedroom, with a bed covered by a brightly colored quilt, and a large bathroom with a walk-in closet. When their paychecks came in that month, she and David repaid the loan.

At that point, at least from the outside, to many it appeared that David and Belinda, along with Evan, their gray cat, Willie, and the brown chow, Shaka, made a nearly picture-perfect family in a picture-perfect house. Soon there was a replay of Comstock Springs, where Belinda knew all the neighbors and always appeared happy to see them. In contrast, David hung back, giving some the impression that he felt those who lived near him weren't worthy of his attention.

For Tammey, the first visible cracks in the Temples' tranquil image appeared over the holiday break, when Belinda complained that David wouldn't let her take Evan to see her parents. By then, while they were playing cards or barbecuing, Tammey had already heard David call his in-laws fat rednecks and white trash.

Tammey urged Belinda to go on her own, saying she had the right to see her parents and that Evan needed to know his grandparents. But, as quickly as she opened up to Tammey about the dispute with David, Belinda made a complete reversal, saying she understood how David felt, and calling him a wonderful husband and father. Tammey listened, stunned. Only years later, would she say, "It was as if Belinda was trying to convince herself that they were happy."

By the spring of 1997, Tammey saw David in a new light. In hindsight, she would wonder how much Belinda understood about David's late nights. More than once she'd said to Tammey, "I don't know why you let Quinton be friends with David."

From the other coaches' wives, Tammey had heard rumors that David was unfaithful. She knew many of the wives didn't want their husbands going out with David. Still, Tammey trusted her husband. "Quinton can take care of himself," she told Belinda.

Then Belinda would say, "If I didn't know David better, I'd think he was fooling around. But he wouldn't be cheating. He couldn't."

That a husband is being unfaithful is a risky thing to tell a friend, and Tammey knew that while the wives were suspicious, it was possible she was hearing groundless gossip. She could never bring herself to tell Belinda of the rumors. In fact, under the circumstances, keeping her mouth shut seemed the kindest option. Yet, as time passed, Tammey wondered even more about David Temple.

One night Quinton returned home with the collar on his heavy denim shirt torn. He explained that he and David had been out at a bar and Quinton wanted to leave. David wasn't ready for him to go, and ordered him to stay. When Quinton attempted to walk away anyway, David grabbed him, pulling him by his shirt. Quinton pulled back, and David pulled harder, until the shirt collar ripped. Although stunned by the encounter, Quinton didn't seem too distressed. He saw David as a good friend, and in the rough, tough world of football, "it didn't seem like a big thing," Quinton said. The following day at school, David acted like nothing had happened.

That was nothing compared to what transpired with another of the coaches at Hastings one afternoon. David and Quinton were in the field house next to the stadium with Billy Kramer, a coach David had picked on unmercifully for more than a year, ridiculing him for what Quinton saw as no reason. With Kramer and people he didn't like, Quinton had noticed that David gave off an aura of sorts, a physical attitude that warned, "Don't mess with me."

Quinton thought that David enjoyed picking on Kramer because he saw Kramer as an easy target. David had made him the butt of his jokes, and Kramer had rigorously ignored the abuse. On this afternoon, the three coaches were in the locker room putting stickers on their players' helmets as "attaboys" for good plays. "David popped off," says Quinton. "And this time [Kramer] didn't take it. He shot back. The next thing, it was like having two bulls in the ring."

David lunged at Kramer, and the two fought. Attempting to break it up, Quinton jumped on David's back, screaming, trying to pull him off. David threw a punch, and Kramer reciprocated, with Quinton screaming at them both to stop. In the end, Kramer sported a busted lip and both had bruises. While no one was seriously hurt, Kramer had had enough. He stayed through the year, but then found a coaching job in another district.

By summer 1997, Tammey was ever more aware of the cracks behind the perfect veneer of the Temple marriage.

David's ten-year high-school reunion approached, and Belinda cried, confessing that David didn't want her to go.

"Well, of course you're going," Tammey responded. "You're going to buy a new dress, and you'll look beautiful."

They talked about it for weeks, and Belinda finally did buy a new yellow dress. When that weekend arrived, David went to the Friday night pre-party alone. That night, many saw him around the bar, flirting openly with his old high-school girlfriend Jimi Barlow.

"Did you have sex with her?" Quinton asked, when David bragged about his exploits.

"Everything but that," David said.

On Saturday night, Belinda went with David to the actual reunion, while the Harlans kept Evan. The next day when Belinda arrived to pick her son up, Tammey opened the door and her friend was again in tears. Once inside, Belinda sobbed, saying she'd been humiliated watching David flirt with the other women, especially Jimi. "I don't even feel pretty anymore," Belinda confided.

"You're a beautiful woman," Tammey assured her. "Don't let all that bother you. Don't let him make you feel bad about yourself."

It would seem that no matter how David treated her, Belinda was determined to forgive. As in the past, she'd soon put the pain of the reunion behind her and move on, acting as if it never happened. Still, Belinda couldn't seem to hide the frustration and disappointment she felt about the way David segregated her from her family.

That summer was the last time that Brian and Jill would see Belinda. She called one Friday to say that she, David, and Evan were driving to Dallas to see David's oldest brother, Darren, and his wife, Lisa. Belinda said they wanted to have dinner with Brian and Jill, who lived nearby. "We're all going to the lake skiing," she said. "But we'll call you and meet you at the restaurant."

They were to meet at Brian and Jill's favorite restaurant, Esparza's. But Saturday came and the phone didn't ring. Jill had Colton, their young son, dressed and ready, excited about seeing Aunt Belinda, Uncle David, and his cousin. They waited and waited, and still they didn't hear from Belinda. As the time passed, the phone remained silent. Finally, hungry and tired of waiting, Brian and Jill decided to pick up dinner and bring it home. They drove past Esparza's and saw Belinda, David, Evan, David's parents and Darren and Lisa drive up. As Brian and Jill watched, the Temples walked toward Esparza's. They were going out, but they hadn't called to tell Jill and Brian to join them.

"We were hurt," says Jill. "Both of us were really hurt."

The following Sunday, Belinda called the house and talked to Jill's mother, who lived with them, claiming she tried to call Brian and Jill but didn't understand she had to dial the area code to reach them. Brian didn't believe her. Darren and Lisa lived in the area, and they would have known how to place the call. Plus, Belinda had called them earlier in the week without a problem.

"It didn't dawn on either one of us that it was David who didn't want to see us," says Jill. "But later, it all made sense."

From that point on, they received photos of Evan in the mail but didn't hear from Belinda. When Brian called, Belinda never called him back.

Although six years had passed since he'd stopped playing college football, David still looked the same, muscular and strong. Nearing thirty, he worked out regularly, and he could still bench-press more than 400 pounds. At Hastings, he was often seen in the weight room, working out with the team. By any measure, David Temple was an imposing figure.

Football season started again that August, and David and Quinton were busy grooming that year's defense for the games ahead. Once the season started, the weeks were filled with obligations. On Monday evenings, the coaches hobnobbed with the school's booster club. In addition to the late practices, on Thursday evenings Quinton had junior varsity games to attend, and their varsity games were on Friday evenings or sometimes Saturday afternoons. Sunday afternoons were spent in the field house with the other coaches dissecting the last week's game and sizing up the coming week's opponent.

"Being a coach's wife is like being a single mom. We hardly ever see our husbands," says Tammey. "Having Belinda to share it with made it easier."

On nights when their husbands worked, they took turns cooking and ate together. One of Belinda's favorite recipes was for hot dogs wrapped in croissants. On Wednesday nights they met at McDonald's, where the women talked while their young ones played on the indoor gym. When the children acted up, Tammey and Belinda joked and said they got their manners from their fathers. Friday nights were spent at the football games, and then the Harlans and Temples did things together on the weekends, everything from barbecuing and cards to shopping and taking the kids to the park.

At Katy High that fall, 1997, Belinda wore a poodle skirt and played a fifties high-school kid in a song-and-dance skit from the Broadway musical *Grease*, for the faculty luncheon. Meanwhile, at Hastings one afternoon, Quinton talked to David about a shotgun he planned to buy. One thing led to another, and soon they had newspaper ads out, comparing prices on different models. They discussed getting concealed gun permits, and David reminisced about goose and duck hunting behind the Katy house, in the rice fields.

"Yeah, our parents gave all of us shotguns for Christmas," he told Quinton.

As close as the two families were, that fall things began changing for Tammey. She'd started growing uncomfortable when David was around. He called Tammey "Little Momma," pointing out how trim she was, even after the three girls. When Tammey looked over at Belinda, who was still struggling to lose all the weight from Evan, Tammey sensed her friend was hurt. And there were those evenings when David laughed, talking about "Belinda's big butt," comparing her to what she'd been like in college, when she worked as an aerobics instructor. She was still an average-size woman, wearing a size twelve, but David implied Belinda had let herself go. "You should have seen Belinda before she had Evan. She looked good," he said as he gave her a slap on the rear.

"You shouldn't let him talk to you like that," Tammey told Belinda later. "Tell David that upsets you. Tell him how you feel."

When Belinda didn't, Tammey began to think of her friend as weak.

In the new house as he had at the old, Shaka moved into the backyard. Evan, a quiet child who had his mother's eyes, rode on the chow's back as if it were a horse, and Belinda often remarked that she appreciated having the dog near. "I never worry about being home alone," she told more than one friend. "With Shaka, I know no one would ever bother us."

It was a different story with non-family members, who she often cautioned to be careful around the chow. When they had guests, David and Belinda locked the dog in a bedroom or outside the house, sometimes in the garage. "She never let the dog loose around any of us," says a neighbor. "I'm a dog person, but I wouldn't approach that animal. It wasn't friendly."

One evening, when she hosted Bunco, a dice game where players rotate tables, Belinda invited a friend into the back-yard to give her advice on planting flower beds. Shaka was in the garage, barking, when the door swung open, and the dog charged out.

"Get back in the house," Belinda shouted at the terrified woman. "Quick."

Her friend did as instructed, slamming the door behind her just before a snapping Shaka lunged at her.

At other times, the dog ran inside along the fence line, growling at neighbors as the children rode bikes down the street or the adults took their evening walks. Shaka so frightened some in the neighborhood that they avoided walking past the Temple house, for fear the animal would break through the gate or fence and charge at them. Even those who had dogs of their own feared Shaka.

On Round Valley, Sheree and her children stopped by, usually while riding their bikes. At other times, she ran into Belinda at the grocery store. That Halloween, Sheree put a "Boo" on Belinda and David's front door, a sign with the word printed across the front. The next time she saw her, Belinda said she'd known it was Sheree from the handwriting. The two women laughed and caught up on news, and Sheree judged the move to the bigger house hadn't changed Belinda. But that wasn't the case for David. When Sheree happened upon him in the neighborhood, David rarely said more than hello before walking on. When Sheree mentioned their old neighbor's coolness to her husband, he shrugged and said, "You don't live next door anymore. He doesn't have to be nice to you."

That fall one of the Temples' neighbors on Round Valley, Mike Schrader, rang the doorbell with two Houston Aeros hockey tickets for David. They'd only nodded in passing a few times, but Mike's wife had spent time talking to Belinda and liked her. Mike had gone over a few times while the women were talking and David was outside. He had never even said hello. This time, David opened the door, took the tickets and nodded at Mike, then closed the door without saying thanks.

Of all of the neighbors, later it would seem that the only ones David Temple did more than barely acknowledge were the Ruggieros, Peggy and Mike, who lived on Hidden Canyon, the side street that bordered the Temples' lot. The Ruggieros' house was one lot down from David and Belinda's driveway, and they talked at times, even sharing a barbecue or two. Mike, an engineer with British Petroleum, would label it a neighborly relationship.

At Katy High, Belinda continued to be one of the more popular teachers. "If you ever need to talk, I'm here," she told a troubled girl that winter. "I want to help." Every morning, she spent time with her suite-mates, Debbie Berger and Cindy O'Brien. It seemed that Belinda perpetually had a new Evan story. She put his picture up on the "Teacher's Brag Board" in the lounge, and there were more family photos on her desk. One morning Belinda talked about how she'd taken Evan to Walmart and he'd picked up a toy. Instead of crying to keep it, he told her, "I'll play with it here and put it back." Belinda was so impressed she gave him the $3 to buy the toy.

At lunch in the teachers lounge, Belinda ate French fries and always had a small pile of chocolate wafer cookies for dessert. She took them apart and licked out the frosting, then finished by crunching on the wafers. If she had an appetite at work, Belinda didn't give up on losing weight. When she wasn't taking Evan to the park after school, she brought him to the gym, where he played in the nursery while she worked out, still hoping to get back to her pre-pregnancy physique. Yet, no matter what she tried, it appeared that David didn't approve. The Harlans heard David ridicule Belinda, embarrassing her by disparaging her family and calling her fat.

More and more that year, 1998, Tammey saw a change in her friend. Belinda away from David remained a happy, fun-loving person. When David arrived, Belinda became quiet, almost sullen. Tammey didn't like to see what the marriage was doing to her friend: "It was like Belinda walked on eggshells around him. It made me so uncomfortable. If I was at their house with Belinda when he came home, I left."

Years later, Tammey would recount an incident but be unable to say whether she saw it or if Belinda described what happened: that David had pushed Belinda into a wall. What gave the memory credence was that, although Tammey had no way of knowing, David had done the same thing to Pam in a hotel bathroom seven years earlier.

While Maureen and Ken Temple were their grandson's usual babysitters, the fall before, a Katy High student named

Ginny Wiley, a pretty young girl with long blond hair, began babysitting for Evan. She and Belinda became friendly, and Ginny rode her bike to the Temples' and played basketball with Belinda. "The woman still had some moves," says Wiley.

When David showed up, he drove into the garage and went in the house without even saying hello.

By then, it seemed that David Temple increasingly had other matters on his mind. He and Quinton continued to go out at night. When they did, David instructed his fellow coach on what to tell Tammey, so their alibis would jibe. But Quinton didn't use David's lies, instead telling Tammey where he'd gone. That spring Belinda found credit-card bills of David's from bars and strip clubs, and when Belinda called Tammey, she verified that was where David had gone. The next day at work, David confronted Quinton.

"You need to keep your woman in line," he ordered, seething. Quinton stared at David, not sure how angry he was or what he might do, but then shrugged it off.

"It was like we were getting pulled into their world, and there was this unbelievable storm we lived in," Tammey would say later. "It was crazy, like everything was unraveling."

With so much going on in her marriage, at school, Belinda talked more openly to Debbie and Cindy, confiding in her fellow teachers about the credit-card bills and the things David said about her family and her weight. "Belinda said that the Temple men talked badly about the women," says Debbie. "It bothered her. She didn't like that."

"Belinda was spunky, but she wasn't tough. She got her feelings hurt," adds Cindy.

One night when Tammey and Quinton were over playing cards, David suddenly stopped in the middle of the game and snapped at Belinda, who'd been jumping up and down whenever anyone wanted a drink. "You've got a big fat ass," he said. Embarrassed, Quinton and Tammey listened as David then railed against his wife for disciplining Evan, something he maintained only he had the right to do, and then brought up another of his pet peeves, Belinda's parents. "They're crazy," he said. "White trash."

Belinda said little.

The discipline issue emerged again and again. Once Tammey was over with Sydnee when Sydnee and Evan had a spat. Belinda put Evan in time out, but when David saw it, he glared at Belinda and talked to the toddler, then let him get up off the chair.

"Why did you do that?" Belinda asked.

David looked furious. "You let me take care of my son," he ordered.

That spring, Tammey Harlan was losing patience with her friend. She urged Belinda to stand up against David and not to let him control her. Belinda agreed, but when Tammey saw them together, she knew Belinda couldn't stand up to David. It was as if David had scraped away all Belinda's self-esteem.

"I hated the way he treated her, and I hated that she let him. I started telling Quinton that David was evil," said Tammey.

While in the beginning David had been obsessive with his yard and his house, over the years he lost interest. He still insisted it was well maintained, but Belinda was charged with the work. On the weekends, Belinda would mow the yard and trim, while David sat inside watching sports on television.

Their neighbor from across the street, Natalie Scott, dropped by often, talking with Belinda in the driveway while the children played. They were both teachers and much of the conversation centered on students. Trying to join in, Natalie's husband, Robert, tried to get them to talk about something else, but usually failed. The Scotts saw little of David. When he poked his head outside or drove up in his pickup truck, Bob Scott would remember David glaring at him. "It was like he was trying to intimidate me," Scott would say years later. "He just had this hard, cold stare."

It was Scott that Belinda asked for a favor one afternoon. She wanted to put Evan down for a nap, and rock and roll music vibrated out of the house next door. The teenager who lived there, Joe Sanders, had his stereo blasting. One of her students from Katy High, Sanders was a laid-back kind of kid, one who smoked pot and cut classes, but he hadn't been in any real trouble in the neighborhood, other than a loud party when his parents weren't home. Perhaps Belinda worried that talking to Sanders alone, without a witness, someone might see her at his house and misinterpret, or that Sanders or his parents could become angry and claim she said things that she didn't. So Belinda asked Scott to stand in her yard, behind the bushes, and listen in on the conversation.

He did, and she left, returning minutes later.

"Everything all right?" he asked.

"Yup. No problem," Belinda said with a shrug. "Joe was really nice about it."

That Christmas, David and Belinda put out their lighted deer and lined the walkway with make-believe candy canes. Belinda asked Ginny Wiley to babysit while she shopped. Wiley drove to the mall with Evan and Belinda in the red Rodeo, then Ginny took Evan up and down on the escalator, with Evan giggling and enjoying the ride, while Belinda searched for the items on her Christmas list.

Over the holidays, Belinda again made the drive home to Nacogdoches with Evan and Shaka. David didn't go. It was getting to the point where much of the contact Tom and Carol had with their youngest child was on the telephone. She visited every three or four months, usually driving up one day and driving home the next. They didn't know that each of her trips home riled David up.

More often, she called on Sundays. "Hi Mops and Pops," she'd say. "It's Number Five." On the phone or during her short visits, neither of Belinda's parents understood what was going on in her life, the turmoil in her marriage. With them, she appeared carefree, never complaining about David.

At Katy High that spring, Belinda cried at her desk one morning when one of the teachers saw her.

"Are you okay?" he asked. "What's wrong?

Belinda just shook her head. The man knew David from his high-school years at Katy and guessed that Belinda's sadness involved a problem at home. He stood beside her and put his arm around her. His wife and Belinda were friends, and he felt sad that all wasn't well. "What's going on?" he asked. "Is there something I can help you with?"

"No," she said. "I'm okay."

Despite her assurances, he wasn't convinced. "I've known you long enough for you to know that I care about you. Is it David?" he asked. "Is there something I can do? Do you want me to talk to him?"

"No, please, don't get involved," she begged.

"Belinda, if he's not doing you right, I will talk to him," the teacher said.

This time Belinda looked frantic. "Please don't say anything. It'll only make it worse."

A few days later, that same teacher saw Belinda and asked if everything was all right. "Things are a lot better now," Belinda said. "We're fine."

The Creekstone area, where the Temples' new home was located, was a quiet neighborhood. It was the kind of place where neighbors leave their doors unlocked and stop to talk or wave as they drive by.

"Nothing much ever happened here," says a neighbor. "It's almost boringly quiet."

That was about to change, and the tremors of what happened would haunt the middle-class subdivision for years to come.

8

"When it came to football, Coach Temple was aggressive," says one of his Hastings players. "You could tell he had a real temper, when things weren't going his way. He cursed at us, but I never saw him hit a kid."

In life, as in sports, there are boundaries that aren't to be crossed. Later, it would seem that 1998 was a dangerous year in the Temple marriage, one in which David continued to pull ever further away from Belinda, putting in motion events that would lead him to violate deeply entrenched mores, the most basic rules that govern society and define family.

That spring, Belinda was in her room at Katy High School, upset about problems at home. Then Belinda called Tammey crying. She'd found more credit-card receipts from bars and strip clubs, and she said that when she'd confronted David, he told her he wanted his own checking account. "I felt bad that I knew about what David was doing, the other women, and I couldn't tell her," Tammey says. "And I was angry at Belinda for not standing up to David. I didn't see her as abused, I saw her as weak."

Tammey mentioned Belinda's call to Quinton, and a few nights later, he and David were in a bar, when David said he was leaving.

"Be sure to get the credit-card bill before your wife does," Quinton prodded. It was the type of jab David gave Quinton regularly, but David apparently didn't like it being directed toward him.

The next day Belinda was on the phone again, frantic, crying and begging Tammey to never again tell Quinton anything she confided in her. "I will never forget that phone call," says Tammey, wiping away a tear. "Belinda sounded desperate."

After school let out for the summer, she called Cindy and Debbie, her surrogate moms from Katy High, and told them there was more trouble. David was so angry that he hadn't talked with her in weeks. "It didn't sound good," Debbie would later say. "I was worried for her. To go a few days not talking was one thing, but not weeks."

When she heard about the latest event in the Temples' marriage, Tammey Harlan was proud of Belinda for standing her ground and not giving in. This was a new Belinda, one who was willing to push back. "Have you and David talked yet?" she'd ask Belinda. When Belinda said they hadn't, Tammey was filled with pride. Finally, her friend was refusing to bow down to her domineering husband.

That summer, there were more calls from Belinda, telling Cindy and Debbie that the situation continued to deteriorate. Debbie wondered if the marriage was ending, and thought that perhaps that would be for the best for Belinda. Debbie had had misgivings early on when Belinda told her whom she was married to; now those fears seemed justified. That summer Belinda told Tammey something else: that she'd begun refusing to go to David's parents' home at times, something Belinda in the past would never have had the courage to do. "She was sick of spending every weekend with them," says Tammey. "In the framework of their marriage, this was big. Belinda was standing up to David. She wanted her own family, just her, David, and Evan. She wanted to do things on their own."

When July came and it was time for the family reunion in

New Braunfels, something years earlier Belinda had looked forward to, she didn't want to go. "Why can't it ever just be us?" she asked. "They're all driving me crazy."

"Don't go," Tammey said. "Just refuse."

"I can't," Belinda said. "I can't not go."

If reluctant to attend, in the photos taken that year, Belinda looked happy. She played in the pool with Evan, and in one, Belinda, with her sisters-in-law Becky and Lisa, who was married to Darren, mimicked their husbands' summer tradition, with cigars in all their mouths, grinning widely.

As he had the year before, Quinton took over duties with Shaka while David and Belinda were gone. As always, Quinton was cautious around the dog. Immediately when he pulled in the driveway and opened the car door, Shaka growled, barked, and jumped against the pine slats that made up the backyard gate. More than once, Quinton shuddered at the prospect that the latch wouldn't hold and the dog would pounce on him. As he approached the gate, Quinton said the dog's name. "Shaka, you know me," he said gently. "I come here all the time. I'm the one who feeds you."

At the gate, he held his hand next to a crack in the slats, so Shaka could recognize his scent. Only after the dog quieted down would Quinton ease inside. As Quinton retrieved dog food out of the garage and refilled its bowl, the dog kept a sharp eye on him. Each time he left unharmed, Quinton sighed in relief.

That summer, 1998, Belinda told Brenda that she and Evan would visit her. Belinda never made the trip to Kansas, where Brenda had moved to work for a poultry company. The middle Lucas brother, Barry, too, was disappointed when Belinda didn't come that summer, as she'd promised. One night while David was at a baseball camp, Belinda did, however, drive to Nacogdoches to see Tom and Carol. No matter how much David ridiculed her parents, the draw was strong and Belinda wasn't willing to lose them.

The weeks passed, and, back home in Katy, David and Belinda continued their silent war, until one morning when she called Tammey in utter despair. As Belinda described it, she was reading Evan a book in his room when David stopped at the door. Belinda looked up and asked him, "Do you love me?"

"I don't know," David replied.

Grieving, Belinda cried as she told her friend, as if David's words signaled an ending to the marriage. Although Tammey knew Belinda's spirits rose and fell with David's moods, Tammey wasn't prepared for what happened the following morning, when her friend called again. Taking up the story where she'd left it off the day before, Belinda explained that she'd cried much of the day after her conversation with David. Then, that night, she was again in Evan's room, putting him to bed. To her surprise, David walked up behind Belinda and kissed her on the back of the head.

"I love you," he said.

It seemed that was all Belinda needed to hear. With those three words, their standoff ended. Despite the pain of the previous weeks, Belinda again sounded head-over-heels in love, raving about David as if he were the ideal man, the only man in the world she could ever love.

The turnaround hit Tammey hard, not so much that they'd made up but that Belinda had made a complete about-face, restoring David to his undeserved pedestal. Feeling that her own emotions, too, had been in upheaval, Tammey made a difficult decision. "I couldn't stay on this roller coaster with Belinda. I had a four-year-old and two babies," she says. "It was eating me up, too. My marriage was suffering. The more time we spent with David and Belinda, the more Quinton and I fought. From that moment forward, I pulled away."

Not long after that Belinda called friends with big news. "She was pregnant," says Cindy. "I was surprised, after things had been so bad between them, and I wondered if Belinda thought another baby would fix the marriage. But she sounded excited, and Debbie and I were happy for her, and we hoped maybe all was well."

* * *

Belinda and David had talked about wanting a baby for more than a year, so it shouldn't have been a shock. Yet after such a stressful summer, the news caught those who understood what Belinda had gone through by surprise. For others, those who only saw the pretense of the Temple marriage—the pretty wife with the football-star husband and the handsome little boy who lived in the well-kept house on the quiet street—there was no reason to greet the pregnancy with anything less than excitement.

When Belinda announced she was pregnant to her friends at the gym, they cheered and laughed, and started singing the old pop hit by the Supremes, "Baby Love." At Katy High School that August, she made the announcement to a wave of hugs and good wishes. And when Belinda told the staff at Evan's day care, Tiger Land, they surrounded her with embraces. There seemed so much to be happy about.

David's parents were in a small town outside of Houston antiquing when they got even more good news. They were both on the telephone with Belinda when she made another announcement; the baby she carried was a girl. The Temples, who had no daughters or granddaughters, were thrilled.

"They were beside themselves with excitement about a baby girl," says a relative. "Maureen and Ken couldn't have been happier."

At first Tammey was shocked by the news, after the difficult summer Belinda and David had had. But then, she thought, perhaps a new baby would help. David was a good father to Evan, obsessively devoted, to the point that Tammey and Quinton joked about him seeing the boy as a mini-David. Now, when David visited the Harlans, he looked at little Avery, with her dark hair and blue eyes, and said things like, "My daughter is going to be like Avery." The prospect of a baby girl, at least in the beginning, seemed to bode well for everyone.

* * *

On Round Valley, there was still a wide disparity between the way neighbors viewed Belinda and David Temple. While Belinda went out of her way to make friends, David continued to hang back with the majority of the neighbors. It seemed as if Belinda couldn't do enough, and David simply wasn't interested.

One of the Temples' across-the-street neighbors, Natalie Scott, was pregnant, too, due in the fall. One weekend a friend was using the Scotts' house to throw Natalie a baby shower. She told Belinda about the event in passing, mentioning that Natalie's husband, Robert, was on a business trip, and that the lawn needed mowing. A short time later, Natalie heard a mower start up and looked outside to find Belinda mowing the lawn.

On yet another weekend, Robert stood on the street in front of his house watching his children, while Belinda and David played basketball. David hit the backstop hard and the ball rocketed off, aimed directly at one of the Scott's young daughters. Without a moment to spare, Robert put out his hand to deflect the ball, but it hit so hard that it split his fingertip. The blood spilled out, but David just stared at the other man. He didn't apologize, and he didn't offer any help. Belinda was the one who ran for a bandage and ordered David to "say you're sorry."

"He mumbled something," Scott would say years later. "But he didn't look in the least bit sorry."

At Tiger Land, too, the disparity between the Temples had people talking. They saw Belinda with Evan, loving and protective. David continued to dote on the three-year-old, but to most he appeared to treat the toddler as older than he was, as if David wanted to train his son to be strong.

They understood that David had high expectations, ones Belinda worked hard to fulfill. Daily, like his father, Evan was outfitted in matching Nike and Tommy Hilfiger clothes, down to his socks and tennis shoes. That fall, Belinda was working on potty training. When she dropped him off at Tiger Land in the mornings, she made the time to take the toddler to the bathroom. As children do, he still had accidents. Prepared, Belinda kept an ensemble of matching clothes at Tiger Land for Evan to be changed into, but one day he went through the extra outfit as well, and his teacher, assuming it wouldn't matter, dressed Evan in clothes the school kept for such emergencies, a pair of coveralls and a shirt. When Belinda arrived, she saw her son and looked worried.

"Oh, Evan, we'll need to go to the mall and buy clothes and change you. We can't bring you home dressed like that," she said. Then, in a cautionary voice, "You know how your father is."

Belinda turned to a woman standing beside her and said, "His daddy gets upset if Evan isn't dressed just right."

At Katy High in the content mastery suite, Debbie hung a big pink bow on a shelf in Belinda's room to commemorate the coming baby. That fall, in her role as the sunshine lady, Belinda sent out e-mails to the other teachers. "I hope everyone has returned prepared to get tired again," she joked in one. In another, later that year, she wrote: "Secret pal people, do not forget your pals!" And then there were the jokes in her e-mails, including one about a three-year-old who put his shoes on by himself, on "the wrong feet." When his mother pointed out his mistake, the child looked dumbfounded.

"Don't kid me," he said. "I know they're my feet."

The boy in the story was as old as Evan, and at the bottom of the e-mail, Belinda wrote: "They're so cute at that age."

Then there were Belinda's customary pearls of wisdom, including "A smile is the cheapest way to improve your looks, even if your teeth are crooked." Most of her missives ended with a cheer for the Katy football team: "Go, Tigers!"

As the school year got under way, it would seem that all was relatively well in Belinda's life. She and David were talking again, and he'd said he loved her. Her pregnancy was exciting for the entire Temple family, including Belinda, who'd ached for another child and always dreamed of a daughter.

There were twins at Tiger Land, and one of them was a little girl named Erin. Belinda's parents had named their children with Bs, and David and Belinda decided that Erin was the perfect name to go with Evan. Before long the baby she carried had a middle name: Ashley.

As painful as the summer had been, the fall held the promise of a better life and a beautiful baby girl named Erin Ashley Temple. Belinda couldn't know that the worst lay ahead.

While Belinda eagerly awaited their daughter's birth, big changes took place at Hastings High School, where David worked. The school had grown to the point where a decision had been made a few years earlier to split off the youngest students and construct a separate ninth-grade center behind the high school. In August 1998, the building opened, and a group of teachers moved into classrooms in the modern facility, with its soaring roof over the entryway. David and Quinton were two of those teachers. Another was Heather DeAnn Scott, a slender, blond English teacher, at twenty-nine a year younger than David. Before long, Heather and Quinton would indulge in a flirtation. At least in the beginning, it all seemed harmless. But that would quickly change, and events would soon spin even further out of control when David Temple became part of a triangle that would end in tragedy.

9

The thing about Quinton and David is that they were so over-the-top competitive," says Tammey. "They were always trying to one-up each other. They were good friends, but at the same time they were rivals, and David always had to be the top dog. David had to be the center of attention, and anything Quinton did, David had to do it better. Quinton laid a stone patio in our yard, and David extended his own patio with brick. David always had to have a better fish story. It was just who he was, and he had to be in control."

Throughout the two years they'd been friends, David had continually tried to show Quinton up at work, David insisting that the coaching ideas were his. When in the fall of 1998 Quinton began flirting with a young teacher named Heather Scott, David was drawn to the same woman. Would he have been interested in Heather anyway? Perhaps. But certainly, his best friend's interest in her didn't dissuade him.

Heather had grown up in Little Rock, Arkansas. Her mother, Sandy, did office work, and her father was a Vietnam vet. After they divorced, Sandy married again, this time to Jeff Munson. When Heather was in the eighth grade, he moved the family to Franklin, Texas, a one-stoplight town of about 1,500.

It would later seem ironic that Heather and Belinda had so much in common. They were both twins with small-town roots. Like Belinda and Brenda, Heather and her sister, Shannon, were best friends. "They were both happy little girls. They're identical but they don't look alike," says Sandy, their mother. "But they're close. They always have been." As girls, Belinda and Heather were both popular cheerleaders in their schools.

Although she'd once wanted to be a flight attendant, Heather majored in English and secondary education at Texas A&M University. Like Belinda, Heather had a boy-friend on the football team. After graduation, she signed on as an eighth-grade English teacher in Hearne, a small town not far from the university. In fall 1998, when she garnered Quinton's attention, Heather had been in Houston one year. She'd arrived the fall before, following a high-school friend, Tara Hall, who taught in an Alief elementary school. Houston must have looked like a good place for a new beginning.

Although not beautiful, and with an angular face, Heather was attractive, with shoulder-length, curly blond hair, and a wide, white smile. At the time she moved into Hall's Perth-shire-Street town house, Heather had only recently ended a long-term relationship. At first, she appeared to devote her time to putting the past behind her. "She was kind of quiet, and she didn't date for a long time," says Tara, with dark, chin-length hair and a matter-of-fact manner. "Heather wasn't like that. She didn't go from man to man."

Instead, Heather developed a close-knit group of girl-friends in Houston, mainly other teachers at Hastings. She was well thought of at the school, considered friendly and smart, and her sister and nieces came into Houston often to visit. For that first year in the city, when Heather went out, it was most often with Tara or her other girlfriends, to happy hours for drinks or out to dinner. During the quiet times, when Tara and Heather discussed their hopes for the future, Heather talked about wanting to have a family, and

Tara always assumed her friend would have children. Sandy thought her daughter would as well, saying, "Heather always loved kids."

One of the things her fellow teachers noticed about Heather Scott was that she dressed impeccably. Like David, she was meticulous about the way she looked. "Heather got dressed up to go to Target on the weekends," says Tara. "It didn't matter what she was doing. Everything she wore had to match."

After a brief time living together, Tara noticed something else about her roommate; Heather didn't take criticism well. Thin-skinned, she became defensive and angry at even the hint of disapproval. Tara thought that Heather didn't have a lot of self-esteem and decided that if they were to remain friends, she couldn't criticize her. "Heather worked hard and tried hard at everything she did, and it bothered her if anyone thought badly of her," says Tara. "She was that way to the extreme."

In the beginning, although they were both young and attractive, there was little exciting going on in Tara and Heather's two-story town house. In fact, Tara describes living with Heather as quiet. Then, once the ninth-grade center opened, the situation changed. A smaller school with fewer faculty members, its teachers quickly bonded into a tight-knit group. The one Tara first heard Heather talk about was Quinton Harlan.

"Heather mentioned Quinton often," Tara says. "I didn't think it was anything serious, but his name started coming up. I'm not sure when I found out that he was married, but I did, and I knew they were flirting."

A few times, Quinton stopped at their town house, sitting in the living room, talking to Tara and Heather. At school, Quinton popped into Heather's room off and on during the day, to carry on the flirtation. Tara liked Quinton. He was fun to talk to, and he and Heather openly flirted. When Tara looked at Quinton, she wasn't surprised; he fit the mold of Heather's boyfriends in the past: tall, lean, and athletic.

Quinton and Heather interacted most often in the confines of the school, in the hallways, visiting each other's classrooms. But then Heather branched out, spending more time off-campus with a group of the teachers. Why not? She was single, free to see whomever she wished. The gatherings were centered on Thursday-afternoon happy hours. Up to a dozen faculty and staff members splintered off after work. At times Tara met Heather, and they went to Pappasito's, a Mexican restaurant with a bar and televisions, a pub called Sherlock's, a microbrewery, and a sports bar, arriving after classes at four or five. Most were on the way home by six or seven.

"I wasn't too sure what was happening between Quinton and Heather, but she started going out more," says Tara. The weeks passed and the situation became even more complicated. "All of a sudden, Heather started mentioning Quinton's friend, David. And then I met David Temple when he showed up at a happy hour."

Later, Quinton would say that he started mentioning Heather to David. "He knew that I was interested in her," he said, remarking that he and Tammey were going through a rough patch. "I guess you could say that it wasn't a good time in our marriage." The conversations came up casually, as the two men sat together in their office in the field house, adjacent to the football stadium. Since they shared a conference period, the two coaches spent time together, much of it talking. Looking back, Quinton would say that Heather's name came up often.

Early in their friendship, Belinda had confided in Tammey that Quinton's relationship with David might prove unhealthy for the Harlans' marriage. At the time, Tammey wasn't worried, trusting Quinton. But as Belinda had predicted, Quinton's friendship with David, with the constant pressure to go out to bars and to rein in Tammey, took a toll. Tammey, who'd been with Quinton since high school, feared they were in dire trouble. "My marriage had started looking like the Temples," she confides, explaining that the pressure was so overwhelming she believed she had no option other than to pull away from both the Temples, including Belinda. Just being with them, Tammey said, made her feel as if she and Quinton were being pulled into chaos. "I had to, to try to save my own marriage," Tammey says. "I had to try."

While Tammey sensed that all wasn't well in her union, Belinda was still in a brief respite after the summer's tense silence. Early that fall, Belinda, five months pregnant, looked happy, rejoicing in the prospect of a baby daughter. In late September, she walked through the high-school gym, where a group of girls played basketball. Despite her blossoming baby bump, Belinda grabbed the ball and dribbled it between her legs, then passed it over her head to the girl standing behind her.

"Gee, Mrs. Temple, you're good," one girl said.

"After the baby's born, we'll play some one-on-one," Belinda promised with a laugh. That afternoon, she left the gym floor looking flushed and content.

Perhaps, at first, ignorance was a blessing.

Meanwhile, Tammey heard about Heather from the other coaches' wives. If any of them knew about Quinton's interest in Heather, the wives didn't mention it. Instead, they talked about Heather as a threat, describing her as a groupie, hanging around the coaches. "They called her the 'Barbie bitch,'" Tammey says. "They said she had a thing for football coaches. At first, I wasn't worried about Quinton."

Looking back, Tara would recall David first showing up at a Hastings happy hour sometime in September. That night, he was gregarious, acting the part of the congenial host, buying drinks and gabbing with his coworkers about school, sometimes complaining loudly about a seminar or in-service training he'd had to attend, calling them a waste of time. "At first, I didn't see David zeroing in on Heather," says Tara. "Then around Halloween, that changed."

They were at Sherlock's Pub, a trendy bar decorated with dark wood and hunter green walls, the night Tara noticed David's attention focused on Heather. On weekends, bands play and the televisions scattered throughout are set on football games. During the week, the pub offers happy-hour drink specials. "I noticed David and Heather kind of pairing up," says Tara. "I didn't say anything to her about it, because she was guarded."

Others noticed, too, as David and Heather sat together at a table or at the bar, talking quietly, off by themselves. On Thursday nights, David could easily stay out, simply by telling Belinda that he was at a junior varsity game watching the up-and-coming class of student football players and assessing their talents for the varsity team. In truth, Quinton was required to attend the junior games, but David rarely showed up. Instead, David sat with Heather, laughing, flirting, and buying her drinks, while Belinda waited at home with Evan.

The storm was building, and the respite in her troubled marriage would be brief for Belinda.

That fall, as Tammey pulled away from her, Belinda spent more time with a young teacher at Katy High, a basketball coach named Stacy Nissley. Stacy had a daughter at Tiger Land with Evan, and on Wednesday nights, as Belinda had once done with Tammey, she now met Stacy and a small group of other teachers at McDonald's, where they ate burgers and watched their little ones on the gym equipment. It was on one such evening that Belinda confided in Stacy that all wasn't well. David was rarely home. "I think we're going through another rough patch," Belinda said. "But I think we'll get through it."

As they talked, Belinda confided that David no longer appeared excited about the baby. At first he'd seemed delighted about the prospect of a daughter, but now, Belinda admitted, she had doubts that David wanted the child at all. Others, including Quinton and Tammey, noticed the same thing that fall. Where in the beginning David had acted thrilled about the pregnancy, he now barely talked about Erin's arrival, and when he did, he acted as if he didn't really want a baby girl.

* * *

Since they were only seen together at school, the other teachers at Hastings didn't realize what was transpiring between Quinton and Heather. Faculty members were, on the other hand, gossiping about Heather and David and what others had noticed at those Thursday-night happy hours. "Everyone was talking about it," says one coworker. "We all knew something was up."

One of the other coaches' wives had her interest piqued when she saw David on a Friday night, after a game. At nearly 11 P.M., when the other coaches left for home, David stood outside the stadium, dressed and groomed, looking ready to go out partying. Later, it became evident that was exactly what he had in mind, and it wasn't with Belinda.

Perhaps she never understood what was behind her husband's actions that fall, why David abruptly decided he didn't want her mixing with the other coaches' wives. In the past she'd gone out to dinner with them before the football games and cheered with them in the stadium. Suddenly, that fall, that was no longer allowed. Belinda told Tammey that David ordered her to instead sit with his parents. Was it that David wanted to insulate Belinda from the gossip about him at Hastings that fall, as word spread throughout the faculty and he and Heather were a couple?

The other coaches' wives wondered, but few asked Belinda why she and Evan no longer watched the games with them. Instead, some stopped to say hello to Belinda, gabbing with the Temples as well. At one of the games, the head coach's wife, Kay Stuart, walked over to say hello to Belinda and ended up talking to David's mother. That night, Maureen confided: "David was a challenge as a boy. We're so thankful about how Belinda changed David."

While the Temples were thankful for Belinda's influence on David, Belinda still struggled, it would often appear, with trying to reconcile the vast differences in her husband: the loving, caring, attentive man who dropped to his knees on the fifty-yard line to propose marriage and the cold, often cruel man, who had turned her, in his presence, from her usual gregarious self into a shadow. Did he love her? Where was he on those nights when she waited for him at home?

"Does your brother come home on Friday nights after the games?" Belinda asked Cindi Thompson one day at school. Darren's old girlfriend was a teacher at Katy High School, and Cindi's brother was a football coach at another school. "Yes, he does," Cindi said, explaining that her brother returned home shortly after the games ended.

"Belinda said that David had told her he was sleeping at the field house," says Cindi.

Tara Hall began arriving home from being out with friends and finding David in their town house with Heather late on Friday nights. Sometimes they were curled up on the couch watching television with glasses of wine. Then, around Halloween, Tara came home and saw David's truck on the street and Heather's purse in the living room, but they weren't downstairs. Instead David and Heather were upstairs together in her bedroom. After that, it happened often.

Years earlier at Stephen F. Austin, David had been generous first with Pam, then Belinda. Now gifts started showing up at the town house for Heather, flowers and perfume, often with little notes. "David treated her well. He was polite and kind to her," says Tara. "I don't think Heather had that in a long time from anyone. Lots of nights, they'd be upstairs when I got home, but by the next morning, David was gone."

At school, Quinton knew that David was interested in Heather, too, but didn't know the relationship had progressed beyond flirtation. Yet remarkably, neither man seemed jealous of the other. Quinton watched David courting Heather and assumed it was all just a matter of the conquest and wanting to get Heather in bed. "The motive for David had always been the sex part," Quinton says. "I never thought he was interested beyond that."

Oddly enough, rather than trying to keep Heather and his rival separated, David pressured Quinton to go out Friday nights with them. He got angry when Quinton didn't go, calling him "pussy" and "henpecked." As always, David played the part of the planner, supplying Quinton with excuses for Tammey. In hindsight, it appeared that David enjoyed watching his friend flirt with Heather, knowing Quinton didn't know that she was David's lover.

At lunchtime, Heather ate with a small group near the front office, and at times she talked about David. He didn't wear a ring, and at first some of her friends didn't know that he was married. "It seemed like everyone realized quickly that something was going on between them," says a coworker. Like Belinda, Heather was a good teacher, well liked by the students. She was creative, once using butcher paper to build a large apple-tree display in the school's hallway, and she had a self-deprecating sense of humor, e-mailing around dumb blond jokes to friends.

Before long, the chatter around David and Heather's relationship spread, as other teachers noticed the two talking in the hallways. Still, there wasn't the rampant gossip that some would have expected. "When Heather talked about David, a lot of us assumed he was separated or something," says one coworker. "They didn't seem to be keeping anything a secret. It was pretty out in the open."

"They were definitely together," says another coworker. "At the happy hours, we started treating them like they were a couple."

As David's tiny daughter grew within her womb, Belinda prepared for Erin's birth. Debbie offered to make crib sheets, a quilt and bumper pad, and Belinda picked out a bright blue-and-white check, with a yellow alphabet print to coordinate. One Monday Belinda arrived at Katy High exhausted, telling the other teachers that all by herself, she'd painted the entire nursery a hue she laughingly dubbed "Big Bird Yellow." Gradually, that fall Belinda, again alone, worked at shelving the nursery closet. Yet there was one thing she wanted David to do, one task she couldn't do alone. She'd seen a decorative shelf in Stacy Nissley's daughter's room, and Belinda wanted one like it in Erin's nursery.

One weekend, while they were out running errands, Belinda brought David to Nissley's house to show him what she had in mind. Stacy opened the door and welcomed them in, but instantly sensed that David had no interest. Shrugging, as if bored, David trekked upstairs behind Belinda to see the shelf, barely grunted, asked no questions about how it was constructed, and then quickly shepherded Belinda out the door.

"He didn't seem interested," Stacy's husband said, stating the obvious. The following week, Stacy thought Belinda looked disappointed when she mentioned that David still hadn't bought the wood.

It was a cool autumn day when Sheree rode her bike in the neighborhood and saw Belinda in front of the Round Valley house. The two women hugged, glad to see each other, and then talked about their work and families.

"Is David excited about a little girl?" Sheree asked.

"I'm not sure," Belinda said, sounding doubtful.

Sheree looked at Belinda. They'd known each other for four years, and Sheree realized Belinda was troubled. To ease her friend's concerns, Sheree remarked that there was a special bond between fathers and daughters, and that David would fall in love with his baby girl. "Our daughter has my husband wrapped around her little finger," Sheree commented. "You'll see."

Despite Sheree's good intentions, Belinda didn't seem reassured.

"Well, maybe after Erin's born, David will be that way, too," she said, sounding as if she harbored misgivings. That day, as she did with so many others, Belinda described her deep disappointment in her marriage; David was rarely home, and when he was, he rarely seemed interested in helping her get ready for the new baby. Belinda had put together the crib, painted the room, and prepared alone. When Belinda mentioned the shelf she wanted him to put up on the nursery wall, she said, "This baby will be in college before David gets it done. I'm not waiting on him much longer."

As she rode off on her bike, Sheree thought it was probably machismo on David's part. "I figured he wanted all boys to play football," she says. "That a little girl was cramping his style."

At work, David, ignoring that Belinda was pregnant, complained to Quinton that she was getting fat. David went on to say she was angry with him for being gone so much. If that were true, he didn't let it change his plans. When Thursday afternoon came around again, he pushed Quinton to skip the JV game and go to happy hour with him. Quinton refused, later estimating that he only went once. That didn't stop David, who taunted him constantly, calling Quinton "henpecked" and telling him to "control your woman."

Unaware his friend was sleeping with Heather, Quinton continued to have feelings for her, and they spent parts of the school day writing e-mails back and forth. Later, it would appear to have been something of a game for Heather, who flirted with Quinton, even kissed him, and then taunted David by repeating what his rival said, as if pitting one of the men against the other, edging up their competition with her affection as the prize.

There seemed little doubt that Quinton and David were battling over the attractive blonde, yet it seemed such a strange situation, hard to understand. Two highly competitive men were vying for the same woman, yet without any apparent animosity. At times, they picked each other up to drive to Heather's apartment and even walked to her classroom together. Perhaps David relished Quinton's ignorance. David was the one bedding her, while Quinton fantasized and flirted.

There was, however, something else; Quinton had a different perspective on his relationship with Heather, at least as far as Tara Hall could see. "It never really looked serious between Quinton and Heather, just a lot of flirting," says Hall. "I never had the impression that either one of them thought it would go anywhere."

Back at the Hastings Ninth Grade Center, the gossip

swirled around David and Heather, as threatening as line-backers rushing an unprotected quarterback. By then, most of the faculty at the Ninth Grade Center realized David was married, and that his wife was expecting a baby. "A lot of us were disgusted," says a coworker. "About how he was a jerk, messing around with Heather while his wife was pregnant."

Acting oblivious to the storm around them, afternoons in the field house, when they had their conference period together, Heather Scott's two suitors sat in the same room at individual computers, e-mailing the object of their attentions. At times, the flirty e-mails flitted back and forth between David and Heather, Heather and Quinton, at rapid speeds. What Tara Hall saw wasn't a woman torn about interfering with two marriages of fathers with children. "Heather seemed flattered by all the attention," says Tara. "She was really enjoying having the two of them both interested in her."

That fall at Katy High, Belinda wore a red turtleneck and maternity overalls on Fridays for the pep rallies before the games, along with funny hats and her red heart-shaped sunglasses. On the night Hastings played Katy High School, Belinda sat in the stands with the Temples. All day long she'd been getting e-mails from coworkers, asking what team she'd cheer for, Katy or David's team. She took it all in stride, laughing it off, even wearing a shirt made of half of a Hastings shirt and half of a Katy High shirt. The weather was cold and windy, and Tammey noticed that despite the turmoil in her life, Belinda cheered wildly for David's team. "You'd never know that so much was going wrong in her life," says Tammey. "To the world, Belinda couldn't have looked happier. And, as always, she was devoted to David."

Yet there were those moments when some friends caught a glimpse of the toll the stress took on her. At a grocery store that November, Evan wet his pants and threw up. Frantic, Belinda left her cart and fled the store, sobbing. "I just lost it," she told a friend. "I don't know what's wrong with me. All I could do was cry."

* * *

When they were together, Heather would later say that David didn't mention Belinda. The only time she'd claim David talked about his family was one night after a football game when Heather brought up the subject, asking if he had children. David told her he had a son and "one on the way."

"I felt sick to my stomach," Heather would say later. Yet that didn't cause her to stop the affair. Instead, it would appear, she continued to ignore the fact that David wasn't a free man, that he had commitments. When he brought her home after happy hours, perhaps she was able to forget about the pregnant wife and the little boy waiting at home.

And at Hastings, the e-mails continued to fly.

At 1:16 on Wednesday, November 4, Heather e-mailed David and Quinton: "What is going on with you two? Anything new? Have a good afternoon. . . . H."

Most of the time, the tone of her e-mails was breathy and casual, and she used ellipses scattered throughout, as if she were in too big a hurry to finish a thought. When David e-mailed back, Heather replied minutes later that she'd heard from an old boyfriend, and that she'd told him "I was dating someone . . . even though I'm not. . . . What is it with you guys?" Perhaps she didn't consider what she was doing with David dating, since they arrived at the happy hours separately.

"Don't compare me with some fool who would let you go, because he is an idiot," David e-mailed back. Later, he asked about plans for that Friday night, wanting to know where they were going after the football game. "It just depends on what you want to do," Heather answered, saying she was looking for someone to go to the game with. "I'll either find someone . . . or I will meet you guys and if you want, just let me know where. Quinton even said he was going out for a little while. I am afraid of what people will say if I do meet you guys out. . . . H."

"I'll be surprised if he actually goes," David e-mailed back about Quinton.

Over a period of twenty-four minutes, David and Heather e-mailed back and forth twelve times. Her last e-mail to David that afternoon, at 1:39, asked, presumably about their sexual liaison, "Does Quinton know anything about you and me?"

One minute later, David responded, "He has no idea."

"Nearly everyone in the Hastings Ninth Grade Center knew David was e-mailing Heather," says Quinton. "I knew about David's e-mails, too, but so was I e-mailing her. I knew for me that it didn't mean anything, and I thought it didn't for David either."

Even if he didn't try to hide the affair, flirting openly in front of others, David appeared to think he could quell any gossip simply by denying it, as on one day at the school, when he asked one of the teachers to make copies for him.

"Ask your girlfriend to do it," the woman responded.

"I don't have a girlfriend," he replied pointedly. "I'm married."

Perhaps it was such an exchange that started the e-mails off on November 5, when Heather wrote David: "I was just going to talk, since you two are deathly afraid to come near me now!!! . . . Tell Quinton [that] it sure is obvious that he is afraid to talk to me. . . . Just kidding!! I guess he should be scared[,] if his wife is getting reports on his behavior!!!!" Despite its serious subject matter, that e-mail ended with a "☺."

Perhaps that e-mail was written after Tammey asked Quinton about the woman the coaches' wives were calling the "Barbie bitch." When Tammey questioned her husband, he responded in a way that raised a red flag; Quinton said the teacher had a good figure and dressed well. "That was something Quinton normally wouldn't notice about a woman, how she dressed," says Tammey. "That was something new for him."

While Quinton may have been concerned about his wife asking about Heather, David admitted to no such qualms. When he e-mailed Heather, he typed: "I'M NOT AFRAID OF ANYTHING."

"What's up for after the game?" Heather responded, and David replied: "A lot of people are going to Sherlock's."

At that, it would seem, their plans were set, and on yet another night Belinda cheered in the stands for her football-hero husband and his team, while Heather watched the game with friends, anticipating going out after with Belinda's husband.

Late afternoon on Wednesday, November 11, of that year, 1998, Belinda and Stacy were at McDonald's with other friends and their children when Ginny Wiley, Evan's babysitter, walked by. Wearing a pink-and-white-striped maternity top, her belly round, Belinda rose to hug the girl. "We have a little girl on the way," Belinda gushed. As they talked, Wiley thought Belinda actually glowed from the excitement of the coming baby.

When Ginny turned to leave, Belinda laughed and said, "Be good, kid."

Only later would Ginny realize those were the last words Belinda Temple would ever say to her.

"Are we having fun yet?" Heather e-mailed David at 8:54 A.M. on Saturday, November 14. An hour later, she e-mailed again, typing into the subject space: "The Truth." Her message was confident: "I would just like to tell you that I am the SEXIEST BLONDE that is in this NEW building."

Minutes later, David e-mailed back. By then, he was most likely at the field house, getting ready for a postmortem of the prior night's game. "Have you been flirting with the maintenance men again?" he asked.

Seventeen minutes later, Heather responded: "NEVER would I flirt to get something I want . . . that is your job. . . . H."

At 11:51, David replied: "You got that right."

The following Wednesday, Heather e-mailed David at 6:36 A.M., sounding disappointed that she'd been out and missed his call the night before. "I don't know what to do about the other situation," she wrote, referring, it would seem, to Quinton. "I don't want to hurt anyone's feelings. . . ."

Heather wasn't the only teacher interested in David, it would seem. Another e-mail came in for David that morning from a woman teacher saying she was sad that she wasn't with him to see his "wonderful body." David forwarded the e-mail to Heather with a note: "Thought you might find this funny." "I think she is really CRAZY!!" Heather replied.

Five days later, they corresponded again.

"... If you need to talk more let me know. I can always make time," David e-mailed to Heather early on Thursday, November 19. "If you want me to talk to Quinton, let me know. I can make it so he doesn't know you have been telling me what he has been saying. I can tell him that I am seeing you away from school, and I think he will back off. It's up to you. All I am interested in is you being happy. Have a great day, and get those papers graded so the kids can have some candy. Where is my piece? D."

"I hope you're talking about a 'piece' of candy!!!!! ☺," Heather replied. In a separate e-mail, she wrote of David's offer to intercede with Quinton: "Let me think about the rest. . . . OK?"

Later that afternoon, more e-mails slipped between them, brief notes that asked, "Are you there?" and "What's up?"

"Nothing. . . . Sorry . . ." from Heather. She had a headache that day, and moaned that her students were getting to her. As always, David made fun of Quinton, this time noting that he hadn't brought his lunch that day "for the first time this year." The reason? David ventured that Quinton hoped Heather would talk to him about having lunch together.

"OK . . . You just made me feel really bad . . . ," she replied.

"I'm sure [Quinton] knew you weren't going. He was just hoping. You need to stop worrying about everything," David wrote in response.

"I'm not . . . you guys have your cake and eat it too. . . . Why shouldn't I . . . just kidding."

David ignored her suggestion that she was viewed differently as a woman, instead inquiring about where they were

going the next evening, but when Heather pushed, reminding him of what she'd said and adding, "You sure need to
keep up," his response sounded peeved.

"What's that supposed to mean?" he asked.

Two minutes later, she e-mailed to say: "Just drop it. ☺"

That afternoon on the Alief computers, they settled on
meeting at Pappasito's, a loud, cavernous Mexican restaurant, after the game, and Heather e-mailed that she wanted
David to come over afterward to her town house. "I just need
to talk to you alone. . . . ☺ I am just so worried about my
reputation."

Less than a minute later, David e-mailed and asked if
someone had said something to her, and inquired why
Heather would be worried if that hadn't happened.

Heather ignored that question but asked: "How do you
feel about me talking to Quinton? Be honest."

"I don't have a problem with you talking to him at all. If
it went passed [sic] that it would bother me. Does that sound
bad? Remember what is important is that you are happy,"
David replied.

"No, it doesn't sound bad. Would you be interested in me
if Q weren't? I don't mean that to sound mean. . . . I'm just
worried about your thoughts of me . . . I don't want you to
think I am available to anyone . . . I really like being around
you. As bad as this sounds, I enjoy e-mailing Quinton . . .
You two just happen to be married . . . that's what makes
everything so difficult. I just don't want to have to choose
between either one of your friendships."

Four minutes later, David wrote to Heather: "I told you
the most important thing to me is our friendship. I wasn't
kidding. I was interested in you way before Quinton was.
That has absolutely nothing to do with my feelings toward
you. What goes in e-mail makes no difference to me. You
shouldn't have to stop doing that no matter what. I would
be happy to discuss my thoughts about you anytime. You
shouldn't have to choose. Are you interested in being with
Quinton?" David asked. "Be honest."

"I am just TALKING to him . . . I just don't want to be the bad guy in this . . . ," Heather replied, then asked, "On what exact day did you become interested? (The minute and hour would be helpful. . . .) Are you and Quinton in the same room?"

"We are on opposite sides of the room. He can't see me," David e-mailed back. "The minute I was interested in you was the first day of school. At that point, I didn't even know you. If it makes any difference, my thoughts of you are great. And I am totally sure that you are not open to just everyone. I totally enjoy being with you, whether it is out or just talking."

Heather replied two minutes later: "OK . . . You got out of that one . . . ☺"

David replied: "Why do you feel like you would be the bad guy?"

When Heather responded three minutes later, she wrote that she wondered if David could see the e-mails she was sending to Quinton, since the two men were in the same room. "So are you reading mine? He might get jealous . . . just kidding. They are harmless."

"As his friend, I am all for e-mail. When he is in the right mood, he is great. He just doesn't spend much time between terrible and horrible, except on e-mail with you," David responded.

"You are too cute," Heather responded. "I am having fun talking to you. . . . I'm glad I can do such a good service for him."

At 3:03 that afternoon, David wrote to Heather: "Well, I gotta go and work. Really not by choice. I really have to go check on my kids and actually do some grades. You made my day better. I am looking forward to tomorrow. Have a great night."

"Bye . . . see you later . . . ☺," Heather responded. After three and a half hours and thirty-two e-mails, they turned their attention back to teaching.

The next day, the Friday before David planned to meet

Heather at Pappasito's, the e-mails that flew back and forth between him and Heather involved Quinton's mood. David wanted to know how his friend was feeling, odd since Quinton was in the room with him, and David and Quinton were discussing what they would do during their lunch hour. Despite his proximity and vantage point to judge for himself, David was filled in by Heather, who e-mailed: "[Quinton] is in a GREAT mood, judging from his e-mail . . . and just think, I don't have anything to do with it . . . he e-mailed me first. . . . ☺"

"So how are you feeling? And, yes, you had something to do with it," David countered.

"Q is in an excellent mood . . . but I can't take the credit . . . I feel pretty good. . . . Are you still going out . . . At least we can talk with ten million people around. I don't even have anything important to talk about . . . just can't ever speak to you at school."

"[Quinton] seemed to be in a good mood when I talked to him earlier. I'm doing great. I'd love to come over later tonight if that is OK with you," he asked at 10:25 that morning.

"Cool . . . I am talking to Quinton right now, too . . . at least you guys aren't side-by-side . . . He said it is hot in his room . . . wonder what he means by that????? ☺"

"You know exactly what that meant," David replied.

"I'm just teasing . . . You don't have to get mad at me . . . ☹ Just remember that's all he gets is e-mail."

"I didn't want it to sound mean," David replied. "I don't care about that. Don't send that unhappy face. It doesn't fit."

"☺ ☺ ☺ ☺ How's that?" she replied.

"That's my girl," he e-mailed. "Much better."

That afternoon, Heather e-mailed that she was counting down the minutes, first to lunch, then to the end of school. At one in the afternoon, David e-mailed, "It feels pretty good, doesn't it. It's almost time for cold beverages."

Heather, however, didn't feel well again, and she e-mailed that she didn't plan on having much to drink, because she was sure that David didn't want to take care of her. "I would love to babysit you," he replied. Then later: "I'll see you at happy hour. Bye."

Perhaps Heather decided to take David up on his offer to talk to Quinton. That month, David called his fellow coach at home. Supplying, as he habitually did, an alibi, David instructed Quinton to tell Tammey that he needed to go to Belinda and David's to help move something. That afternoon, Quinton did as told, but brought his middle daughter, two-year-old Avery. Once he got to the house, Quinton and Avery left with David to drive around while David talked.

"What are your intentions with Heather?" David asked.

"I don't know," Quinton replied.

"Would you be willing to leave your wife for her?" David pushed.

"No," Quinton said. "What about you? Would you leave Belinda?"

David hesitated just a moment and then said, "I'm not sure."

10

The holidays approached, and Brenda called Belinda late that fall, 1998, and said she wanted to come from Kansas for Christmas. Belinda loved Christmas, and the house was always decorated, but what Brenda wanted was just to spend time with Belinda and see three-year-old Evan open his presents. In a sense, Brenda's visits were a tradition. Throughout their lives, she'd spent the holidays with her sister, including celebrating their joint birthday on December 30. This year it seemed even more important, since the sisters were turning thirty, entering a new decade of life. Making plans for her sister's stay, Belinda sounded excited that Brenda was coming. But then, days later, Belinda called back and said, "I'm sorry. David doesn't want you to come for Christmas. We're going to be busy with his family. Why don't you come after for our birthday?"

Disappointed, Brenda agreed. She could tell that it bothered Belinda to have to tell her that she couldn't come, and she missed her. Belinda sounded upset on the telephone, but Brenda had no way of knowing how much was going wrong in her sister's life. Since childhood on, Belinda had protected Brenda, and even now, with so much turmoil in her life, Belinda didn't say anything about her problems to her sister.

Late that year, going into the seventh month of her pregnancy, Belinda often arrived at work appearing worn out. Cindy and Debbie pampered her, bringing over a chair so she could put up her feet and rest. Always loving to tease, Belinda sat back and relaxed. They called her their East Texas beauty queen, and she acted the part, ordering them around to do her bidding.

Going with the joke, Belinda's surrogate moms teased and said that once Erin made her appearance, they'd sit back and issue orders to Belinda. At such times, the women laughed, discussing the excitement ahead, how soon Erin would arrive.

Yet, at other times, Belinda was quiet and serious. One afternoon, she walked through the parking lot with Debbie and said, "David doesn't seem interested in me or the baby. I don't think he wants the baby." Crying, Belinda admitted, "I think he's having an affair."

Debbie tried to comfort her, but began to think that perhaps once the baby was born, she and Cindy needed to sit Belinda down for a serious talk, one where they explained to her that she had the right to be happy, and that maybe life with David Temple wasn't worth so much pain.

But then, as always, Belinda backtracked, belittling her suspicions. "I don't know, maybe I just feel this way because I'm pregnant," she mused.

"Maybe so," Debbie agreed. In her heart, she couldn't believe any man would be unfaithful to Belinda. Why would he?

As the year began drawing to an end, Belinda expressed those same worries to Stacy Nissley, this time admitting, "I think my marriage is ending."

Overcome with sadness, Belinda cried, but Stacy told her that she could hold her head high, that she knew Belinda had tried hard to keep the marriage together. Then, Belinda confessed what she'd already told Debbie: "I think David is having an affair, but I don't have any proof."

Football season ended for the year, but David was still rarely home. One who saw them often would later remember how David hardly ever looked at Belinda, treating her as if she weren't even there. Yet Belinda still didn't seem ready to admit defeat. "Belinda was in love with David, even then," says Stacy. "She would have done anything for him, even walked away from the marriage, if that was what he wanted."

As the Christmas break approached, Belinda sent e-mails to the Katy High faculty. First, she had finally given up on getting David to put up the nursery shelf, and she wanted a referral for a handyman. Second, she wrote: "As most of you know, I'll be delivering a little one real soon." What Belinda needed was a recommendation for a good substitute teacher to take over her work with her students. She worried about them, and wanted the teacher who replaced her to do the same.

Getting ready for the holidays, Belinda happened upon Staci Rios, her college roommate, at the mall, Christmas shopping. Belinda was in Victoria's Secret looking at a maternity thong. "Belinda, you have no business wearing a thong now," Staci teased. The two women laughed until they both cried.

Staci was pregnant, too, due any day, and they talked about their pregnancies and made a promise to get together soon.

At her Bunco game that month, Belinda and her friends, including Tammey, talked and laughed while they ate dinner. That was always a big part of the event, enjoying the hostess's specialties, sometimes lasagna or a piping hot bowl of homemade chili with a salad and bread, followed by a fast-paced game with plenty of opportunity to catch up on each other's lives. That evening, a few women noticed that Belinda looked anxious. Usually, she was the life of the party, cracking jokes and fighting to grab the dice and steal the Bunco when someone on the opposing team threw three sixes. Once she'd tackled the dice so aggressively, she'd scratched one of the other players. But this night, Belinda had little appetite and then played quietly.

As the holidays approached, Sheree, too, saw Belinda at the mall. She looked tired, and Sheree wasn't surprised when Belinda said, "I'm ready. I can't wait to have this baby girl and hold her in my arms."

Appearing worried, Belinda talked about all the shopping she had yet to do. Sheree said she envied Belinda's holiday break, nearly two whole weeks, but Belinda said she didn't have enough time. She wanted to make Evan's final Christmas before the baby arrived perfect, but she was feeling worn out.

"Evan's only three," Sheree pointed out. "He won't even remember."

"Oh, I just want this to be a special Christmas," Belinda said, looking increasingly uncomfortable. She complained that the pregnancy was taking a toll on her, that her feet swelled and her back hurt.

"I don't want to keep you here standing," Sheree said.

"I'll call when the baby comes," Belinda assured her.

That year, Christmas arrived surrounded by controversy. Just before the end of school for the year, Katy High was thrown into turmoil. The football team had done well, and they were still playing, winding their way through the play-offs. But at one of the final games, a teacher in the stands saw one of her students playing. Unbeknownst to the coaches, the teenager had been given a progress report stating that he was failing, which presented a problem. A Texas law called "no pass/no play" required that students needed to be passing all classes to be eligible to compete in extracurricular activities.

A couple of weeks later, the team won a berth in the state championships. After a rousing pep rally, as the excited football team loaded gear onto the bus to go to the big game, spirits were high. The team was strong and expected to win. It was then that one of the coaches received a call from the principal. Because of the infraction, the Tigers were disqualified from the championship. Minutes earlier revved up for the big game, the players departed the bus shoulders sagging, more crestfallen than if they'd been trounced. That year the Tigers' season ended in disappointment and disgrace. In a town that worshipped football, many were irate over the teacher who'd reported the violation.

That Christmas, Tara Hall wasn't around the town house as much as in the past. By then, she and Pete Engler, a teacher at Hastings she'd met through Heather, were dating. Pete didn't care for Heather, so Tara spent more time at his place than at hers. Yet, from what she did see, it appeared to Tara that the relationship between David and Heather was escalating, perhaps even becoming serious, as when over the holidays David dropped in to give Heather her Christmas gift, a beautiful gold necklace. "She looked pleased," Tara would say later. "Heather hadn't had a relationship in a long time, and David was really caring. I think he made her feel special."

Later, Belinda told friends that David didn't buy her anything that Christmas, explaining that they had agreed to forego big gifts for each other to save money for baby expenses. Evan had a full helping under the tree, however, including a brand-new bicycle with training wheels.

As always, Belinda and David spent Christmas at Ken and Maureen's house, starting out with breakfast and going through the day. It was around the holidays that Belinda heard David talking about getting a vasectomy. "Belinda was really upset," says a friend. "David had never mentioned it to her."

Two days after Christmas, on the morning of Sunday, December 27, Belinda, David, and Evan drove to Cleveland, Texas, halfway to Nacogdoches, to meet Tom, Carol, and Brenda. The plan was to pick up Brenda and drive her to Katy. On the phone earlier that week, Belinda had told Brenda that David didn't want to make the drive, but Brenda insisted Belinda had to make him. She didn't want her sister, so far into her pregnancy, to drive alone. Besides, Tom and

Carol had asked to see David and Evan. It had been a long time since they'd all gathered together.

That afternoon, they met at a McDonald's, ate lunch, and talked briefly. Evan sang the song "B-I-N-G-O," and everyone laughed. When he sang the alphabet, he seemed especially excited about the letter "S," because Belinda had taught him the song "You Are My Sunshine."

"S is in sunshine," Evan said, beaming, and they all reassured him that he was absolutely correct.

At one point, Evan walked over and kissed Belinda's round belly, smiled and then started singing to his mother's wide girth. "That's Erin inside," the toddler told Brenda.

After lunch, Brenda put her suitcase in Belinda's red Isuzu, and Tom and Carol headed north to Nacogdoches, while David and Belinda drove west, bringing Brenda to their house in Katy for a five-day visit, including a celebration of the sisters' thirtieth birthday. They arrived at the house about noon, and David carried Brenda's suitcase upstairs, to the nursery, where they had a bed for her, and Belinda showed off all she'd done, including painting the room.

Much at her sister's house seemed changed to Brenda on this visit. With Belinda pregnant, Willie, the gray cat, was relegated to the outdoors. To give it a place to sleep, Belinda had put a blanket in the garage, along with a litter box and bowls for cat food. Shaka, too, spent more time outside than Brenda remembered. But what struck Brenda from the first night of the visit were the elevated tensions in the house.

While David and Belinda had sometimes sniped back and forth, it always seemed no different than most married couples. Now, however, they argued, more than Brenda had seen before. And David didn't appear to understand when to back off.

"Look at her big butt," he said ruefully, on Brenda's first night with her sister and brother-in-law. "Your sister's got a big butt."

"David, I'm pregnant," Belinda said, appearing hurt and upset.

But David didn't stop. Over and over again he mentioned it, until Brenda finally looked at him and said, "Shut up, David. Don't say that." Only then did he let it go. David had never ridiculed Belinda in front of Brenda before.

That evening, they went out for Chinese food, and afterward, Brenda was in the den while Belinda and David were in the adjacent room, the kitchen. Brenda didn't hear what David said, but she heard her sister's reply. "You're not happy about having this baby girl," Belinda snapped.

"If you say that again . . ." David warned, but Brenda looked up and her eyes met his. He paused and suddenly went quiet.

Football season was over at Hastings and the staff was on vacation, yet the next day, David left early in the afternoon, saying he had to meet with the coaches. Belinda said nothing, but she appeared upset. "There was no arguing with him," says Brenda. "Belinda let him do his thing."

The following morning, a Tuesday, Brenda and Belinda drove to Walmart. Belinda had been stocking up on diapers with each paycheck, and they bought more supplies for the baby. At home, a few hours later, Belinda, bulky and uncomfortable from the pregnancy, twisted her ankle. "Clumsy," Brenda heard David say under his breath. Belinda said nothing.

That afternoon, they headed toward downtown Houston, exiting at the Texas Medical Center, a 1,000-acre maze of high-rise hospitals off South Main Street. One of David's cousins had been severely injured in a car accident, and Brenda waited outside in the hospital corridor with Evan while Belinda and David went into the room for a visit. Afterward, they stopped at the Houston Zoo, a short distance away, and pushed Evan in a stroller, wandering through the winding paths that took them from the monkeys to the lumbering elephants and growling lions.

The following day, the third of Brenda's visit, would be busy. That morning, Brenda sat in the waiting room at the obstetrician's office, thumbing through magazines, while

Belinda and David talked to the doctor. Afterward, Belinda filled Brenda in, saying Erin was growing, and the doctor thought the baby might make her appearance earlier than the official mid-February due date.

From there, they drove to a Department of Public Safety office to renew Belinda's driver's license, which expired that day, on her birthday. David didn't want to go and was in a foul mood. When he saw the long lines, he insisted they leave, but Belinda stood up to him, saying she had to stay. His attitude deteriorated further when, after the tedious wait in line, Belinda hit a glitch. Although she wore glasses to drive, she'd never before needed them for the vision test. This year, for the first time, she couldn't pass without her glasses. The catch was that Belinda had left them at home.

All the way back to Round Valley, David smoldered, and he and Belinda argued. When they arrived, Belinda grabbed her glasses and left, returning to the DPS station alone. The pressure in the house was palpable, and Brenda had never before seen things so strained between Belinda and David.

Later that afternoon, Brenda went with Belinda to the beauty salon. While Belinda had her hair cut, Brenda shopped in the small stores in the surrounding strip center. She felt bad for Belinda, who'd looked depressed, and Brenda found something she hoped would cheer her sister up, a small gift for their birthday, a statue with two angels, one blond like Belinda and one with dark hair like Brenda's. She also bought a pink plastic bank for the baby and a few toys. When Brenda gave Belinda the gifts, she appeared excited, and at the house she showed them to David, but he stared vacantly at the television, hardly looking. Brenda never saw David give Belinda a birthday present that year, and she wondered again but didn't ask what was wrong.

As they did every year on their birthday, that evening they all drove to meet David's parents. Belinda had chosen Los Cucos, her favorite Mexican restaurant, a short drive from the house. In the noisy restaurant, they sat around the table and talked, and for the first time, Brenda heard of David's plans for the next day, New Year's Eve.

"I'm going hunting," he told his parents, saying he was leaving the following afternoon and would be gone for two nights, returning on Saturday.

Belinda looked surprised, and Brenda wondered why her brother-in-law was hunting on a holiday, especially when his wife could have a baby at any moment.

"Have you got a warm jacket?" his father asked. David insisted he did.

From the restaurant, they drove to the Temples' home on Katy Hockley Road, the one that backed up to the rice fields where David had hunted birds as a boy. Maureen had a chocolate cake for Belinda and Brenda, and they lit the candles and sang "Happy Birthday," and then blew out the candles.

Belinda's excitement spilled out as she talked about the baby's approaching birth. She told the excited grandparents that her doctor had said she could be early, and she was beginning to feel ready. That evening, Evan entertained them all, singing his favorite songs, including "You are My Sunshine." Although a quiet little boy, he appeared as excited as his mother was about Erin. Belinda had taught him to write his name, and she'd shown him that both his name and Erin's started with an E and ended with an N. All he had to do, she explained, was change out the V and the A for an R and I to write *Erin*.

As the others talked, Ken retrieved a jacket of his for David to wear hunting, insisting his son needed something warm. But when David put it on, the jacket wouldn't close around his muscular body, and they all laughed at how silly it looked straining to cover his shoulders. David again assured his father that he had everything he needed, and before long, David, Belinda, Brenda and Evan were on their way home.

The next morning, New Year's Eve day, Brenda helped Belinda take down the Christmas decorations, while David sat on the den couch, transfixed by a football game. Brenda watched him, staring at the television, not offering to help.

Afterward, Brenda and Belinda carried the boxes of decorations upstairs to the master bedroom and into the large walk-in closet, where they piled them on the floor. The attic access was in the closet ceiling, and Belinda wanted to pull down the stairs and carry the boxes up.

"Let David do that," Brenda insisted, disgusted at her brother-in-law's unwillingness to help. "He can do some of this."

After lunch, David put Evan in bed for his nap. When David returned, dressed and ready to leave for his hunting trip, Brenda and Belinda were in the den. Belinda looked wary as her husband kissed her good-bye. He then turned to Brenda, reminding her that she would be gone by the time he returned. "So this is good-bye," he said.

They hugged, and he was gone.

Cell phones weren't common in Katy in 1998, and Belinda had the only one in the family, a large, bulky black model. David took it with him, and for the coming days that phone was the only way his eight-months-pregnant wife could reach him. Brenda never heard David tell Belinda where he was going hunting or whom he'd be with. He didn't even say if he'd be hunting deer or birds. After David left, Belinda looked sad, and Brenda thought that her sister couldn't go on this way, having to carry the load with the house and the children. "You have to put your foot down with him," she advised Belinda. "He's going out too much. He has a wife, a three-year-old and a baby on the way. He should be home. He doesn't need to be going out all the time."

Belinda looked upset but said nothing.

Instead of sitting at home depressed, Belinda announced they were going to Walmart and the Home Depot, to buy some things for the house. The sisters returned hours later with blinds for the living room, and Brenda feared the worst when her sister, with her round, pregnant belly, climbed a ladder to hang the blinds herself, saying that she knew David would never get around to it.

That evening, a warm night, Belinda brought Brenda and

Evan to the Nissleys to welcome in the New Year. Stacy and her husband grilled and the women sat in lawn chairs in the backyard and lit fireworks, as Belinda talked about how disappointed she was that David would leave her to go hunting on the holiday. "I can't believe he went, but what can I do?" she asked. When Brenda wasn't around, Belinda confided in Stacy again, saying she feared her marriage was ending. "I know we agreed we'd be careful with money, with the baby coming, not buy anything big, but David didn't even get me a small Christmas gift."

Perhaps wanting to comfort his mother, Evan rubbed Belinda's belly and talked to his sister, calling, "Erin. Erin."

"He was such a sweet child," says Brenda.

When Brenda and Belinda arrived home shortly after midnight, they put Evan to bed, and then checked messages. Maureen had called and left a frantic message saying she and Ken were worried about Belinda, wondering where she was so late. Kenny, Maureen said, was on his way over to check on them. A short time later, David's father stood on the front porch ringing the doorbell. When Belinda answered, Brenda noticed the older man looked worried.

"Where did David go hunting?" he asked.

"I don't know," Belinda said. "I don't know who he's with or where he is."

Brenda thought Kenny looked upset, but he said little more and quickly left.

The planning for the New Year's Eve party at Heather and Tara's town house had gone on for a couple of weeks. That afternoon, the two women cooked and decorated, and the guest list included friends from both their schools. As they prepared, Heather talked to Tara off and on, worried that her coworkers would sense that she and David were a couple. Perhaps she didn't understand that many on the staff already knew. The anxiety appeared to take a toll on her, and she began drinking early.

When David arrived, they stood around eating and drinking and talking to the others at the party. He laughed, telling the other guests how he'd pulled one over on Belinda, that he'd lied and told her that he'd gone hunting. "I have my guns and my hunting gear in the truck," Tara heard him say. "My wife's not stupid."

The guests had a good time, but by 10:30, her early start had taken a toll on Heather. Not feeling well, she retreated to her bedroom. For the rest of the evening she was in bed, and Tara and David took turns checking on her.

Late that night, David drove Tara's boyfriend, Pete, home. On the way, David repeated again what he'd said earlier, that he had his guns and hunting gear in the truck, so Belinda wouldn't catch him in his lie. Afterward, he returned to Heather and Tara's town house, where he spent the night in Heather's bedroom.

New Year's Day can be cathartic, the sweeping out of the old year with its frustrations, replaced by resolutions not to make the same mistakes in the year ahead. In hindsight, Belinda must have viewed 1998 as a disappointment, a year filled with tension, including those weeks when she and David lived like strangers. Even her characteristic optimism might not have been enough to assure her that the coming year would improve her marriage. Belinda woke up New Year's morning alone in the spindle-framed bed. She didn't know where her husband was or who he was with, but she must have realized even more acutely that her marriage was in trouble. With only a month until Erin's birth, perhaps Belinda thought she could wait out the storm in her marriage, and that once the baby came, 1999 might bring peace along with the happy family she prayed for.

The first day of that nascent year fell on a Friday. Brenda had an early flight to Kansas, where she had to report to work the following Monday. The sisters rose at 6 A.M., and Belinda didn't look well. She seemed weary and depressed and Brenda suspected her sister hadn't slept. At the airport,

Belinda parked the car and then walked Brenda and Evan inside the vast and already busy terminal. A bit of a worrier, Brenda didn't care for flying, and this flight was on a small plane, a commuter jet. All morning she'd had a strange feeling, as if something awful lay ahead. All she could think of was that there might be something wrong with the flight.

As they waited for boarding, Brenda looked at Belinda and thought again about how worn out she looked. Without saying anything about her own building anxiety—the unsettling feeling that all wasn't well—Brenda said, "You should go home, Belinda. Take Evan and go home, try to get some rest. I'll be fine here."

Although in the past Belinda would have insisted on waiting with Brenda, on this morning Belinda didn't argue. The sisters hugged good-bye, and Belinda turned to leave, leading Evan by the hand. As Brenda watched her sister and the toddler walk down the long, austere hallway that led to the main lobby and the parking garage, Brenda had the unmistakable impression that she'd never see Belinda again.

Chastising herself to be reasonable and not to worry needlessly, Brenda boarded the airplane. Still she couldn't shake the premonition, and as she waited for liftoff she wondered if the plane would crash. It never occurred to Brenda that she wasn't the one in danger. Belinda was.

When Brenda arrived safely in Kansas City a few hours later, after a smooth ride through calm blue skies, she shook off her misgivings. Relieved, she dismissed her fears as senseless worry. She could never have imagined the horror that was now only days away.

That New Year's Day, Belinda drove home from the airport with Evan and, undoubtedly, spent the rest of the day working in the house, caring for her son and worrying about her husband's absence. Late in the pregnancy, Belinda's feet were swelling, and she complained to friends that she felt uncomfortable and achy, carrying so much extra weight. But the most upsetting aspect must have been her worsening relationship with David, the uncertainty and the fear that her marriage might not survive.

Meanwhile, fifteen minutes away by car, Heather and David made love and lounged on the town-house couch, watching football. Perhaps Heather never thought about Belinda at home, eight months pregnant, alone on the holiday with David's three-year-old son. Or perhaps Heather was so delighted to have David to herself that she simply didn't care. It obviously didn't worry David that his wife could deliver their daughter at any time. Later, cell phone records would show that he called Belinda only once during his three days with Heather, on Sunday afternoon, when he was on his way home.

Did David and Belinda argue when he arrived home? Was Belinda angry?

That Sunday evening, about 6 P.M., Bill Norwood, one of the other Hastings coaches, and his wife, Marianne, were at Los Cucos, when they noticed Belinda and David with Evan at a table across the dining room. From the moment she saw her, Marianne thought Belinda looked upset. It seemed odd that David and Belinda sat silently across from each other, not talking. When they finished dinner, Belinda took Evan to the restroom, and David walked across the restaurant to say hello to the Norwoods.

A few minutes later, Belinda returned from the restroom and joined them, holding Evan by the hand. "I'm still teaching," she told Marianne. "I'm trying to save all my sick days to use when the baby comes." While she talked about Erin, Belinda rubbed her belly, as if caressing her unborn child. Minutes later, after the Temples left, Marianne remarked to her husband that Belinda Temple had looked incredibly sad.

"I wonder if something's wrong," she said.

At Hastings that first week of school in 1999, a rumor floated around. As some heard it, David Temple had told people that his wife, Belinda, was the schoolteacher who reported the infringement of the rules and caused the Katy football team to be disqualified from the state championship. That wasn't true. Later, some would wonder why David wanted the teachers to think it was Belinda. "Football was everything in Katy, and the team had to forfeit a championship game," says a teacher. "People were saying that David said a lot of people in Katy were really mad at Belinda."

At Katy High, the teachers later strained to remember if anything odd happened that first week of school, but Belinda appeared well, if tired. The following weekend, on Saturday, Belinda was still trying to finish Erin's nursery, and the sticking point was the shelf she'd tried unsuccessfully to get David to hang. He had worked around the house over the holiday. For Christmas, Maureen and Kenny had given David and Belinda the materials to build a small pond next to the back door. Perhaps David had mentioned wanting one. Quinton had just built one in his backyard a few weeks earlier, and David was not one to be outdone. However it happened, the pond was finished, but the nursery shelf Belinda had been begging for remained undone.

Frustrated, Belinda had a handyman give her an estimate on putting up the shelf early that week, but she told a friend the price the man quoted was high, and she'd decided to do it on her own. By then, one of the teachers had given Belinda a shelf that wasn't being used. Later, it would appear that Belinda didn't care for the brackets it came with, because on that Sunday, January 10, Belinda drove to the Home Depot on I-10, about eleven minutes from their house, and purchased a set of replacement brackets.

That same Sunday afternoon, Natalie Scott saw Belinda in the garage, working on the shelves she'd been installing in the nursery closet. Amazed that at such an advanced stage of pregnancy Belinda was still doing physical labor, Natalie walked across the street to talk about the baby shower she'd offered to host for Belinda. Over the two years they'd lived nearby, Belinda and Natalie had become friends. Her own baby had arrived two months earlier, and Natalie had already brought her maternity clothes to Belinda to wear. That afternoon the women talked, and Belinda invited Natalie inside to see what she'd done to the nursery.

When they walked through the den, Natalie saw David sprawled out on the couch, watching television. When they got upstairs, Belinda confided in her neighbor that David had done little to get ready for the baby's arrival. As if to illustrate that point, the wall shelf with the old brackets lay on the nursery floor. Yet, despite her frustration, as Belinda talked about Erin's arrival, saying it might now be only days or weeks away, "she looked really happy," says Natalie. "She was so excited about having a baby girl."

The following morning, Monday, January 11, Maureen Temple called Belinda around 6 A.M., while she and David dressed for work, to say she'd cooked a pot of homemade soup. "Come over and get some after school," she offered.

That morning, David and Belinda's house on Round Valley was particularly hectic.

During the night, Evan brought his pillow with a big red truck on it and crawled into his parents' bed, curling up under the brightly colored quilt. Exhausted, Belinda slept soundly, only to awake and find that the three-year-old had become ill during the night. He was running a low-grade fever and looked lethargic, so Belinda gave him Motrin. Not wanting to use up her sick days before the baby arrived, Belinda dressed her son for day care, while David left for work at Hastings.

Despite her worries about Evan, Belinda showed up at Tiger Land with a wide smile and Evan riding on her back. That morning Belinda had on a black maternity top and black-and-white-checked leggings, with black socks and low-heeled shoes with elastic bands across the top.

When Belinda walked in the door, Ida Sivley, one of the teachers, called out, "Girl, you better put that boy down or you'll have that baby right now!"

"No, he's my baby, too," Belinda replied with a laugh.

After taking the toddler to the water fountain for a drink and to the restroom, Belinda talked with Evan's teacher, filling her in on the rough night he'd had, and telling her that while Evan wasn't currently running a fever, he might not make it through the day. "If his fever goes up or he gets ill, call me," Belinda said. "David has agreed to come get him so I can finish the day."

The teacher agreed, and Belinda left. It was less than a week after David and Belinda's seventh anniversary, and a beautiful winter day in Houston, with afternoon temperatures predicted to be close to seventy.

Just after seven that morning, Belinda was at school in her room with Debbie and Cindy. Her ankles were swollen, and Belinda sat on a chair the other teachers brought out for her. Cindy massaged Belinda's ankles and they listened as Belinda repeated her account of the turmoil of the night before, talking about how guilty she felt for sleeping through the night while Evan was ill. Debbie and Cindy told her that she had a right to be exhausted, since she was eight months pregnant, working and chasing a toddler. They talked about the baby and the doctor's prediction that it could come early. "You know, I don't have much of an appetite," Belinda said. "I didn't even feel like eating breakfast."

"Maybe that's a sign that the baby is coming," Debbie suggested.

Belinda laughed and said, "Maybe." Then she asked Debbie and Cindy to let her know if Tiger Land called. If Evan's temperature went up again, she had to contact David to pick him up.

That morning, Belinda sent out her morning e-mail to the staff, a joke: "Can people really predict the future?" a little boy was asked.

"My mom can," he replied. "She takes one look at my report card and tells me what will happen when my father gets home."

She signed the e-mail: "Have a great Monday!!! Belinda."

If Belinda could have predicted the future, she would have been terrified.

Later, Debbie and Cindy would describe that morning as like any other, until about 11:40, when the telephone in their area rang. Debbie talked to the woman in charge at Tiger Land. Evan's temperature was above 100.6 degrees, the highest they allowed at the day care. Someone had to pick the toddler up.

As soon as she hung up, Debbie called the teacher's lunchroom, where Belinda got on the line. A few minutes later, Belinda was in her classroom, on the phone, calling David at Hastings. He didn't answer. She called once, twice, three more times from her cell. "I can never find David when I need him. I ought to get him a beeper," she told Debbie. Belinda appeared irritated, as she gathered her things to leave. "I need to pick up Evan, but as soon as I can reach David and get him home, I'll be back."

From her room, Belinda detoured to talk to Margaret Christian, one of the administrators, to tell her of her plans. Belinda had a meeting scheduled with Christian and a parent at two that afternoon, and Belinda assured the other woman there was no need to cancel. David would care for Evan, and she'd be back in plenty of time. On the way out the school doors, Belinda saw Stacy Nissley. Complaining that she could never find David when she needed him, Belinda told Stacy about Evan's temperature. Recounting that afternoon, Stacy would say that was the most upset she'd ever seen Belinda. Later, Belinda's cell records showed that in addition to the attempts from her room, Belinda called David five times on her cell phone. "What's wrong with him?" she said. "Where is he? I'm going to end up missing the day."

At Tiger Land, Belinda walked in and saw Eileen Lang, another of the teachers, in the lobby. Eileen was pregnant, too, albeit not quite as far along as Belinda. While someone went to fetch Evan, the two women talked about their plans, comparing baby bumps. Putting her open hand on Eileen's swollen midsection, Belinda grinned happily and remarked, "You're getting so big!"

"I know," said Eileen proudly.

With that, Belinda ran her hands over her own wide belly and said, "Erin will be here any day now, and your baby is right around the corner."

When Evan's teacher came to the front carrying the toddler, asleep and wrapped in his blanket, she explained that the usually energetic child appeared tired all morning and, while he nearly always ate two or three portions of lunch, barely touched his food. He'd refused to play, and had spent most of the morning with his head down. He'd even refused to sing the ABCs, one of his favorite events. At lunch, the teacher touched his forehead and suspected his fever had gone up, a fact confirmed with a thermometer.

Visibly worried about Evan, Belinda gathered his backpack and took the toddler wrapped in his blanket from the other woman. He was asleep in her arms as she carried him from the day care, saying she wanted to take him home for a nap.

Later, it would appear that at some point during one of her nearly back-to-back phone calls, Belinda had connected with David. He left Hastings around noon, and they met at the house, where, on the counter in the kitchen, Belinda recorded when Evan had last taken medication on a Post-it note: one and a half teaspoons of Motrin at 12:15.

Just after one, Debbie saw Belinda walk back into her classroom at Katy High. Both the women were busy, and they didn't talk, but Debbie didn't sense that there was anything wrong. One and a quarter hours later, at 2:30, their last student left for the day, and Debbie walked out of the room with Belinda, who was on her way to the parent conference meeting. Debbie had made the bumper pad, sheets and pillows for Erin's crib, and she'd brought in the final pieces, some pillows, that afternoon. Before leaving her room, Belinda straightened up her desk and put everything in order, including leaving instructions in case she wasn't in the next day. "Maybe I'll need a substitute tomorrow if I have this baby tonight," Belinda said with a laugh.

"Maybe," Debbie said. "It'll be soon."

On the way to the meeting, Belinda crossed paths again with Stacy in the hall. When she asked how Evan was, Belinda looked frustrated. "David's home. I'll tell you about it later," she said, then closing the conversation as she ran down the hall with an exasperated, "Men!"

Margaret Christian would later say the meeting went well that afternoon, the student's mother agreeable to the school's plan to change his class schedule. Before finishing, the women briefly shared pregnancy and childbirth stories. From Christian's office, at approximately 3:20, Belinda left in a rush, eager to get home.

In her classroom, Belinda grabbed her purse and car keys and the new baby pillows. On the way out the door, a woman security guard saw Belinda, so heavily pregnant, struggling to carry everything, and offered to help. By then, Belinda appeared exhausted. "She was dragging," says the guard.

"Why don't you stay home until the baby comes?" the woman asked, leading Belinda to explain once again that she only had so many sick days and needed to save them to have time with Erin after her birth.

From Katy High School, Ken Temple would later say his daughter-in-law drove to his home on Katy Hockley Road to pick up the homemade soup Maureen called about that morning. When Ken saw Belinda pull up, he brought out the container. In Ken's recounting, he and Belinda talked briefly about Evan being ill and her suspicions that little Erin would be coming soon, and Belinda hurriedly left.

That evening promised to be busy for Belinda, so her rush wouldn't be surprising. In addition to being eager to check on Evan, that Monday was Belinda's Bunco night. She'd told friends she still hoped to go. The monthly game was one of her favorite pastimes, and that evening the hostess was serving enchiladas, one of Belinda's favorite dinners.

At 3:32, Belinda made another cell phone call, this one

to the Round Valley house. David and Belinda talked for a mere thirty seconds, and David would later say that Belinda called to tell him that she was in the car, on her way home. Later, David estimated that Belinda arrived home about thirteen minutes later, at 3:45.

After traumatic events, it's not unusual for family, friends and neighbors to reconstruct what they saw or knew. Later, those close to Belinda and David would commit to memory what they were doing that afternoon, tracing back their steps. At 3:15, for instance, one neighbor, Barbara Watt, arrived home briefly after work, then left to pick up her children at school. Watt returned home with her children about 3:50. Her dogs were barking in her backyard, but she didn't hear or see anything unusual. She saw no strangers or unknown cars on the street.

About that same time, Mike Schrader, a CAT scan technician who lived across the street from Belinda and David, pulled up in his car. He, too, wouldn't recall anything unusual taking place. The Temple house, a couple of doors down from his, appeared quiet.

At 4:38, the telephone rang at 22502 Round Valley, but neither David nor Belinda answered. Brenda was calling; she needed to talk to Belinda. Their paternal grandfather had fallen and hit his head on a concrete birdbath, and he was being airlifted in critical condition from Nacogdoches to a trauma center in Tyler, Texas. Tom and Carol were in their car rushing to Tyler with Tom's mother.

All that day, Brenda had felt antsy, uncomfortable, like something bad would happen. With the news of her grandfather's fall, Brenda assumed she knew why. She worried about the old man and wanted to reach her sister. Disappointed when Belinda didn't pick up the telephone, Brenda left a message, asking Belinda to call.

About forty-five minutes later, the telephones inside 22502 Round Valley rang again. This time the caller was Ken Temple, inquiring about his sick grandson. David's father's call, too, went unanswered. Like Brenda, Ken left a message: " . . . I was calling to check on Little Man."

Later, that silence seemed like the proverbial calm before the storm, for as the afternoon ended, as the day flirted with the first signs of darkness, something happened that changed lives forever.

Just before 5:25, Angela Vielma walked along Hidden Canyon, the street that ran along the side of David and Belinda's home. A pretty eighteen-year-old with long dark hair, Vielma had argued with her boyfriend over how to cook sloppy joe sandwiches. She'd left after *Oprah*, hoping to ease her anger by walking to a friend's house. As Vielma approached the Temples' garage, a blue truck pulled up. David was behind the wheel, and Vielma saw no child seat but thought she saw a young child in the front passenger seat. Vielma stopped and waited as David drove past her. He pulled into the garage, and, as the overhead door descended, she heard the truck door open. As she walked past the driveway, she saw a man's legs. Thinking little of the event, she continued on to her friend's house, just doors away on Round Valley.

About that time, Peggy and Mike Ruggiero, the neighbors David had casually befriended, were at home after returning from an afternoon walk. It seemed like any other day, until, suddenly, someone was at their front door, pounding.

"Mike, Mike, open up!" a man shouted. "Open up!"

Ruggiero, a wiry man with a monk's fringe of dark hair, a mustache, and glasses covering round eyes, peered through his front door's peephole.

"Mike, Mike, it's David, let me in," Temple shouted.

Recognizing his neighbor, Ruggiero opened the door. Immediately, David thrust Evan at Ruggiero. "Someone has broken into my house!" he said. "Take Evan!"

Instantly, David turned and ran, as fast as if sprinting across a football field, heading for the gate into his backyard. Ruggiero called for his wife, and Peggy ran to the door, not understanding the drama unfolding. He quickly handed Evan off to her, told her someone had broken into the Temples' house, and ordered, "Call 911." Within seconds, Mike Ruggiero was running behind David, shouting, "Wait up. Wait."

No matter how loud Ruggiero shouted, David didn't stop. He never looked back. David reached the gate just steps before his neighbor, swung it open and pulled it closed behind him, then barreled full-speed toward the house. Ruggiero reached the gate just in time to see David run through the back door, closing it behind him. Ruggiero worried. What if the burglar was still inside? What was David walking into? One look at the back door and Ruggiero's concern mushroomed. The glass in the lower right-hand panel was shattered, cracks spiraling out from a hole above the knob. It appeared as if someone had broken in.

Intent on helping his friend, Ruggiero opened the gate to follow David, when from somewhere in the backyard, Shaka charged, teeth bared, growling. Ruggiero slammed the gate to prevent the agitated chow from attacking him. Unable to do anything else, Ruggiero strained to hold the gate shut, worrying that it could give way, as Shaka pummeled himself against the pine slats.

What's going on inside the house? Mike wondered. What happened?

11

The 911 call came in at 5:36 that afternoon, January 11, 1999.

"Somebody's broken into my house and my wife has been shot," David said, his voice breaking. " . . . Oh, my God . . . Oh, Jesus."

Outside the Temple house, Mike Ruggiero struggled to hold Shaka at bay, to keep the dog from bursting through the gate. Inside the house, David waited while the operator patched the call through, assuming the caller needed medical personnel and an ambulance. In her office, in Katy, Shannon Tuttoilmondo-Buell, an EMT who also worked as a dispatcher, came on the line asking, "Fire and ambulance. What is your emergency?"

"I've just walked in on my wife. I believe she's been shot. It's got blood everywhere," David responded, sounding calmer. When asked if Belinda was breathing, he gasped out, "No. I don't believe so. . . . Her brain is on the floor. I think she's already dead."

The next statement hit Tuttoilmondo-Buell especially hard. The dispatcher was expecting a child and couldn't help but feel the impact when David said, "[My wife's] eight months pregnant."

Despite the blow of those words, Tuttoilmondo-Buell had

been trained to remain composed. "Okay, sweetie," the dispatcher said. "Just stay on the phone with me, okay?"

David said nothing, but could be heard crying.

"Is there any way that you could see if she's breathing for me?" she asked, after a short pause.

"I can check, I think," he responded.

With that assurance, Tuttoilmondo-Buell asked if David would kneel beside Belinda and see if she was breathing. David didn't reply, but moments later could be heard at a distance, saying, "Honey. honey."

"Are you there, sir? Sir?" the dispatcher asked.

After a pause, David said, "She's dead." His voice was low, committed.

"Okay," Tuttoilmondo-Buell replied.

The dispatcher then asked questions, attempting to determine how long Belinda might have been dead. In response, David said, in a calm, quiet voice, that he'd left the house several hours earlier and just returned to find Belinda in the closet. He didn't know what she'd been "hit with or shot," but, he repeated again, " . . . her brain. Part of it's out."

Minutes earlier David had sounded in control, but again, in the background, he could be heard crying as the dispatcher assured him help was on the way. "Oh, God," he said, sounding as if he could barely contain his agony. "Ooooh, Jesus Christ."

"You say half of her brain is on the floor?" Tuttoilmondo-Buell asked.

"She's got part of it or part of something," he said. "I can't even tell. She's down in the corner."

"She's eight months pregnant?" the dispatcher asked again.

"Yes," David said.

Again, Tuttoilmondo-Buell asked questions, this time if David had seen anyone in or around the house when he had arrived home. Again, David's voice calmed, and he said he'd been with Evan, and that he'd taken the child across the street when he saw the back door window shattered.

"Just hold on the phone," Tuttoilmondo-Buell said. "Let's see if we can do anything for her, okay?"

"Oh, God," David said yet again. While he waited, the dispatcher could be heard in the background. Later, she'd say she was asking questions about what could be done for the baby, if the unborn child Belinda carried, nearly full-term, could be saved. Tuttoilmondo-Buell again turned her attention to David, "Are you there?"

"Yes, oh shit," he said. " . . . I can't breathe."

The dispatcher asked a second time if David would check Belinda, to make sure she wasn't breathing and confirm if she had a pulse. But David replied that he'd already done that and concluded, "She's gone."

"Okay, okay, what about the baby, sweetie?" she asked. Even though Belinda was dead, there remained the possibility that her baby could be still be viable. All hope of saving Erin hinged on how long the baby was deprived of oxygen. With that in mind, the dispatcher tried again to pin down the time frame, to determine how long ago Belinda might have been shot. This time in response to her questions, David said he'd been gone at least two hours. "Somebody's entered my house," he said. "The back window is broken, and my back door is still wide open."

Again, Tuttoilmondo-Buell asked if Belinda was eight months pregnant. David suddenly changed his mind. His wife, he said, wasn't eight but seven and a half months pregnant. Tuttoilmondo-Buell replied, "Seven and a half is okay. Okay. Is there any way that maybe you could . . . ?"

"What do I need to do?" David asked. "Tell me, and I can do it."

The dispatcher asked if David knew CPR, and he said he did. "I want you to do CPR for that baby," Tuttoilmondo-Buell said, undoubtedly thinking about her own unborn child and how she would want to give it every chance to live. David agreed and moments passed, but then he said, "I can't. Her head is just gone. . . . Oh, Jesus Christ . . . Oooooh."

The dispatcher spelled out the situation for David, explaining that if he did CPR on Belinda, he might keep oxygen circulating and save little Erin. Then Tuttoilmondo-Buell asked again, "Is there any way that you can do this?"

David moaned and cried, and said he couldn't. "There's . . . she's . . . there's . . . just no way. She's got her brain is just bloody. It's covered on the floor."

Reluctantly, Tuttoilmondo-Buell replied, "Okay."

Moments later, David, sounding calmer, said he'd seen two squad cars pull up to the house. The police had arrived. Tuttoilmondo-Buell assured him that an ambulance was also on its way. But she wasn't willing to give up. She kept thinking about the baby Belinda carried, nearly full-term. Every second the baby went deprived of oxygen threatened its survival. In a last effort, Tuttoilmondo-Buell asked David to try to give Belinda CPR.

"Okay," he said, but then the dispatcher heard nothing more.

12

A t the same time David cried into the telephone and listened to Shannon Tuttoilmondo-Buell urge him to give CPR to his dead wife to save his unborn child, in the side yard, Mike Ruggiero wrestled with the gate, fighting to keep Shaka from breaking through, fearing for his own safety.

Other neighbors began to notice that something odd was going on. Natalie Scott drove by, wondering why Mike was at the Temples' gate. She stopped, lowered the window and shouted, "What's going on?"

"Someone broke in," Mike said. "I'm trying to keep Shaka from getting out."

"Where are Belinda and David?" Scott asked, instantly concerned. "Are they okay?"

"I don't know about Belinda, but David's inside the house," Ruggiero answered. "Evan's at my house."

When Ruggiero told her Peggy was calling 911, Natalie continued on to her own home, a house away, to see if she could find a leash to help Mike control Shaka.

A few minutes later, Peggy ran across the street, wanting to help her husband. She'd left Evan coloring with their twelve-year-old son, and she had a cordless phone in her hand. She'd just hung up with 911, reporting a burglary at 22502 Round Valley Drive.

"Call David's house and see if he answers," Mike instructed his wife. Peggy did and the phone rang, but no one picked up. Since Shaka had always been better with her than with Mike, Peggy offered to take over the gate. Mike agreed, and Peggy held the gate and began talking to Shaka, attempting to calm the dog. It worked, and Mike ran around the front of the house to see if he could see David. Just then, a squad car pulled up in front of the Temples' redbrick colonial. Sam Gonsoulin, a sergeant with Precinct Five, the local constable's office, got out of his squad car with his revolver in his hand. Seconds later, another squad car arrived, this one with Deputy Kathleen Johnson inside. She walked briskly from the car to join Gonsoulin. They'd been on a call five minutes away and the time Johnson recorded as their arrival was 5:49, eleven minutes after the 911 operator answered David's call. The initial report was a burglary, but on the brief drive to the house, Gonsoulin had been notified that the incident had been upgraded to a shooting. According to the dispatcher, someone inside the house had a gunshot wound to the head.

"Who's inside?" Gonsoulin asked Ruggiero.

"The guy who lives here, David Temple. He's a big guy, a football coach," Ruggiero explained, then giving more details, including the broken glass in the door.

Ruggiero shadowed Gonsoulin and Johnson as they made their way around the house to where Peggy held the gate. When they told her to, Peggy let go and stepped back, and Gonsoulin and Johnson approached. Almost as a reflex, they slammed it shut as Shaka once again charged the gate, baring his teeth.

"A chow," Johnson said, knowing the breed to be fierce. Yet she and Gonsoulin had been told someone inside the house was injured, and they knew that they had to move quickly. Shaka snarled and barked, protecting his territory from the intruders, as they discussed what to do. All the while, the dog pummeled himself against the gate, the latch so loose the deputies pushed to hold it shut.

Shouting above the shrill barking of the dog, Johnson and Gonsoulin discussed alternatives. Quickly they agreed they had no other options. Someone was injured, and there might be an intruder. If the chow wouldn't let them pass, they had to shoot it. Gonsoulin gave her the nod and Johnson raised her gun, preparing to enter the yard. If the dog attacked, Johnson would shoot the chow in self-defense. Then, as the gate opened, a large, muscular man in a yellow T-shirt and black shorts opened the back door with the broken glass and walked out of the house.

"That's David," Ruggiero said. "He lives there."

"Secure your dog," Gonsoulin shouted.

As ordered, David called the dog, then grabbed Shaka's collar in a thick hand and walked it to the garage, opened the door and released it inside, closing the door after it. With the chow finally secured, Johnson and Gonsoulin entered the backyard.

The first thing David said was, "My wife's dead."

With that he hung his head, as if deeply troubled.

"Where is she?" the sergeant asked.

"Upstairs," David said, explaining that Belinda's body was in the master bedroom's closet. Gonsoulin instructed him to wait with Deputy Johnson while he went inside. For the next few minutes Johnson stood on the patio outside the back door with David Temple, waiting for Gonsoulin to return. Later, she'd say what struck her as odd was something Gonsoulin would also notice: that David Temple didn't look as upset as she would have expected. His wife was dead, but Johnson didn't see any tears in David's eyes.

An ambulance arrived as Sergeant Gonsoulin exited the back door. Dispatch had told those on board that there was an injured pregnant woman, and paramedic Maria Meijida and her fellow EMT rushed from the ambulance loaded with gear, but Gonsoulin stopped them before they reached the door. Meijida listened as the officer explained the situation. There was a pregnant woman inside, apparently deceased.

They didn't yet know what had happened to her, and Gonsoulin instructed that only one of the medics could go inside. Meijida volunteered, and Gonsoulin ordered her to put her hands behind her back. As they entered, Gonsoulin put his hand on her shoulder and led her to the right, through the kitchen, to the front of the house, and upstairs.

On the second floor, they walked past the nursery Belinda had so lovingly decorated, Evan's room with his name on the door, and the bathroom with the lively jungle decorations. They continued into the master bedroom, with Evan's truck pillow and the quilt on the bed, past the dresser and into the master bath, until they stood at the open closet door.

"Don't touch anything," Gonsoulin cautioned. "And be careful where you walk."

On the right, inside the closet's sliding door, lay what remained of Belinda Lucas Temple, on her stomach, turned slightly to the side, just enough so the sergeant and the paramedic could see she was well into a pregnancy. Belinda's left hand was crooked awkwardly beside her, the top of her head beneath a low-hanging rack of slacks and blue jeans, in a corner next to a rack filled with tennis shoes, flip-flops and boots. Her right arm was hidden from view beneath her.

There was no need for Meijida to bend down to take Belinda's pulse, no longer any chance that either she or little Erin could be saved. Brain matter covered the floor next to Belinda's head and her left hand, and Meijida could see that the blood had already begun to congeal. Unborn babies had been known to survive up to half an hour inside a dead mother's womb, but Meijida realized from the condition of the body and blood that more time than that had elapsed between the 911 call and her arrival on the scene.

Belinda Temple and her unborn child were dead.

Gonsoulin and the paramedic stood at the closet only long enough for Meijida to be certain Belinda and Erin were beyond hope. Then the would-be rescuers retraced their steps, down the stairs, to the door and out to the backyard. Sadness surrounded them as they talked, and Meijida asked

Gonsoulin if the dead woman's husband was on the scene. He nodded at David Temple sitting on a bench. As the others had before her, Meijida assessed the bulky young man with the clear blue eyes and didn't see a single tear.

As Meijida left, Deputy Johnson strung yellow tape across the front of the Temples' house. Once that was done, she took her post, guarding the door. Sam Gonsoulin did the same at the back door. He'd already asked dispatch to notify Harris County Homicide that detectives would be needed at the Temple house, ASAP.

About that time, 6 P.M., down the block on Round Valley, Barbara Watt was cooking dinner when her children ran in from playing to tell her that there were police at the Temple house. At first she didn't believe them, but they all walked outside and Barbara saw the yellow tape and the squad cars. Natalie Scott was also on the street. She watched the ambulance arrive and then leave without taking anyone. Natalie thought about what that meant. She saw David in the backyard. She knew Evan was at the Ruggieros' house. "That left Belinda unaccounted for," says Scott. "I knew it had to be Belinda inside the house, and that the ambulance left without her . . . that wasn't good news."

The call came into the Harris County Sheriff's Office homicide division on Lockwood Drive at 5:50. Precinct Five constables were on the scene of a suspicious death in a quiet neighborhood off I-10, near Katy. Which of the stable of detectives was sent out to a scene was the luck of the draw, influenced by what time a call came in and who was on duty. On the night Belinda Temple died, the evening shift supervisor sized up his roster of detectives and chose two who were in the office, Chuck Leithner and his partner, Mark Schmidt. They quickly left for the scene in individual cars.

Minutes later, another call went out, this one to Dean Holtke, a crime-scene investigator who lived in the Katy area. Leithner and Schmidt had an hour's drive ahead of them, while Holtke was at home, just minutes away. In his county car, Holtke arrived at the scene at 6:35, just under an hour after David Temple dialed 911.

A tall, muscular man with an olive complexion and dark hair slicked back, Holtke has a wide, white smile surrounded by deeply etched dimples and a well-trimmed mustache. He'd grown up wanting to be a cop. When he applied, the sheriff's office needed crime-scene investigators. "I figured, what the heck," he says. Holtke signed on and found he enjoyed the work, piecing together the evidence. On this night, he arrived on Round Valley and found Sgt. Gonsoulin, who filled him in on what he knew about the woman dead inside the house. Holtke asked where the husband was. Gonsoulin pointed at Temple, who was sitting on a bench near the garage. David had his head in his hands, but, like the others before him, Holtke noticed that the victim's husband wasn't crying.

"Put him in a squad and keep him there," Holtke instructed. By then, other deputies had arrived, and Gonsoulin ordered one to escort David to a squad car. Then Gonsoulin and Holtke began a walk-through of the scene. Entering the house, Holtke wasn't sure what waited inside. All he knew was that there was a dead pregnant woman in the master bedroom closet, and his job would be to collect and catalogue the evidence, to help determine how she died.

At the closet door, Holtke looked down at Belinda's corpse, so obviously pregnant, and the blood. Not wanting to disturb the scene, he and Gonsoulin quickly left. On the way downstairs, Holtke wondered if the death could be a suicide, and if the woman's body was lying on top of the gun.

David Rossi, a senior crime-scene specialist, was the next to arrive. An affable man, he'd grown up in the central Pennsylvania city of Hillsdale. He'd seemed to be destined for police work when, as a young boy, he discovered three dead bodies, one a woman with a pigeon jammed into her mouth, presumably the victim of a mob killing. Holtke and Gonsoulin explained the situation to him, and Rossi, an average-sized man with short dark hair and expressive brown eyes, thought about David Temple in the squad car.

"Do an absorption test on the husband," ordered Rossi, the lead CSI officer on the scene. Holtke nodded, and, while they waited for the homicide detectives to arrive, he walked across the street to where David Temple sat in the backseat of a Precinct Five squad car to do an atomic absorption test for gunshot residue, to determine if he fired a weapon. Holtke explained what he was doing, and David quickly agreed, putting out his hands to be swabbed.

"Sorry for your loss," Holtke said, wondering again if the woman upstairs, perhaps in the throes of the hormonal ups and downs of pregnancy, had taken her own life.

"Yeah," David said.

While he worked, Holtke realized he knew who David Temple was, remembering him from his days as a star player at Katy High School. "My ex-wife went to Katy High with you," Dean mentioned.

After Dean mentioned her name, David nodded, saying, "I think I remember her."

With that, Dean walked away thinking the same thing that Gonsoulin and the others on the scene had, that for a man who'd just lost his wife and unborn child, David Temple looked remarkably calm.

"Could be a suicide," Holtke told Leithner, when he arrived. The street was filling with county vehicles, from squads to unmarked cars, as deputies and detectives arrived to assist in the investigation. The clock was ticking. Statistics show that homicide cases not cracked within the first forty-eight hours have a high probability of never being solved. They didn't yet know what they had, but until they were sure, they would treat the case like a murder, flooding it with person-nel. Chuck Leithner had already been assigned as the lead investigator on the case. One of the sergeants on the scene took a position on the street to direct the deputies arriving to set up a perimeter and to handle traffic.

A cocky man with a round chest and thinning hair, Leith-ner had a mixed reputation in homicide. Some viewed him as overly confrontational with suspects, more likely to try to bully instead of finesse a confession. Yet he was also seen as "a stand-up guy," says one coworker. "He'll tell you when he thinks you're doing something wrong."

As he was being brought up to date on what was known so far, Leithner looked out to the street and saw a muscular young man talking to two people, an older man and woman. Early on Ruggiero had asked Gonsoulin if he should call David's family. Gonsoulin had told him no. Ruggiero, however, ignored the order and decided to notify Ken Temple, telling him something had happened at David and Belinda's house. Ken and Maureen rushed to the scene, screeching to a stop in the middle of the street, across from David's garage. Running up to their son, they embraced him. Later, the deputy standing nearby would say that he heard Maureen ask her son, "What happened?"

"I don't know," David replied. "Belinda's dead."

Ken asked about baby Erin, and David shook his head.

Hysterical and screaming, Maureen held David.

After Gonsoulin pointed out David as the dead woman's husband, Leithner suggested that the sergeant ask Temple to sign a COS, a consent to search form that gave police permission to enter the scene and collect evidence. Then, the detective explained, he wanted David kept segregated, in a squad car, until they were ready to talk to him. While Gonsoulin did as requested, Leithner turned his attention to Mike Ruggiero, to hear firsthand what David's neighbor witnessed.

Leithner heard from Ruggiero about the knock on the door and the barking chow, while out on the street, Gonsoulin explained the COS form to David. At 6:46, a little more than an hour after calling 911, he signed it. Minutes later, Leithner's partner, Mark Schmidt, arrived.

While Leithner had been in homicide for thirteen years, Schmidt was a new addition. A nineteen-year veteran with the sheriff's office, including stints in narcotics and child abuse, Schmidt had been promoted to homicide only nine months earlier. With a dark brown flattop, blue eyes with the hint of a twinkle, and a slight slouch to his walk, Schmidt had the appearance of a favorite uncle. Yet looks could be deceiving. Schmidt was so methodical and determined that one coworker called him the "Boy Scout." On the job, the detective had a quiet, shy manner, but somehow it worked. "People liked to talk to Mark," says one coworker. One night on patrol, when Schmidt stopped a truck for a moving violation, the driver blurted out: "I've got stolen car parts in the back."

That night Schmidt recovered three cut-up Suburbans, but rather than reveling in the collar, Schmidt would simply shrug and say, "just at the right place at the right time."

In anticipation of entering the scene, Schmidt returned to his car to get a pair of gloves. While he was there, one of the deputies approached him, saying that David wanted to talk to someone in charge. Schmidt walked over and bent down to talk to David in the backseat of the squad car. The sun had set, and the streetlights had come on. The evening was cool, and Schmidt had put on a jacket.

"How long am I going to have to sit here?" David asked the detective.

Schmidt looked at the man, thinking he seemed only vaguely interested in what was unfolding around him. "My partner may want to talk to you, to take a statement," Schmidt explained. "You'll have to wait here, maybe go downtown with him."

"Why would he need to take a statement?" David asked, appearing agitated.

Schmidt again thought that David didn't appear to grasp the seriousness of the situation. "We need to know what your wife did today, to figure out what happened," he said. With that, Schmidt turned and left.

On the patio, Schmidt joined Rossi, Holtke and Leithner, listening as Gonsoulin, who had the signed COS in hand, described the scene that awaited, preparing for what they'd find once they entered the Round Valley house. Then Gonsoulin led the way, giving his third tour of the evening, this time to the men who'd be in charge of the investigation.

Through the back door, Gonsoulin led the detectives to the right, into the kitchen instead of left toward the den. "We had to be careful," Holtke would later recount. "There was some glass inside the house in front of the door, but not as much as we expected. Most of it was off to the left, scattered on the den carpet. So we avoided it, didn't want to disturb it, and walked to the right, to the stairs, and then up to the bedroom."

As they walked through, it appeared to be a typical, middle-class home, albeit unusually immaculately kept. Photos were scattered throughout, including on the refrigerator, depicting David, the woman who lay dead upstairs, and their three-year-old toddler, all smiling for the camera, looking like any other attractive, happy young family.

Upstairs, the four men followed Gonsoulin into the master bedroom. At the walk-in closet, they peered in at Belinda Temple's body, lying facedown on the carpeting. It was Holtke who decided to investigate. At one point, while considering the possibility of suicide, he wanted a closer look. Wondering where the entrance wound was, he leaned down beside the body. If it were a suicide, the most likely scenario was that the entrance wound would be in the front or sides. With a gloved hand, Holtke parted Belinda's hair, starting at the side and moving slowly toward the back. There the thick strands fell open to reveal a gaping wound, bloody and angry. Meanwhile, Rossi spotted lead pellets mixed into the brain matter on the carpeting. Someone, it appeared, had held a shotgun to the back of Belinda Temple's head and pulled the trigger.

No longer was there a question of suicide. Belinda Temple was murdered.

13

At Bunco, the women were beginning to wonder. Belinda loved the game so much she was habitually one of the first to arrive. When she wasn't there by 6:30, half an hour after the start time, Tammey wondered if her friend had gone into an early labor. The phone rang when Tammey called the Temple house, but no one answered. They ate the enchiladas Belinda had so looked forward to, and waited, but she still wasn't there. Belinda's friends sat down at the tables spread across the living and dining rooms. As the time neared seven, Tammey and one of the other women decided to drive to Belinda and David's house to see if all was well.

For some unknown reason, Tammey felt panicked. On the drive to Round Valley, she prattled nervously on, describing herself as a "terrible friend to Belinda," for pulling away in the previous months. When they arrived, she felt sick as she took in the scene: the yellow tape, the crush of neighbors and police officers, and David in the squad car.

"Oh, my God," Tammey whispered to her friend. "David killed Belinda."

Fearing to know but needing to understand, Tammey spotted David's parents in the crowd and ran up to Ken. "Belinda's gone," he said. Releasing a small scream, Tammey threw her hands up to her face and sobbed. Kevin and his wife, Becky, had already arrived, and Tammey walked over to Becky and leaned on a tree. Becky and Belinda had been closer than sisters-in-law, truly good friends, and Becky cried as hard as Tammey.

"But David was home," Tammey said.

"What?" Becky asked.

"David was home. Evan was sick," Tammey said.

Becky ran and Tammey heard her tell Kevin what she'd just said.

After Holtke discovered the entrance wound in the back of Belinda's head, headquarters was called and the investigation officially became Harris County Sheriff's Office case number 99-0111-2596. From that point forward, everything collected, every note taken would be labeled with that designation. The detectives now knew they had a homicide scene to process. Starting in the master bedroom and bath, they went slowly through the house, assessing the overall picture.

The broken back-door glass suggested a burglary, but much of what they saw upstairs challenged that assumption. One of the first things Schmidt noticed was Belinda's jewelry box, sitting in plain view on her dresser. Through the glass top, he could plainly see money and jewelry. They saw no evidence the box had been disturbed. On top of the five-drawer chest was a television. Next to it, Rossi spotted a dish with David's watch, wedding ring, a gold necklace, and his heavy, carved gold championship ring. If a burglar broke in, if one was in the bedroom, why didn't he take the jewelry?

Holtke noticed something else, the duck design on the dish holding the jewelry. There were more duck decorations on the lamp, and downstairs there was a sign with ducks that read "David's Roost." It seemed obvious that David Temple enjoyed bird hunting; if so, it wasn't a stretch to think that Belinda's husband owned a shotgun.

Leaving the bedroom, the investigators deliberately and slowly retraced their steps through the house. On a stair,

Rossi pointed out a set of keys. It seemed odd. Who would leave keys discarded on a step halfway up a staircase? Especially in a house with a toddler, who might find them, play with and lose them? Rossi made a mental note to photograph the keys on the step, and they continued their way down the stairs.

In the dining room, drawers gaped in a buffet, but on closer inspection nothing inside appeared in disarray. Someone had apparently opened the drawers but hadn't rifled through them, looking for valuables. Why not? Wouldn't a burglar have wanted to see what was hidden beneath the linens?

"Look at that," Schmidt said.

In the den, the detective stood, hands in his pockets, looking at a bulky, black fifty-pound television. The TV was on its side on the floor, in front of the stand. Why? Had someone attempted to move it? What seemed strange was that the television was still plugged into the power and the cable outlets. Wouldn't a burglar have pulled out the plugs before attempting to carry it off?

On closer inspection, Holtke noticed scrapes on the front of the TV stand, where wood had been knocked off. Crouched down, he spotted splinters on the carpet, as if the damage was fresh. To Holtke it didn't look like someone had tried to pick up the television but rather wanted to slide it down to the floor. "It looked like someone used the stand as leverage while the TV was going down," Leithner would say.

This wasn't a scene any of them expected to see at an attempted burglary. Burglars ransack houses, wanting to get in and out quickly, before anyone walks in and surprises them. They don't usually open drawers and leave the contents undisturbed, and carefully set televisions down. They don't leave behind easily seen jewelry.

Then there was the back-door glass.

"If the door was closed when the window was broken, shouldn't the glass be in front of the door, not off to the left in the den?" Holtke asked.

Schmidt looked at Leithner and all the investigators understood what the others were thinking. The entire scene seemed off-kilter. Even the time of day was odd. Burglars rarely struck in late afternoon, when neighborhoods were busy with families returning from work and school. They also didn't usually carry shotguns. The weapons were bulky, hard to conceal, and carrying such a large weapon made it difficult to lug out valuables.

"We were looking around thinking the scene looked staged," Schmidt would say years later. "Between all of us, we'd seen hundreds of burglaries, and this one didn't look the way a burglary scene was supposed to look."

The night yawned before them, one filled with tension. They had Belinda Temple's husband outside in the squad car. What pieces of the puzzle could he supply? The detective in charge, Leithner, told Schmidt to stay on the scene, to supervise while Holtke and Rossi documented and collected the evidence. "Chuck said he'd take David Temple in for questioning," Schmidt said. "They needed to have a talk."

Out on the street, Leithner asked David to accompany him to the Clay Road Substation to make a statement, filling in what he knew about Belinda's activities that day. David agreed. Moments later, Leithner was on his way to Clay Road, following the squad car that transported David Temple. His parents drove behind them in their own car, and Detective Tracy Shipley, who'd been asked to interview David's parents, followed in hers.

Later, some would see this decision of Leithner's as a mistake. At Lockwood, homicide's headquarters southeast of downtown Houston, waited special interview rooms, eight-by-eight white-walled quarters, each equipped with only a table and a few chairs. The prevailing theory of the best way to conduct an interview was to get a drink and use the restroom before starting, then keep the witness or suspect for as long as necessary, up to hours at a time, answering questions. To avoid all distractions, the optimum setting was a bare, blank room, with nothing to distract.

Instead, Leithner had chosen to conduct the interviews at

one of the outlying substations, closer to Katy, on Houston's west side, where phones rang and people walked through the hallways. Years later, some would say that night might have ended differently had that one decision been different.

At Bunco, Tammey had returned and told the other women what they'd witnessed, that Belinda was dead and that police had David in a squad car.

"He did it, didn't he?" another of the coaches' wives asked Tammey.

"Yeah," she said. "David killed her."

From Bunco, Tammey called Quinton, who was feeding the younger girls in their high chairs. Weeping, Tammey told him what happened and then said, "That S.O.B. murdered her. David murdered Belinda. I know he did it!"

For a moment, Quinton thought it was possible, but almost immediately dismissed the possibility. "No," he said. "David wouldn't do that. He wouldn't."

"Yes, he would. I know he did it," Tammey insisted. "David murdered Belinda."

After they'd arrived on the scene, Ken Temple attempted to call Belinda's parents in Nacogdoches. He didn't know about Tom Lucas's father, or that Tom and Carol were on their way to Tyler for another family emergency. When no one answered, he waited and tried again. When there was still no answer, he dialed Brenda's number. He hated to tell anyone what had happened, but especially Brenda, knowing she'd be alone in Kansas City. The phone rang and Brenda answered.

"Brenda, I have some really bad news," Ken began. "It's about Belinda."

When she heard, Brenda screamed so loud neighbors in the surrounding apartments ran to find out what was wrong. She sobbed out that her sister had died, and then she thought about whom to call. She knew her parents were in Tyler, at the hospital with her grandfather, but she couldn't bear to tell them, so she dialed her oldest brother's phone number, and Brian answered.

"Belinda's dead," Brenda said. "Someone shot her."

Brian threw back his head in agony, and the first thought that entered his mind was, *David did it.*

David Temple would later describe those first hours after his wife died as being "in total shock. When you have something that traumatic . . . it's incapable of putting it into words how you feel . . . Sometimes it felt like an eternity and sometimes it went quick. I can remember having trouble walking."

Yet at the Clay Road Substation, others thought the victim's husband appeared less than disturbed. Once they arrived, Chuck Leithner took David to the main reception area for the sheriff's department, off to the side of the main corridor, and told him to wait on a bench. A husky young deputy was seated nearby in his uniform, working in a cubicle. The man said little to him, not wanting to do anything to jeopardize the interview that was about to take place. By then, he'd asked and been told that the man on the bench was the victim's husband. Like others, the young deputy was struck by how "unemotional" David Temple appeared. As he waited, David looked about the room with a sullen expression, when he suddenly turned to the deputy.

"Hey, did you play high-school football?" he asked.

The deputy shook his head, no, he hadn't. He said nothing.

David shrugged at him, and then stared back down at his hands.

In Tyler, the doctor gathered the Lucas family and told them that he didn't know if Tom's father would make it through the night. The blow to his head had been severe and he'd had seizures.

"Can we see him?" Tom asked.

Tom still hadn't heard about the horror unfolding in Katy. Brian had called twice trying to tell his father about Belinda, but couldn't find the words. When Tom got on the telephone,

Brian instead asked about his grandfather. But now, as Tom walked toward the ICU to see his father for what he believed might be the last time, a nurse rushed forward and said, "You have an emergency phone call."

Tom picked up the telephone, and heard a familiar voice. "Tom, Belinda's been murdered," his sister from Houston said.

For a moment Tom Lucas went silent, unable to speak. Then he fell to his knees and cried. Carol ran toward him, and for moments couldn't understand what he was trying to tell her.

14

Detectives are taught the circle theory, that in a homicide the most likely suspects are those closest to the victim. When they work a case, unless evidence or circumstances suggest otherwise, the most common approach is to first look within a victim's inner circle, at family and close friends. Then, if no solid suspects emerge, they widen the circle, expanding it to include neighbors and coworkers. If there are still no viable suspects, the circle gets even bigger, including acquaintances and strangers.

To eliminate individuals from a list of suspects, investigators weigh multiple factors: physical evidence, possible motives, truthfulness, if an individual is cooperative, and alibis.

Late that evening Kevin and Becky reclaimed Evan from the Ruggieros and drove the toddler and Shaka to Maureen and Ken Temples' home on Katy Hockley. Meanwhile, at the Clay Road Substation, Chuck Leithner explained to Tracy Shipley that he wanted statements taken from both of David's parents. An affable woman who doesn't have the air of a hardened detective, Shipley understood. Although she, like Mark Schmidt, had only been in homicide for a matter of months, Shipley had been in law enforcement for thirteen years. She'd begun as a civilian employee, a dispatcher, and then took the test and hired on as a deputy, working in narcotics and vice. With long brown hair and expressive eyes, for a time Shipley had worked as a prostitute decoy, propositioning men while her fellow deputies caught the evidence on videotape.

"I had to learn not to react when a man said they wanted me to perform some pretty bizarre acts," she says.

On one such night, a man told her, "I like girls. I won't hurt you. I just want you to pee on me."

Although stunned, Shipley simply smiled and said, "Okay. I can do that."

As the others left for Clay Road, Mark Schmidt and the crime-scene officers, Holtke and Rossi, stayed at the scene. Schmidt began by conducting a preliminary search of David Temple's garage, inspecting the blue truck and the red Isuzu. He noted the close quarters between the vehicles, so tight he had to turn to walk between them, and saw a bag of cat food inside the truck. Evan's car seat was in the Isuzu, along with a Home Depot bag containing a receipt and brackets, the kind used to hold up a shelf. Those items didn't strike Schmidt as odd at the time, but later, after he and Leithner were able to pull the threads of David's activities that night together, they would take on added meaning.

Inside the house, Holtke and Rossi mounted a methodical search, starting on the first floor and working their way up. They first shot a video, preserving the scene the way it was that night on film. Even rooms where nothing appeared out of place, such as the nursery and Evan's room, were videotaped. The sheriff's department would only have control of the scene for so long before it would be released to David's custody. Once that happened, there would be no possibility of reconstructing what they found inside 22502 Round Valley on the night of the murder.

Before they'd left for Clay Road, Gonsoulin had asked David if there were any weapons in the house. He told them about two rifles, a 30.06 and a .22, both in the master bedroom closet. When the time came, Rossi laid them on the bed, taking them out of their cases. It seemed unlikely that either one was the murder weapon, since the pellets found in the closet suggested the fatal shot had been fired by a shotgun, not a rifle, but both weapons were dusted for fingerprints and photographed.

Her sister-in-law called Debbie Berger that night at home, to tell her that she'd heard that Belinda Temple had been murdered. Debbie immediately dialed Cindy O'Brien, who listened politely but then said, "I don't believe it." That would be the first reaction for many of Belinda's friends, that it was inconceivable that anyone would kill Belinda.

After Cindy hung up the telephone, she called Stacy Nissley, who knew nothing about the night's events but offered to run over to the Temple house and check on her. Half an hour later, Stacy called Cindy back, crying. "It's true," she said. "Belinda is dead."

"It was impossible. I just couldn't believe it," Cindy would say later. For all three of the teachers, their first thoughts were of David.

"I knew he did it," says Debbie. "Absolutely knew."

At 8:35 that evening at Clay Road, Leithner and Gonsoulin escorted David Temple to an area used by traffic officers, not an interrogation room where David would have nothing to look at but bare beige walls. "It was a mistake," says a longtime homicide investigator. "When you're interrogating, you want no distractions, no ringing phone, nothing but your questions and God in the room."

Leithner offered David a drink and the use of a restroom, but David turned him down. The veteran detective began by removing a blue card from his pocket and reading David his Miranda rights, saying he was entitled to an attorney and warning him that anything he said could potentially be used against him in a court of law. On his written report, the detective noted what David wore: tennis shoes and white socks, black shorts and a yellow T-shirt. Leithner then explained to David the circle theory, where investigators begin by looking at close family and friends. The reason he was talking to David, Leithner said, was to collect information, and in the process, perhaps, eliminate him as a suspect.

When the investigators asked questions, David described the history of his marriage, explaining that he met Belinda in college and that they had one child, Evan. That morning, David said that he'd left the house before Belinda and gone to work at Hastings. He told how Belinda had called around noon, and said he'd gone home early to care for Evan while Belinda finished out her day at Katy High School. Around 3:30 she'd called him on her way home and arrived at the house on Round Valley at 3:45.

As David Temple talked, Leithner looked him over for cuts or scratches. With the broken glass in the back door, it was possible the killer had been injured. Or Belinda could have fought her killer and left scratches behind to help identify him. But Leithner found nothing on David resembling a fresh wound. "I decided to take my son to the park for a while," David said. Afterward, he said that he'd taken Evan to a grocery store to buy drinks and cat litter, and then to the Home Depot. When they arrived back at Round Valley, he left Evan "to play on his bicycle" in the garage. The first time he realized something was wrong, he told the detective, was when he saw the broken window.

After David talked, Leithner typed David's account into an official form on his computer called "a statement from a person not in custody." Finished, he ran off a copy and asked David to review it. David found two details he asked to change. The first: Leithner had typed that Belinda and David married as teachers, when it should have said while they were in college. The second: David asked to change the passage describing what Belinda was doing when he and Evan left the house that afternoon. Leithner had typed that Belinda was sleeping. As David requested, Leithner retyped the report to read that Belinda "was resting."

After he saw the broken glass and brought Evan to the Ruggieros, David said he'd returned to the house. When he found her in the closet, he said he "walked up to her and shook her briefly, but she didn't move." David said he'd checked for a pulse, as the 911 operator asked him to, but didn't find one. Belinda was "all balled up," David said, and he pulled on her legs to straighten her out.

"The operator also told me to try to give her CPR. I tried to move Belinda, but only succeeded in rolling her on her side . . ." The statement ended: "I know of no one who would want to cause harm to me, my wife or my son. We moved to the neighborhood as we felt it was a good and quiet neighborhood. We felt safe in the neighborhood."

While David read the statement over, Leithner left the traffic room to find Tracy Shipley. He needed to know how she'd fared with David's parents.

On Round Valley, as the video of each room was completed, Dean Holtke moved in with a still camera. Before the age of digital photography, Holtke used a standard 35 mm to shoot multiple angles of each room, getting close-ups of anything that appeared potentially important. Only when that was done did he and Rossi turn their attention to Belinda's body. At about 8:25 that evening, they'd progressed far enough to call an assistant medical examiner. The woman arrived on the scene a little more than an hour later to inspect and transport the body. As Holtke shot photos before the body was moved, he wondered where the blood spatter had gone. There didn't seem to be enough on the slacks that hung above Belinda's head for such a large wound.

When Holtke had enough photographs of the body, still clothed in the black-and-white-checked pants and black top Belinda had worn to school that day, still wearing her shoes with the elastic bands, the medical examiner laid out the red body bag, and Rossi and Holtke helped roll Belinda over. Strands of her long hair caught in the clothes hangers above her, and they had to untangle them. Once she was on her back, they could see that the carpet underneath her upper body was soaked in blood, and for the first time, get a look at the full injury to her face. The shotgun blast had entered her head left back and exited in the front, on the right side of her face. The damage was catastrophic. Much of the right side of Belinda's face, including her eye, had been utterly blown away, leaving a bloody crater. Shattering her skull, the shotgun blast left Belinda's face distorted, elongated and narrowed, and her mouth open, as if perpetually screaming in agony.

As they would throughout the night, Rossi and Holtke bantered back and forth about the burglary theory. They'd already documented Belinda's apparently undisturbed jewelry box on the bedroom dresser and David's jewelry, including his heavy gold ring, sitting out in plain view. On Belinda's corpse, they found more jewelry. The assistant M.E. removed a silver bracelet and necklace, and put them in an envelope. From Belinda's left hand, the physician slid the beautiful diamond engagement ring David had given Belinda seven years earlier on the fifty-yard line.

The red body bag was closed with Belinda's cold, lifeless body inside. Traveling with it to the Harris County morgue would be other evidence. One red plastic bag held brain matter collected from the floor. Another contained shotgun pellets and wadding found near the body, and Belinda's broken glasses. She still had them on when the shot was fired.

As they assessed the scene, Holtke and Rossi were puzzled. Once they'd been able to take a good look, they realized that the shotgun blast had virtually emptied Belinda's skull. Why wasn't there more blood splatter near the body? Holtke thought again that there should have been more debris on the slacks hanging over Belinda's head. At his side, Rossi had the same thoughts. "It didn't look right," he says.

Rossi looked around the closet and didn't see any blowback, blood spatter on the opposite wall caused by the vacuum created by the gunshot. "I figured we were looking at a contact wound and her hair had absorbed the little there was," he says. "Otherwise, with a shotgun, we should have seen something."

With the body removed, Holtke was finally free to take a closer look at the closet. Using a gloved hand, he pushed back the slacks hanging on the rod. Once he did, the wall behind them was exposed. It was there that he found what he'd been looking for: the missing brain matter. The lower closet wall was covered in blood and tissue.

As Holtke considered the position of the brain matter, he had only one explanation. At the time of the gunshot, the slacks must have hung off to the side, exposing the wall. Later, someone, presumably the killer, rearranged the hangers, hiding the brain matter and blood that covered the wall.

With this new evidence to consider, Holtke and Rossi discussed the angle of the shotgun blast and what they observed on Belinda's body. They'd seen lividity, purplish areas under the skin where blood had settled after death, on Belinda's knees and shins. That, coupled with the blood and brain matter splattered low on the wall led them to conclusions about her position at the time of the fatal shot. "Because all the blood spatter was low on the wall, she had to have been on her knees, facing the closet wall, when the shot was fired," says Rossi.

Why would a burglar take the time to rearrange the hangers? "It smacked of someone who was ashamed of what they'd done," says Holtke. "It was like they were trying to cover it up."

At ten that night, the local news came on television, and teasers at the beginning of the broadcast urged viewers to stay tuned to see a segment on a crime in Katy, the murder of a pregnant high-school teacher. In her living room, Staci Rios saw the brief mention and turned to her husband and said, "Belinda is dead."

A minute later, she called her mother and told her what

she'd just heard and that she was sure the dead woman was her college roommate. Staci's mother protested, saying Staci couldn't be sure.

"It's Belinda," Staci said, thinking back to those college years and her first impressions of David, mostly bad. She wanted to be wrong, but she couldn't fight back the certainty that her friend was dead, and that David Temple was responsible. As Staci talked to her mother, she continued watching the broadcast, and soon saw footage of Belinda's house and David in a squad car.

"Oh, my God, it is her," Staci told her mother. "Belinda is dead."

Ginny Wiley, Evan's babysitter, saw the news that night, too. Just that day, she'd sent Belinda a card, wishing her good luck with the baby and telling her to call after Erin was born. Now she thought it couldn't be true. Belinda couldn't be dead. But she was. That night she slept fitfully, waking repeatedly, crying and wishing that it were "all a horrible nightmare I'd wake up from."

Leithner's decision to interview David and his parents at Clay Road, a brown brick, flat-roofed building across from a Sonic Drive-in that housed a justice of the peace court and a smattering of county offices, wasn't proving beneficial. When Tracy Shipley arrived, she searched around for a place to question David's parents. The only place she found was a secretary's desk on the west side of the building, one without privacy. Having no other options, she showed Ken to a nearby chair and seated Maureen at a desk across from her. Shipley then opened up a laptop computer Leithner had given her to use, to type up Maureen's statement.

From the beginning, the lack of seclusion proved to be a problem. "We were in an environment we couldn't control," Shipley would say later. "We needed to be on our own turf, even if it meant a longer drive downtown."

That night, Shipley asked Maureen questions. The matronly woman with the helmet of precisely arranged pale blond hair answered, only to have her husband periodically rush to her side to correct her. It seemed that from his perch, David's father listened to every word, apparently concerned about what his wife might say. "Every time Maureen said something, Ken Temple jumped up like a jack-in-a-box and came around and answered for her," Shipley would say later. "It was frustrating."

That night, Shipley tried to stop the interference. "Please don't interrupt," she asked David's father. "This is your wife's statement, and it needs to be in her words. You'll have your opportunity to say what you want in your statement."

But only moments later, it happened again; Ken rushed through the door, contradicting Maureen and insisting Shipley change his wife's words. Throughout the lurching process, Shipley felt the older man didn't understand that in this situation, she was the one in charge, not him. In Shipley's estimation, the older man was condescending, treating her "like a disrespectful youngster."

By then, Ken Temple had worked for more than a decade for the county government, as a supervisor in the computer department, setting up classes for county personnel. That night while she took Maureen's statement, Detective Shipley ran into minor problems using the borrowed computer, and more than once Ken Temple snapped, "You need to take some classes."

The fitful situation staggered on, Shipley asking questions, Mrs. Temple answering, and Mr. Temple sporadically barging in. Unaware that at the scene suicide had been ruled out, Shipley asked if Belinda had been depressed or experienced hormonal problems, if her death could have been a suicide.

"Oh, no, that's not possible," Maureen said, clutching a tissue in her hand, one Shipley never saw the older woman use. "Belinda was a happy person, and she was excited about the baby."

"Did your daughter-in-law have any enemies?" the detective asked.

"No, Belinda was liked by everyone," Mrs. Temple said.

Then something extraordinary happened. Maureen Temple buried her face in her hands, and Tracy Shipley heard the older woman say in a troubled, mournful voice, "I just could not have raised a son who would kill his wife."

Ah, now there it is, Shipley thought.

Yet she said nothing. As she had with johns interested in kinky sex more than a decade earlier, Shipley consciously made her expression noncommittal, and said, "Mrs. Temple, I didn't mention anything about your son." She started to ask a question: "Why would you think he might have killed his wife?" But Shipley never got the chance.

Before she could form the words, Ken Temple charged toward the desk, furious, chastising Shipley like a superior correcting an errant teenager and insisting, "My wife didn't mean that." From that point on, Ken refused to leave the room, standing at attention next to his wife. When Tracy went to talk to Leithner, to tell him about the problems segregating David's parents, Leithner came out briefly to talk to Ken Temple.

"She asked if David killed Belinda!" Ken charged, indicating Shipley.

"I never said that," Tracy responded.

At the house on Round Valley, after the video and photos were finished, Holtke again started on the first floor and worked his way upstairs. He drew a sketch of the crime scene, marking X's where the broken glass lay, a small amount in front of the back door but most of it on the carpeting in the den. There wasn't any on the blue couch positioned just feet in front of the door. Instead, the glass had scattered to the left of the doorway into the den. Holtke and Rossi inspected the door, not finding any signs that it was damaged except for the glass. "Simple physics said the glass shouldn't have been where it was if the door was closed when the glass was broken," says Rossi. "It just wouldn't work that way."

Once Holtke finished his diagram, he and Rossi bagged evidence, including Belinda's keys found lying on the step.

Holtke collected the sheets off David and Belinda's bed, and then picked up a blue towel he found in the master bathroom, near the bathtub. It was damp, as if recently used. On the rug in front of it were some of Evan's superhero figures, toys he played with in the bathtub.

As Holtke and Rossi made their way through the bedroom, they found three jewelry boxes, none appearing to have been disturbed. Rossi had already discovered Belinda's purse in a first-floor closet, under the stairs. It seemed an odd place for it, and they'd bagged it and taken it in as evidence. Before turning it in to the lab, he pulled out an address book and set it aside for the detectives. It would have the names and phone numbers of Belinda's friends and coworkers, potential witnesses.

When the crime scene officers finished in the bedroom, Mark Schmidt entered wearing latex gloves, taking in the scene. He turned his attention to a black cordless telephone found lying near the body. Had Belinda grabbed it off the cradle on the dresser, as she ran to the closet, to call for help? After the telephone was photographed and tested for fingerprints, Schmidt pressed the REDIAL button. The last call on that particular telephone, it would turn out, had been to the Ruggiero residence, the neighbors David had run to with Evan. Why would Belinda call a neighbor rather than 911 if she were fleeing a burglar?

Schmidt then picked up the telephone next to the bed, one with a cord anchored into the wall. He hit redial on this phone as well, and this time 911 answered. Since he knew David had called 911 and there was no record of Belinda calling, that phone, he surmised, was the one David used. As he looked about the bedroom, Schmidt, like Rossi and Holtke had before him, thought about the undisturbed jewelry boxes and the glass scattered across the den. He and the others had examined and reexamined the door and the glass. The only way they could envision that glass pattern was if the door was already open when the windowpane was shattered.

"A whole lot of what we were seeing didn't make a whole lot of sense," says Schmidt.

Lastly, Schmidt checked the answering machine, pressing the PLAY button. He listened to the messages David's father and Brenda had left early the prior evening. When finished, he popped the top of the machine open and removed the micro cassette, then slipped it into an evidence envelope, numbered and sealed it.

As the investigators worked in the house, it seemed odd. They were in a quiet, middle-class neighborhood processing what appeared, from the photos scattered throughout, to be a happy home. Upstairs, hidden in the master bedroom, was the horror of what had transpired that afternoon, the puzzle that had to be pieced together to find Belinda Temple's murderer. Yet much of the house appeared undisturbed.

In the kitchen, Maureen's homemade soup sat in a container on the counter, as if Belinda hadn't had time to put it in the refrigerator. Next to it were Post-it notes. The first lay next to a digital thermometer and recorded the time Evan received medication for his fever: "1½ tsp of Motrin @ 12:15." Next to that were notes asking Belinda to call her aunt in Houston. As if he'd just walked in from day care, Evan's backpack hung over the back of a kitchen chair. About eleven that night, Rossi finally went home to sleep for a few hours. He'd be back in the morning.

On Clay Road, after midnight, tensions were rising.

When Leithner returned to the traffic room, he asked David for more information about his activities that afternoon. David had said that when he left the house, he took Evan to the small park in his neighborhood. But this time, David changed his account, instead saying that they had gone to Mary Jo Peckham, a large park with a lake, near the Katy police station. He then gave Leithner the name of a grocery store he said he'd gone to, Brookshire Brothers, on Franz Road, about seven miles from the house.

After they finished filling in the holes, Leithner began

The Lucases had nearly given up on having a girl when the twins were born. *Clockwise from left*: Tom Lucas, Brian, Carol, Barry, Brent, Belinda and Brenda.
(Courtesy of Brenda Lucas)

Belinda, in her bedroom, seemed to have it all: She was bright, pretty, athletic, with a sunny smile.
(Courtesy of Brian and Jill Lucas)

At Stephen F. Austin University, David, a remarkable football player, set records that would endure. *Left to right*: Ken Temple, David and Maureen Temple.

When they dated in college, David and Belinda were called the Golden Couple. They appeared that way in this engagement photo. (Trial exhibit)

On her wedding day, Belinda glowed with the anticipation of marrying a romantic, caring man, who appeared to worship her. (Courtesy of Brian and Jill Lucas)

The twins, Belinda and Brenda, weren't identical, but they'd always have a special bond. (Courtesy of Brenda Lucas)

David bought Shaka, a brown chow that resembled a bear, in college. Early on, the dog earned a reputation for being aggressive. (Trial exhibit)

Belinda and David were both so devoted to Evan, some said David was nearly obsessive. (Trial exhibit)

Every holiday, here Christmas, was spent with David's family. Belinda is on the far right. In Nacogdoches, Carol and Tom missed their daughter but said nothing. (Trial exhibit)

Heather Scott would later testify that she moved into the Hastings Ninth Grade Center in fall 1998 to teach English.
(Steve Ueckert / Courtesy of the *Houston Chronicle*)

The shattered glass in the Temples' back door made it appear someone had broken in. (Police photo)

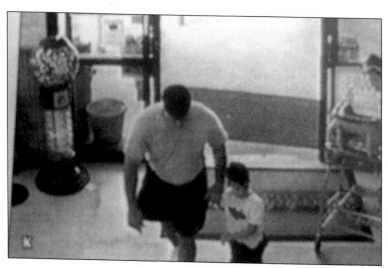

An image from the surveillance cameras at Brookshire Brothers showing David and Evan walking into the store. (Trial exhibit)

The detectives working the case never gave up. *Left to right*: Dean Holtke, Tracy Shipley and Mark Schmidt. (Photo by Kathryn Casey)

As the lead forensic specialist on the scene that first night, David Rossi saw many things that didn't make sense. (Photo by Kathryn Casey)

On a dish decorated with a duck motif, like many of the decorations throughout the house, David Temple's jewelry sat in plain view. (Police photo)

Two rifles were found in the closet at the Temple home, but the murder weapon was a shotgun.
(Police photo)

Her habit was to kick her shoes off when she walked in the door, but that afternoon Belinda still had them on. (Photo by Kathryn Casey)

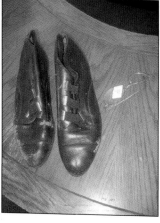

An odd thing, the detectives thought: Why were Belinda's car keys found lying on a step?
(Police photo)

Belinda's bloody glasses found near her body inside the closet. What did they tell police about when she was murdered?
(Police photo)

Inside the garage, officers found little room for Evan to have been riding his bike, but there were dishes and a blanket that David said explained where Shaka was that terrible afternoon. (Police photo)

Kelly Siegler was a top prosecutor, not only in Houston, but also the nation. Even those who didn't like her methods called her a great lawyer.
(Steve Ueckert / Courtesy of the *Houston Chronicle*)

The Temple family banded protectively around David, as they had throughout his life. *Left to right*: David, Kenneth, Maureen, Darren and Kevin Temple. (Steve Ueckert / Courtesy of the *Houston Chronicle*)

In the courtroom, Dick DeGuerin was a lion, yet some wondered about his strategy.
(Steve Ueckert / Courtesy of the *Houston Chronicle*)

The Lucas family listened to painful testimony in the courtroom, at times walking out when it became overwhelming.
(Steve Ueckert/ Courtesy of the *Houston Chronicle*)

Over the years, David had aged and gained weight.
(Steve Ueckert/ Courtesy of the *Houston Chronicle*)

An exhibit from the trial, an aerial photo of Katy, Texas, showing the route David said he took that day.
(Photo by Kathryn Casey)

Another exhibit, this one a diagram depicting the position of the body in the closet.
(Photo by Kathryn Casey)

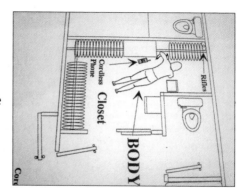

pointing out inconsistencies between David's statement and the physical evidence, from the glass in the den indicating the door was open when the window was broken to the staged look of the crime scene. One big problem with David's story, as the detectives saw it, was Shaka. The chow was ferocious when defending its yard. Although he knew the animal, Mike Ruggiero had been afraid to enter the yard, and the dog snapped and barked, flailing itself against the gate, to get at the first officers on the scene. Deputy Johnson and Sgt. Gonsoulin had been so fearful of the dog they were ready to shoot it.

"It's odd that an officer couldn't get past that dog but [a burglar] could go in there, just walk by that dog," Leithner remarked.

David didn't respond, and the detective would later note that the victim's husband looked "irritated." Throughout the interview, Leithner would later say, David never looked him in the eye. Instead, he fidgeted in the chair. David was hesitant in his answers and, Leithner judged, uncooperative.

During a break in the interview, Leithner talked with another detective, Bill Valerio. Leithner mentioned that David Temple had said he didn't own a shotgun and that there weren't any found in the house. It seemed odd for someone who grew up bird hunting in Katy, a man who had duck decoys and plates, plaques and boxes with ducks on them scattered throughout the house.

"Did you ask his father about that?" Valerio asked.

Leithner said he hadn't, and Valerio said he'd go and ask Ken Temple.

A short time later, Valerio returned and talked to Leithner again, this time telling him that Ken said he'd bought each of his three sons a shotgun while they were in high school. Yet, what the officers didn't get from Ken Temple was something that would prove important as the investigation progressed: the gauge of the shotgun.

Perhaps more than anything, David's demeanor seemed off to those who saw him that night. Throughout the interview, David never shed a tear. His eyes weren't red. Leithner would later write in his report that at times David bowed his head as if trying to look upset, but there were none of the usual physical signs of sorrow. As the interview became increasingly confrontational, David Temple stopped talking. He didn't ask how the investigation would proceed and never expressed any urgency for the detectives to find the man who'd killed Belinda.

As the interview drew to a close, Leithner again told David that he was trying to rule him out, take him off the list of suspects. If David wasn't involved in the murder, a quick way to take the spotlight off of him was to take a polygraph. While not admissible in a courtroom, they were used routinely by investigators, who believed the tests to be useful in gauging cooperation and truthfulness.

It was then that David became openly defensive, Leithner would later say. Refusing to take a lie detector test "under any circumstances," David announced, "I want a lawyer."

Before they parted company, Leithner said again that David's account of the events didn't match the physical evidence. "I'll have to consider you a suspect," Leithner said.

After finishing with David, Leithner checked in with Shipley, and then took Ken's statement himself. David's father said that his son and daughter-in-law had a good marriage, and he recounted Belinda's stopping at the house that afternoon to pick up Maureen's homemade soup. "She was in a hurry," he said. "Evan had been ill."

By then, others had arrived at Clay Road, including the pastor of the church the Temples attended and family— Maureen's brother and sister and their spouses and children. The main entry filled with people, and Shipley would remember the night as being "out of control."

After he had the statements recorded, Leithner, along with Shipley, talked to Maureen and Ken about the situation as it stood that morning, less than ten hours after Belinda's murder. Their son's version of the events didn't match the evidence, the detective explained, and David wasn't cooperating. He'd refused the polygraph test.

The Temples appeared upset, but seemed to take in the information, when Leithner told them, "We cannot eliminate your son as a suspect."

Ken assured Leithner that they would talk to David that night, and that the following day, David would take the lie detector test, that he would do whatever he needed to do to prove his innocence.

At that point, Maureen left for home, and Leithner went into an office to call the district attorney's office. On intake that night was a man many considered to be one of the Harris County District Attorney's top prosecutors, Ted Wilson, chief of the special crimes unit. Tall and scholarly, Wilson was known as a man who enjoyed mentoring young prosecutors. He'd started at the D.A.'s office in 1974, because he enjoyed being in courtrooms. He stayed on because he found the cases exciting. "When you get up in the morning and watch the six-A.M. news, a lot of times you've already consulted on the case with the police the night before. It's fun being on the inside."

Some of his cases were legendary. Wilson had successfully prosecuted Woody Harrelson's father, Chuck Harrelson, for the 1979 murder of U.S. District Judge John Wood, and tried a murder case without a body and gotten a conviction.

On the phone, well after midnight, Leithner explained the Temple crime scene, the evidence and the events that had unfolded that night. Wilson listened, asking questions.

"Can we arrest him?" Leithner asked when the prosecutor had all the facts.

"No," Wilson replied. "We need more."

"What do I need to do?" Leithner asked.

Wilson replied, "Find the murder weapon."

Minutes later, Shipley and Leithner watched as David walked out of the Clay Road substation with his father. There was nothing the detectives could do to stop him.

* * *

Finished at Clay Road, Leithner returned to Round Valley and the crime scene. Rossi had left, but Holtke and Schmidt were there, sifting through evidence. They discussed what had happened at the substation, including David Temple's statement. Much of it didn't make sense, including that he'd left Evan in the garage to ride his bicycle. The two men stood and looked at the Temple garage, where there was barely enough room to walk between the cars, making it all but impossible for the toddler to have ridden a bike.

When she arrived, Shipley couldn't stop thinking about what Mrs. Temple had said: "I just could not have raised a son who would kill his wife."

"Is the husband a suspect?" she asked.

The others filled her in on what they'd seen, the shotgun blast to the back of Belinda's head, and the physical evidence that didn't match David's story, from the ferocious chow that wouldn't let a police officer in the house to the shards of glass indicating the door was open when the glass was broken.

The detective listened, thinking about Belinda, eight months pregnant, executed by someone cold and callous enough to put a shotgun to the back of her head and pull the trigger. Despite everything she'd seen in her years in law enforcement, Tracy Shipley wondered: *Could a husband really do that to a wife, to his unborn child?*

15

L ate that night, one of David's uncles called Paul Looney, a Houston criminal defense attorney the uncle knew from church. Soon after David arrived home, Looney, a man with a high forehead surrounded by a fringe of white, a firm jaw and an expressive voice, hopped in his Porsche and drove to Maureen and Ken's house on Katy Hockley Road, arriving sometime after 1:30 A.M. He talked briefly to David's family, and then was escorted outside to where David sat on a bench, his head buried in his hands.

When it came to Looney's client list, most were relatively low profile, with the exception of a brief stint as the attorney of Timothy McVeigh, the Oklahoma City bomber, and one of the Branch Dividians caught up in the David Koresh case in Waco, Texas. At one point, Looney represented convicted sex offenders in their bid to better their chances of parole by asking for surgical castrations. Looney was used to cases being highly emotional, but he'd later say that the Temple case seemed even more so, and that when it happened it "rocketed through the Temple family."

In the dark, cold backyard that night, Looney asked David's brother, who'd accompanied him, to leave them alone, and then talked to David briefly, telling him that it wasn't a good time to discuss the case fully, but that he didn't want him talking to police without him from that point forward. "Don't say anything precipitously. Don't do anything precipitously," he ordered his new client.

David agreed, but seemed preoccupied. Looney couldn't seem to get him to focus on what he was saying, and he worried that David wasn't getting the message. "He had an overwhelming concern for what he would tell his son," remembers Looney.

On his way back through the house to leave, the defense attorney listened to Maureen and Ken Temple's account of their encounter with the detectives at Clay Road, saying that Leithner had told them, "You need to get used to the idea that your son killed his wife."

That sent Looney to the backyard again, this time to ask David if detectives had accused him of murdering Belinda.

"He confirmed that had happened, repeatedly," Looney would say later. "At that point, I told him no polygraph." Looney made arrangements for David to meet him at his office early the following morning, and then left the house. Later, Ken would say that none of the family slept that night, and he'd describe his son as stunned, as if in shock.

The first *Houston Chronicle* article on the murder bore the headline: PREGNANT WOMAN FOUND SHOT TO DEATH IN HER HOME. The reporter said that David M. Temple told deputies that he'd returned home to find the body of his wife, Belinda, about 5:40 that afternoon, in the bedroom of their house. Belinda was described as a popular teacher at Katy High School, and it was noted that the School District planned to bring in counselors to work with the faculty and students.

Heather was the first one up at the Perthshire-Street town house that morning, but by the time the phone rang, Tara was getting ready for school. Heather picked up the telephone and talked to a friend, who told her to turn on the television and watch the news. She did, and moments later, Heather and Tara saw the reports of Belinda's murder. In some of the news footage, David could be seen sitting in the back of a squad car. "Heather became hysterical," says Tara. "She cried, 'Oh, my God,' and got extremely distraught."

Also up early that morning, Debbie Berger arrived at Katy High School and found the principal in the midst of a meeting with counselors and a few of the teachers. Berger poked her head in the office to listen, but was there only moments when she began to cry. The other teachers gathered around to console her. "I felt like all of us were grieving and at the same time in a state of disbelief," she says.

Before school began, the school psychologist talked to Debbie and Cindy, the teachers closest to Belinda. Both were crying and upset, but then many were on campus that morning, as students arrived with tears in their eyes. "The kids wanted to know who would do such a horrible thing," says Debbie. "We couldn't tell them."

Meanwhile, at Hastings that morning, an e-mail went out to the staff from the principal: "Give our sympathy to Coach Temple. His wife was brutally murdered last night." There were many whispers that day on the campus, much of it about David, as his coworkers wondered if he was behind Belinda's murder. When Heather showed up, she went to the principal's office and spent much of the day there.

At the Alief field house, where David officed, early that morning, a teacher's wife called to try to find out if anyone had talked to David. One of the other coaches, Mike Slater, answered the telephone. He sounded upset and said that he'd only heard about the murder on the news that morning, on the car radio on the way to work.

Later, the woman would recount her conversation with Slater, a conversation the coach, who was a good friend of David's, would deny took place: "Mike Slater said he couldn't believe that it had happened. Then he said that David must feel really awful, especially since when David had to leave school early to take care of Evan that afternoon, he was cussing Belinda up and down. David was furious with her."

* * *

At the Temples' house, Ken would later say, the day began with David going into Evan's room to tell him of Belinda's murder. Later, David would say he lay down beside the toddler and told him that "some bad men had broken into the house and momma's heart stopped, and that she's gone to be with Jesus, and she won't be with us anymore."

Later, a relative would say that Evan asked a lot of questions, including a recurring one: "Why isn't Mommy here?"

Afterward, David arrived in Paul Looney's seventh-floor office, off the Katy Freeway, with his parents and brothers. It would seem that the family often did things as a tribe, but the defense attorney asked to talk to his client alone. Behind closed doors, Looney still had a hard time getting David to focus on Belinda's murder. All David wanted to talk about were concerns about Evan.

What David didn't appear worried about was the investigation. He barely seemed interested in anything Looney had to say about what police might be doing. Still, there were things Looney needed to ask. Some defense attorneys don't want to know if a client is innocent or guilty, believing that knowledge can tie their hands in the courtroom. For instance, codes prohibit an attorney from putting a client on the stand if they know he or she will lie.

"I tell my clients that the only thing I want is to keep them out of trouble," says Looney, with all the certainty of a convert preaching the gospel. "I don't give a damn if they did it or not. I don't approach a case any differently if my client is Charlie Manson. I have a moral calling to keep everybody out of cages. . . . But don't let me be surprised with the evidence."

The defense attorney would say that years earlier he'd used that same speech on Timothy McVeigh after the Oklahoma City bombing, and McVeigh, without hesitation, told him of making and planting the bomb. "I can be very persuasive," says Looney.

It was after such an impassioned introduction, Looney

would say later, that he asked David if he'd murdered Belinda. "David said, 'Of course not, and I'm not sure I can keep you working for me if you're going to keep asking that kind of question.'"

Early that morning Ginny Wiley drove to Katy High, where she'd graduated a year earlier, to see her old teachers. She felt alone and needed to talk about the murder. At the school, Ginny listened to the morning announcements, at the end of which the principal told the students about Belinda's death. Some of the teenagers cried, and many hugged and held hands.

Afterward, Ginny drove home and changed clothes, then bought flowers. She drove to Round Valley, where police cars were still out on the street and an officer sat in his squad car watching the scene. It was a windy day, and Ginny bent down and put her flowers with others that were collecting in front of David and Belinda's house. They blew away, and she ran after them and replaced them. Then she stood on the street and looked up at the redbrick colonial Belinda had been so proud of, sadness surrounding her.

Others made the same pilgrimage that Tuesday, including Tammey Harlan and Kay Stuart, the wife of Hastings' head football coach. They laid their flowers beside the others, and throughout the day the memorial grew, some with small notes written by children on the block and Belinda's friends.

Something about this particular murder touched so many; perhaps it was the memory of Belinda's enthusiastic smile or the thought of an innocent infant who would never be born. When Detective Tracy Shipley thought about why it touched her, she thought of all the cases detectives handled where the victims were known to be at risk by their families and friends, victims involved in drugs or crime. Belinda wasn't someone who'd lived a risky lifestyle that would have portended a violent death. "Her murder pretty much killed everyone's innocence," says Shipley.

* * *

At 7:30 that morning, Detective Chuck Leithner received a call from the medical examiner's office. Belinda's autopsy was scheduled for nine. It's not unusual for homicide detectives to attend autopsies, to collect evidence and hear firsthand the impressions of the physician. Leithner called his partner, Mark Schmidt, and made arrangements to meet him at the county morgue, a commonplace-looking brick building not far from the miles of hospitals that make up Houston's Texas Medical Center.

When they arrived at the Joseph A. Jachimczyk Forensic Center, on Old Spanish Trail, Dr. Vladimir Parungao, the assistant medical examiner who'd conduct the autopsy, told them that Belinda's body had already been examined under ultraviolet lights, searched for hair and fiber evidence. When they walked into the morgue, her naked corpse lay on a metal gurney in an autopsy suite, the right side of her face a gaping, bloody, raw hole. Two bags held other evidence, including brain matter, her broken glasses and the lead shot fragments from the shotgun shell. The clothes she'd worn that final day rested on a tray underneath the gurney. Although he'd seen much in his years in law enforcement, Mark Schmidt looked at Belinda's body, swollen in the final month of pregnancy, and felt overwhelming sadness.

As Parungao examined the body, he pointed out bruising on Belinda's knees, consistent with her having been in the position Holtke and Rossi suggested, crouched down, perhaps kneeling at the time of the fatal shot. Examining the body, Parungao measured her hair, twelve inches long, and noticed Belinda had lividity, the settling of blood by gravity, on both sides of her body.

"She was rolled over?" Parungao asked the detectives.

"Yes," they confirmed. "We rolled her over at the scene, when the assistant M.E. arrived."

That settled, Parungao made the initial incision into the body, a "Y" cut, starting at the clavicle and, at the end of the sternum, straight down through the abdomen. Once he'd spread the skin back, he examined her internal organs. Belinda was a healthy woman, only thirty years old, and he found nothing out of the ordinary, until he reached her abdomen.

Mark Schmidt had been in the delivery room when the younger of his two daughters was born, and it was a "fantastic moment." He would never put behind him the memory of Parungao cutting through Belinda's cold uterus, opening it up and bringing forward the corpse of a perfectly formed baby girl. Erin was eighteen inches long and weighed six pounds. The umbilical cord was still attached to the placenta, but the baby was ivory white and eerily still. The sight of the dead infant made Mark Schmidt shudder.

From that day forward, Schmidt would say, "I could never forget it. We want to solve every murder, but what made Belinda Temple's death stand out was the baby." Even years later, Schmidt would tear up at the memory of that day.

After extricating the dead baby from her mother's womb, Parungao took a blood sample from Erin's heart to run tests on, including paternity. Could the baby somehow be a motive for Belinda's death? Was there another man in her life? The blood tests could answer those and other questions.

Leithner and Schmidt remained nearby watching, as Parungao then turned his attention to Belinda's neck, examining her hyoid bone, at the base of her throat. The bone remained intact, suggesting that she hadn't been strangled.

With that, he turned the body over, and inspected the entrance wound at the back of her head, on the left-hand side. To gauge the size of the bullet hole and examine it more closely, Parungao stitched together the area around the wound, reconstructing the hole, four inches below the midline of her head. The wound, the physician estimated, was three quarters of an inch in diameter, a contact wound. Belinda's murderer had pressed the gun against the left backside of her head and pulled the trigger.

When Leithner assessed the wound, he concurred with Parungao's assessment; gunshot residue in the wound suggested to both the detective and the physician that the shotgun had been flush against Belinda's skull.

With Belinda's body again on its back, Dr. Parungao examined the exit wound. The damage to Belinda's face was catastrophic. As it entered, the force of the blast had shattered much of her skull, emptying it and blowing out the right side of her face, centered on her eye. Belinda's teeth were still in place, but her jaw was broken. "The cranial cavity was empty of any brain tissue," the physician noted. "The blast shattered the entire cranial cavity. . . . The brain exited on the right side of the face."

On his report, Parungao listed his conclusions. First: the trajectory of the blast was left to right. Second: the cause of death was a contact wound to the head. Third: the manner of death was homicide. Based on the size of the wound, the diameter of the contact area, the murder weapon was a .12-gauge shotgun.

The autopsy continued, and Schmidt stayed with the coroner. Meanwhile, Leithner took the elevator to the fifth floor, bringing with him the remains of the shotgun shell recovered from the scene and the body. Once there, he met Matthew Clements, a firearms expert. Carefully, Clements examined the wadding and lead fragments. Based on the weight of the pellets, it didn't take Clements long to evaluate the type of shell used. "It was double aught, not birdshot but buckshot, a type of shell used for hunting deer," says Schmidt.

There was something else about the shell's remains. Examining the wadding and pellets and comparing it to samples he had, Clements was able to determine that the shotgun shell wasn't factory manufactured but rather a reload, a recycled cartridge that had been refilled with pellets and wadding for reuse. Even more interesting, the wadding was of an unusual type, one Clements had never before come across.

"We now had an idea of the murder weapon and the shotgun shell," says Schmidt.

* * *

The first morning after the murder turned out to be a hectic one for the detectives on the case. As they finished at the M.E.'s office, a call came in. Paul Looney had faxed a letter withdrawing consent to search. That meant that the sheriff's department no longer had permission to process the Round Valley house, now known as the Belinda Temple murder scene. Assistant D.A. Ted Wilson had already been notified, and he wanted Leithner in his office to help write a search warrant. While within David's rights, withdrawing permission made the prosecutor and investigators look even harder at him. Says Wilson, "I'd never known anyone who'd done that who didn't have something to hide."

At the D.A.'s office late that same morning, Wilson listened as Leithner detailed the discrepancies between David's statement and the evidence at the scene, including the broken glass and the dog that wouldn't let police enter the yard. The detective thought that perhaps he had enough evidence to book David while they continued the investigation. The prosecutor wasn't swayed. "What Detective Leithner told me was highly suggestive that the victim's husband was the killer," says Wilson. "But to take it into a courtroom, I needed more evidence."

At Tiger Land day care that morning, the teachers gathered, many upset, talking about the news reports. "Her husband did it," one said.

Another replied, "Do you really think so?"

"I know he did," a third said.

When the mothers and fathers came in, many were curious about David as well. Some remembered him from his years as a student at Katy High, where stories of bullying and violence circulated about him. Still, everyone's primary concern was the children. The teachers were cautioned not to show emotion. Most made it through the morning, but by break times, some sat in the lunchroom, their heads on the table, crying.

* * *

After interviewing his client and pinning down his alibi, Looney called Wilson. David had told his defense attorney that he had left the house the evening before and gone first to the park, then to a Brookshire Brothers grocery store on Franz Road, followed by a stop at the Home Depot on the Katy Freeway. Looney figured both of the stores had surveillance cameras. "I knew the cameras were probably on a loop, and I wanted the prosecutor to get them before the tape was erased," says Looney. "I didn't want them to be lost."

Looney also put something else in action that morning. He called Mark Hatfield, Ph.D., a psychologist who specialized in treating children. David was worried, concerned about Evan and how to handle his grief and confusion over his mother's death. Hatfield said he would see the toddler and made an appointment for David to bring him in that afternoon.

At the Round Valley house that morning, all work had stopped.

The CSI officers had predicted that would happen.

Early that morning, David's brothers, Darren and Kevin, had shown up twice, the first time wanting a prescription medicine and a jacket for Evan and a suit for David to wear to Belinda and Erin's funeral. The next time they'd come looking for Evan's bike, a yellow two-wheeler with training wheels that Holtke had to get down off hooks from the garage ceiling. Holtke had followed orders and given them what they were looking for, but saw one of the brothers in the garage writing down the VIN numbers off the Isuzu and David's blue pickup truck. In Holtke's opinion, it seemed like David's brothers were on a fishing expedition, looking around to see what the crime-scene investigators were doing.

So when the sergeant called around 11 A.M. to say the consent to search had been revoked, Holtke shrugged as if it were expected. As ordered, he and Rossi vacated the house, standing out on the street, guarding the property while they waited for Leithner to obtain a search warrant. An hour later, the confirmation came in. Holtke and Rossi walked back into the house, this time under the authority of a search warrant signed by a judge.

The work resumed at 22502 Round Valley. In the laundry room Holtke collected a shirt, one with a golf pattern they'd call the "rules of golf" shirt. On the front they saw a spot that resembled blood. They bagged the two Post-it notes from the kitchen counter, the one documenting when Evan had his last Motrin and the note asking Belinda to call her aunt. In the master bedroom, Rossi claimed as potential evidence a gray warm-up suit, including the jacket, which had been draped over the back of a chair, just inside the door. The reason it caught his attention was that the matching pants were on the bed, as if David had just taken them off. The damp towels, too, went into an evidence bag, and a call was put out to a serology expert, asking her to respond to the scene to test for blood evidence that might have been missed.

The crime-scene unit worked throughout the day. That afternoon Dean Holtke and David Rossi threw finely ground black fingerprint powder, covering the doorways, doorknobs, parts of walls, and much of the back door with the broken glass, hoping to find a clue to the identity of the killer. At the morgue, Belinda's fingerprints had been recorded. In the end, many of the prints found in the house were small, indicating they'd come from a child, presumably Evan, and all the others tied back to David and Belinda.

In the garage, Rossi processed the Isuzu, taking into evidence the Home Depot bag. At the back door, Holtke saw a pair of tennis shoes on the patio and bagged those as well.

When the serology expert showed up late in the afternoon, she sprayed luminol, a chemical made of nitrogen, hydrogen, oxygen and carbon. When mixed with hydrogen peroxide and lit with an ALS, an alternative light source, in a darkened room the chemical glows when reacting to iron found in blood. Holtke and Rossi went through the house, pinpointing areas to test. The "rules of golf" shirt they'd bagged in the laundry room tested positive, and upstairs in the master bedroom, Holtke asked the woman to spray the backs of the mirrored doors on the closet, looking for blowback from the shotgun blast. Although sections of the closet glowed when the ALS was turned on, including the wall in front of where Belinda's body had lain, the backs of the doors, where blowback should have been found, didn't react. There was no indication that the blast had scattered blood and brain matter behind Belinda, in the direction of the killer.

"Our thought was that the blowback was small and, if the shotgun was tight against the victim's skull, it would have been sucked up back into the barrel," says Holtke.

In the bathroom, however, another area did react. When the serologist sprayed luminol in the sinks, one drain glowed. When Holtke dismantled it and removed the P-trap, the U-shaped pipe below the drain that fills with water to prevent sewer gases from entering a room, it, too, lit up with luminol exposure. He bagged the pipes to be sent in for more testing.

As they searched, both Rossi and Holtke knew the importance of the evidence, especially if it turned out that a stranger had broken into the Temple house and killed Belinda. Unexplained fingerprints or blood could point to a possible suspect. On the other hand, if David was the killer, they also knew that forensic evidence could be difficult. In domestic homicides, where both victim and killer live in a house, it's not surprising to find their fingerprints and DNA present. It would be more unusual if they didn't leave behind evidence of their presence in the form of fingerprints, hair, fibers, and DNA, even blood.

At the district attorney's office, Wilson met with another of the A.D.A.s, Donna Goode, a tall, thin woman with long dark hair. Goode, who'd been born on Galveston Island, had been a social worker before law school. While they worked on the search warrant, Leithner and Wilson had discussed Evan, wondering if the toddler heard or saw anything during the murder.

"I'd like to get the boy to give a statement," Leithner suggested.

Wilson thought it over, agreed, and called Goode, who as a social worker had worked with children. In the past, Goode and Wilson had worked closely together, including on the Laura Smithers case, that of a twelve-year-old girl who disappeared while jogging not far from her home. Wilson thought they complemented each other well, that he was better at the big brush strokes, while Goode worked well with details.

While Leithner was at the D.A.'s office, Schmidt returned to homicide on Lockwood to make phone calls. His first was to Precinct Five constables' office, where he asked for a copy of all the dispatch tapes for the officers who'd made the scene the evening before. Afterward, he called the 911 telephone center and asked for tapes of David and Peggy Ruggiero's calls. He picked them up and brought them back to the Lockwood station, where a group of the detectives gathered around, Shipley among them. On the 911 call, they heard David talking to the dispatcher and then the EMT, who tried but failed to convince him to give Belinda CPR for the sake of the baby.

The first time they listened, it was hard for the detectives to take it all in, so they played the tape a second time. It was then that they noticed David fluctuated from sobbing to sounding calm, and how he stressed that the back-door glass had been broken. "It was like he was saying, 'You stupid cops. Don't miss this!' " says Shipley.

The more they listened to the tape, the less believable it sounded to the investigators. Considering that they viewed themselves as skeptics, they decided to bring in others who worked in the department, gathering the clerical staff together, and again played the tape. Their reaction mirrored the detectives' take on the tape.

"That doesn't sound right," said one woman. "He doesn't sound real."

Afterward, Schmidt planned to head back out to the scene, but then his desk phone rang. An officer with the Alief Independent School District said, "I just wanted you to know that Mr. Temple has been seeing a woman teacher."

"Oh, really?" Schmidt replied.

As the officer talked, Schmidt wrote down an address and a woman's name: Heather Scott.

16

That afternoon, the first day after Belinda's murder, David and Ken brought Evan to the Harlans to play with Sydnee while they went to make funeral arrangements. Ken sat in a chair and talked to Tammey, who was torn up inside wondering if David murdered her friend. When she looked at David, she was struck by how calm he looked. His eyes, as they were the night before, looked clear, as if he'd hardly shed a tear.

After David and Ken left, Evan came into the kitchen.

"My mommy is in heaven," Evan told her.

Evan didn't seem to truly understand, and appeared confused when Tammey cried.

The bell rang at the back door of Katy's Schmidt Funeral home. With so much press surrounding Belinda's murder, the undertakers hoped to protect the Temple family from being seen walking in the front door. Richard Lenius, a former firefighter, worked part time as an embalmer, and he looked out and saw David, appearing calm and at ease.

In the back room, Lenius had been working on Belinda, trying with little success to repair the damage to her face. His efforts would go on throughout the afternoon, into the evening and much of the night. In all, Lenius spent twelve hours attempting to disguise the damage done to Belinda Temple's face, but could do little. "There were too many missing pieces," he says.

When he finally gave up, Lenius wrapped gauze around Belinda's head. After arranging Belinda in the coffin, he wrapped Erin in a soft blanket and placed the dead baby next to her mother.

Late that afternoon at the Temple house, Kay Stuart arrived. The wife of David's boss, Hastings' head football coach, Kay intended to pay her respects. She wanted David and the family to know that she and her husband gave their sympathies. But when she walked in the house, Darren and Kevin flanked David, as if protecting him, and David appeared so unemotional that Kay wondered what was wrong with him. Her husband, Bobby, had said he'd meet her at the Temple home, so Kay sat with Maureen and waited. Understandably, David's mother's conversation was disjointed and emotional. Over and over, she talked about the call from Mike Ruggiero the night before, the one that began her nightmare.

"Maureen thought he was calling to say Belinda had gone to the hospital, to deliver the baby," says Kay. "She thought it would be a happy call, and that she'd be going to meet her first granddaughter."

The women talked, and Maureen mentioned that they'd hired an attorney for David, lamenting the cost, which she set at $30,000. Kay said nothing but wondered why David needed an attorney. Then Maureen glanced up at her and said, "Kay, surely I didn't raise a murderer."

Those words sent a shiver through Kay.

A little while later, the evening news came on, and David watched reports of Belinda's murder, still showing no emotion. As far as Kay could tell, he didn't shed a tear. When one of his sisters-in-law got up to put Evan in bed, she fussed over him a bit, and Kay heard David say, "Oh, you're just going to make a sissy out of him."

* * *

Heather Scott and Tara Hall were home late that afternoon with a friend named Beth when Leithner and Schmidt rang the bell at the town house on Perthshire. After a quick interview with Heather, during which she described her relationship with David as "more than friends," Leithner asked if Heather, Tara and Beth would follow them to Clay Road for a longer interview. The women agreed. Once there, Schmidt talked to Tara, while Leithner splintered off with Heather.

During the interview, Heather labeled her relationship with David as "casual and romantic." She talked about their meetings at happy hours, and insisted that he wouldn't and couldn't have murdered his wife. Off and on, Scott stopped talking, wondering out loud if Alief would find out about their relationship.

"We won't disclose this to your employer," Leithner assured her.

Scott said that David told her he was married and never indicated that he'd leave his wife, and that he never said anything derogatory about Belinda.

"Does he ever talk about hunting?" Leithner asked.

"No," she said. "He never talks about hunting, and he never talks about guns."

When Leithner finished typing, he gave it to her to read. "For the past three months or so, David and I have been sort of seeing each other once a week at happy hours," Heather's statement read. David, she said, drove her home, but they weren't alone. Sometimes he came over on weekends and watched movies. Then she mentioned something that caught the detective's interest, that six days before Belinda's murder, Heather had told David she didn't want to continue "with the way our relationship is going."

David responded that was fine with him, she said, yet the conversation "didn't really mean anything, however, as we still talk to each other at school and it seems that we are the same as we were."

When Leithner asked, Scott described David as a passionate person, with many friends, who seemed close to his brothers. The last time she'd seen him on the day of the murder was at 10:30 A.M., when he walked down the hall, "and said, 'Hey,' to me, but didn't stop to talk." An hour and a half later, David Temple left school early, after Belinda called about Evan's illness. Just hours later, Belinda lay dead.

After Heather initialed each page and signed the end of her statement, Leithner asked her to take a polygraph, and Heather agreed. An examiner was brought in, and the test was given. When he finished, the polygraph examiner told Leithner that the test results suggested Heather Scott could be withholding information.

Meanwhile, in another part of the substation, Tara felt uneasy. She wanted to tell Schmidt what she knew about David and Heather, but at Clay Road, without interview rooms, he questioned her in front of the woman who'd accompanied them, Beth. "I knew whatever I said, Beth would tell Heather," says Hall. She also knew of Heather's inability to accept criticism, how ultrasensitive she was to others talking about her. So when Schmidt asked questions, Tara said little, other than that David and Heather were dating and that they went out with a group of other teachers to happy hours.

Approximately two hours after Heather and Tara arrived, Leithner and Schmidt said good-bye, and the women left the substation. On the way home in the car, Heather was anxious and upset, insisting she couldn't understand how they could think David was involved in Belinda's murder. "She felt she really knew him and there was no way he could have done it," says Tara.

"They don't know what they're talking about," Heather insisted.

All day Tuesday, the day after their youngest child's murder, Tom and Carol Lucas waited with Tom's sister, Lorraine, at her house in Houston, hoping for news. David and his family never called. Tom and Carol did call the Temples, but David never returned their phone calls. Belinda's parents hoped they'd be consulted on funeral arrangements, but that didn't happen. For seven years, they'd never had a Christmas or Thanksgiving with Belinda. They'd never been included for Easters. Now, their daughter was dead, and the Temples never called to ask what they wanted for Belinda's funeral.

That evening at the Round Valley house, the crime-scene investigators were finishing their work. Rossi and Holtke stood looking at the den television, the one on its side next to the wooden stand. They'd already picked up the splinters of wood that appeared to have been knocked off when the television was slid down off the stand and onto its side on the floor. One of the men suggested they put the television back on the stand and turn it on. What that might tell them was how roughly the set had been handled. Was it dropped when Belinda surprised a burglar, or had someone put it down gently, so as not to damage the set? If so, it seemed logical that it was someone who planned to use the set in the future and didn't want it ruined.

Rossi and Holtke lifted the television and replaced it on the wooden stand. "We hit the button, and it started right up," says Holtke. "The picture was fine."

David's 1991 Chevy pickup and Belinda's red Isuzu had already been towed to the impound lot to be more closely inspected. Put in to evidence from the Isuzu was the Home Depot bag with the shelf brackets and Belinda's cell phone with its charger. On the records, it was again noted that there was no car seat in the blue truck, the vehicle David said he'd taken Evan out in the afternoon of his wife's murder.

After dark, the two crime-scene investigators finished with the house and notified their office that they were leaving. Paul Looney was called and told that they were releasing the house back to David.

When a homicide takes place, the detectives who investigate it take a new, clean, black three-ring binder out of their department's supply closet. Each day, they type up their notes, recording what they've done, where they've been and whom they've interviewed. That binder, along with any others generated over the course of the investigation, is known as *the murder book.*

On that Tuesday evening, approximately twenty-eight hours after he'd responded to the crime scene, Leithner ended his report for the day, the report that would be printed and placed in the Temple murder book, with four words: "Disposition: Investigation to continue."

17

That Wednesday, the *Katy Times* ran its first piece on Belinda Temple's murder. The headline read: INVESTIGATORS PUZZLED BY TEACHER'S MURDER. The paper reported that the scene at the Round Valley house appeared odd, not as chaotic as detectives expected in a burglary, and that there'd been no evidence the dog had been drugged, and therefore no explanation as to how a burglar could get past an animal so vicious it wouldn't let police into the yard. "Lots of things didn't look good for David Temple, but we were trying to be open-minded," Schmidt later said, with a frown. "We didn't want to get tunnel vision on this thing. We had a case to investigate, and no one wanted to arrest the wrong guy. We had to look at all the possibilities."

By then, detectives were checking out a report of a man jumping fences in the Cimarron neighborhood hours before Belinda died. A neighbor reported the incident, thinking the man she saw could be the murderer. What police discovered was that he was a utility company meter reader. After a few calls, investigators confirmed that the man had remained on schedule throughout the afternoon and was miles away from Round Valley when Belinda was murdered.

* * *

Early that morning, Schmidt and Leithner left Lockwood and drove to downtown Houston, to the Harris County District Attorney's office, to meet with the prosecutors overseeing the Temple case, Ted Wilson and Donna Goode. Once they arrived, they briefed the two A.D.A.s, giving them a rundown on what they knew about Belinda's murder. Then Leithner asked again about having an expert interview three-year-old Evan.

Goode, who'd taken over that task, explained that she was in the process of finalizing arrangements for Dr. Bruce Perry, a psychiatrist who specialized in childhood trauma, to meet with Evan. As soon as they had everything lined up, including a court order signed by a judge, a date would be set.

From the courthouse, Schmidt and Leithner drove to the Hastings Ninth Grade Center, where David worked, and met with the principal, who'd arranged for them to use the main office boardroom to interview faculty members. That morning, many of the coaches at Hastings reported to talk to the detectives. Few offered anything that helped. One coach recalled a conversation with David regarding hunting, but couldn't say if David mentioned using any specific type of weapon. They all insisted they'd never heard David talk negatively about Belinda. Going through the records, they found that David had only reported having problems with two students, one over a pot-smoking incident and the other when a student broke the windshield on David's pickup truck. Neither incident appeared worthy of more investigation.

When they left that day, the detectives had little information, other than the knowledge that rumors were flying at Hastings over Heather and David's relationship. "Well, I heard he might be seeing someone," more than one teacher had admitted. But when asked if they'd heard of any threats against David, if anyone was angry with him for any reason, the detectives heard: "No." "No." "No."

Meanwhile that afternoon, Tracy Shipley and another detective met at Katy High School to interview Belinda's coworkers. When they walked through the hallways, the school was oddly quiet. "The kids almost looked sedated from the sadness," says Shipley.

The morning began with Shipley talking to a Katy ISD police officer, asking for any complaints Belinda had made against a student or reports of any incidents involving Belinda on campus. When the Katy officer looked through the files, he found nothing to turn over. Afterward, Shipley and her fellow detective interviewed teachers. With each, Shipley explained that they were under no obligation to talk, and, when some asked, she said that David hadn't been ruled out as a suspect, but that he wasn't the only suspect. They were looking at other possibilities, including a burglary. The first interview was with Margaret Christian, the administrator at the parent conference with Belinda just two days earlier, her final duty before leaving the campus around 3:20 that afternoon. Christian recounted what others would, including how anxious Belinda had been to get home to check on Evan.

At Katy High, Shipley noticed that many of the men appeared to be in shock, while the women cried. At first, few said anything other than that David and Belinda appeared to have a happy marriage. The two closest to Belinda were Cindy O'Brien and Debbie Berger. While the other detective talked to Cindy, Tracy sat down with Debbie, asking her about Belinda. Debbie sobbed, describing Belinda as a wonderful woman and a great teacher, but she said little that helped, too frightened to focus. "I was petrified," Berger would later recount. "I told that detective, you're going to find my fingerprints all over the baby's crib. I just finished making all those linens."

Afterward, Tracy talked to the other detective and learned that he'd fared better with Cindy. Rather than frightened, O'Brien was angry. She wanted the detectives to know that David and Belinda's marriage was far from the happily-ever-after stuff of fairy tales. Instead, Belinda worried that David might be having an affair, and just that summer, David and

Belinda didn't talk for weeks. One of the things O'Brien asked was, "How could anybody get past that dog?"

With that information, Katy High's wall of secrecy fell. Citing what she already knew, Shipley reinterviewed teachers. This time she started out by saying, "I hear Belinda's marriage wasn't happy." Looking relieved at not being the first to tell, they slowly opened up. One was Stacy Nissley, who repeated Belinda's suspicions that David was having an affair and her sadness at thinking the marriage might be ending. It was Nissley who first told Shipley about New Year's Eve. "David left Belinda home over the holiday," she said. "He went hunting and never even called to check on her."

Other teachers recalled how, when they visited Belinda's house, she warned them not to go into the backyard where Shaka was kept. "Belinda said the dog was protective," said one. "She said it might attack."

Still, others defended David, including the coaches, some he'd known as a student and others he'd coached against at Hastings. They called David a good guy and, what Tracy heard over and over was, "David was a great Katy football player."

"It was like David Temple was the hero of Katy, Texas," says Shipley. "We didn't care what he was like on the football field. We just needed to hear the truth. We needed to know what we were looking at."

Before she left the campus that afternoon, Shipley confiscated the hard drive from Belinda's school computer. The department's computer experts would inspect it in hopes that it might lead to sources or perhaps even a suspect.

Back on Lockwood, Shipley wrote her report. When she finished, she took out a pen and paper and drew a timeline, recording what she'd learned about where Belinda Temple was at what time on that final day. She now knew from the teachers at Katy that Belinda left school sometime around 3:20 that afternoon. The 911 call came in at 5:38. The question all the investigators had to answer was, What happened in those two hours and eighteen minutes?

* * *

To their surprise, Schmidt and Leithner read in the *Katy Times* that Paul Looney said jewelry had been stolen from the Temple house. The detectives thought back to the scene and the jewelry boxes they'd seen that night, none of which looked as if it had even been disturbed. And then there was David's jewelry, sitting out on the top of a chest of drawers, in the open, including a heavy gold ring. Ted Wilson contacted Looney, inquiring about the report, and Looney faxed over a list of the items that included, among others, a silver necklace, sapphire and diamond earrings, and a bracelet with the letters EVAN. Everything on the list was Belinda's, nothing of David's.

About ten that morning, after talking with detectives, Cindy O'Brien and Debbie Berger left Katy High and drove to the Temple house to pay their respects and talk to David. Many of Belinda's coworkers were asking about setting up a scholarship fund for Evan. Although it was a cold, drizzly day, when they arrived, they found Belinda's sisters-in-law, Lisa and Becky, in front of the house, along with David's aunts, uncles, and cousins. Cindy and Debbie walked up, said how sorry they were about Belinda's death, and then asked why they were outside.

"Mrs. Temple is at the beauty salon, getting her hair done for the funeral," Becky said, appearing upset. "And the men are having a meeting inside."

Cindy had called earlier and talked to one of the Temples, and she said, "But we had an appointment."

"I'm sorry," one of the sisters-in-law replied. "They asked everybody to wait outside."

Later, David's father would say that at that time, while the women and other relatives waited, he was inside the house asking David, "Is there anything we need to know?"

At first, David denied he had anything to tell his father and brothers. But Ken asked a second time. In response, David admitted that he'd been with another woman.

While inside the house David was confessing to his infidelity, outside, on the driveway, Debbie and Cindy waited patiently with the others. The minutes ticked by, the women shivering from the cold and rain. After fifteen minutes or so, Maureen Temple arrived. She parked her car and rushed into the house. More time passed, during which David's mother would later say that her son told her what he'd just confessed to his father and brothers, that he'd been unfaithful to his murdered pregnant wife.

Outside, those waiting had no idea of the drama unfolding within the Temple house. But the conversation between mother and son must have been brief, for only minutes after she arrived home, Maureen, her cap of hair freshly styled for her daughter-in-law's funeral, opened the door and invited all of them in. "She had a smile plastered on her face," says Cindy. "She looked like she was welcoming us for tea and crumpets."

Inside the house, David stood in the living room with his father and brothers. Debbie walked over and hugged him. "I'm so sorry," she said, but David didn't answer. Although he wasn't crying, David appeared subdued and perhaps, Debbie thought, a bit "bored."

The two teachers stayed about twenty minutes, offering their sympathies. When Cindy asked David what to do with the scholarship money, he replied, "Give it to me. I'll take care of it."

The Temple household was a busy place that Wednesday. As is customary in the South, family and friends filtered in and out, coming to pay their respects to the grieving family. That afternoon, Quinton and Tammey arrived to see David and his family. When they walked in the door, Quinton approached David and embraced him, and both men cried. The Harlans stood and talked to David and his family for a while, and then David and Quinton went to the kitchen. Once no one was able to overhear, David asked, "How's Heather? Is she okay?"

"She's okay," Quinton said. "Are you going to tell your parents about her?"

"I already did," David said. "I didn't want them to read it in the newspaper." Then David advised Quinton to tell Tammey about his own flirtation, "Because it's going to come out."

At the district attorney's office, Ted Wilson heard from Looney that David had taken his son to a psychologist. Eager to find out what the toddler said, Wilson drew up a search warrant for Evan's records. That afternoon, the prosecutor interviewed Dr. Mark Hatfield, who said that he'd heard nothing from the toddler that led him to believe Evan had experienced anything traumatic, certainly nothing that suggested he'd witnessed his mother's murder.

While Wilson talked with the psychologist, another warrant was being executed. Leithner and a physician from the medical examiner's office met David at his attorney's office, where David submitted to a full body examination. Inside Looney's private office, replete with Southwestern art and leather furniture, David stripped naked. The physician pulled out magnifying equipment and examined him, inch by inch, searching for any scratches or cuts that could have resulted from either breaking the door glass or a struggle. "He looked in every cavity, even under David's eyelids," says Looney. "The doctor took forever, but he told me and Leithner that he didn't find anything."

Before he left the office, while alone with his attorney, David admitted to Looney what he'd already confessed to his parents and brothers, that he'd been having a relationship with another woman at the time of the murder. "Belinda's family doesn't know," David said.

"It's better that you tell them than someone else," Looney advised him.

Meanwhile, Tara Hall fretted over her interview with Detective Schmidt the day before. When she finished teaching for the day and returned to the town house, she called someone she'd dated in college, a lawyer, and filled him in on the situation. "He urged me to be clear with the detectives about everything I knew," says Hall.

After she finished talking to the attorney, Hall asked Heather if she wanted to discuss anything with him. Heather did, and Tara left her alone, to talk to the attorney privately. Whenever she thought about Belinda's murder, Tara worried about her friend, hoping for Heather's sake that David wasn't the killer.

Later that same day, Hall's attorney friend put in a call to Schmidt. "Tara would like to talk to you again," he said. "She may have more to tell you."

When Tara Hall voluntarily returned to Clay Road, this time she met with Tracy Shipley, and the two women were alone. "I told her that there was more to the relationship between David and Heather than I'd said earlier," says Hall. "I told her about coming home and finding them upstairs, in Heather's room, that he'd given her a gold necklace for Christmas, and that David had stayed at the apartment over the New Year's holiday."

There was something else Tara Hall told Detective Tracy Shipley: "A few days before his wife's murder, Heather told me that David said he'd totally fallen in love with her."

While Shipley interviewed Hall, Leithner was at Evan's day care, Tiger Land, talking to the toddler's teacher and the others who'd seen Belinda that last afternoon. What he learned was that Belinda had been a doting and devoted mother. The teachers described Evan as sick that morning, running a fever, not eating and not playing with the other children. When they called Belinda, she said David would come for him, but she was the one who rushed over to pick him up. One teacher said, "Evan was sound asleep when Belinda carried him out."

If Evan had been ill, why would David have taken him to a park?

When one coach's wife heard David took Evan out after

he'd been sent home with a fever from day care, she called one of the detectives: "I told him there was no way Belinda would have let David do errands with Evan when he was sick. Belinda wouldn't even take him to the games with a runny nose."

18

I n a *Houston Chronicle* article that ran three days after the murder, Paul Looney railed against the sheriff's department, claiming that David and the Temples were being treated "bad beyond description." David's attorney was on the offensive, charging that the investigators weren't sensitive to a grieving family.

A vast city that sprawls, Houston had more than four million residents in 1999, but Belinda's murder was becoming big news. A suburban woman, pregnant, a beloved teacher with no history of risky behavior, she wasn't the usual murder victim. Television news reporters were camped outside Tom's sister's house when Tracy Shipley arrived on Thursday morning. Belinda's visitation was scheduled for that evening, and the Lucas family was gathering in Houston, giving the detectives the opportunity to conduct interviews without traveling to Nacogdoches.

One of the first things the detective asked about was the note found on the kitchen counter, asking Belinda to call her Aunt Lorraine. Tom's sister explained that she'd called Belinda to let her know her grandfather had been taken to the hospital. While she talked with David, Lorraine heard Evan in the background. What Lorraine couldn't pin down was the time of the phone call.

When Shipley interviewed Tom and Carol, the detective was surprised that they offered so few answers to her questions. Belinda's parents seemed disconnected from their daughter. The more Shipley questioned them, the more apparent it became that the Lucases knew little about Belinda's life with David Temple. "The Lucases thought it was a matter of the physical distance and their lack of financial resources to visit often," says Shipley. "They were on a fixed income and couldn't afford long-distance phone calls."

When Carol said Belinda always came alone to visit them in Nacogdoches, Tom defended his son-in-law, saying it was because of David's demanding coaching responsibilities. When Shipley asked why David didn't come in the summers, Tom shrugged and answered, "I guess he's just too busy."

Confiding that her lack of contact with her youngest child had been a grave disappointment, Carol said, "David and Belinda spent every holiday with the Temples. It hurt my feelings, but I never said anything to Belinda about it."

Shipley pushed, asking if anyone had seen any evidence of problems in the marriage, but Carol insisted they hadn't. In fact, Brenda had been with Belinda and David just weeks earlier. "Everything was fine while Brenda was there," Carol said, unaware of much of what her surviving daughter had witnessed.

Recounting their history with David, Tom told of his son-in-law's popularity in Nacogdoches, how he'd been a football star, and told the story of how David had been respectful during the courtship, even asking Tom and Carol for Belinda's hand in marriage. "He was very gentlemanly," Tom said, with a sense of pride.

"Have you spoken to David since Belinda's death?" Shipley asked.

"No," Tom said. "We called the Temple house and talked to his mother, but David never called back."

The interview continued, and Shipley asked about Shaka. Carol and Tom had only been to David and Belinda's house in Houston once, but the dog wouldn't let them in the backyard until Belinda came outside to control it. "Belinda said she liked having the dog in the yard," Carol said. "It made her feel safe when David was gone and she was home alone with Evan."

In hindsight it would appear that in the wake of Belinda's murder, both the Lucases were protective of their son-in-law. Their feelings were natural; they had always liked David and neither had ever seen him anything but loving with their daughter. David had always appeared to Belinda's parents to be a good husband and father. Adding to the tension was that Tom had heard from Ken Temple that the police were being less than professional. Seething, David's father had insisted that detectives weren't investigating the murder, instead focusing solely on David. The situation was so bad, Ken fumed, that David had to hire a lawyer, because "the police aren't looking for the real killer."

Sympathetic, Carol and Tom hadn't even considered the possibility that Belinda's husband could be responsible for her death, and Tom spelled that out clearly for Shipley, telling her they knew their son-in-law couldn't and wouldn't have hurt their daughter and his own unborn child.

At her aunt's house, while Shipley interviewed her parents, Brenda hung back, saying little. But at one point, Belinda's twin pulled the detective to the side. "We should talk, but not with my parents," Brenda said. "I'd like to talk to you separately."

Brenda gave her a phone number, and the brief exchange ended. In the end, Shipley would say that whatever Tom said, Carol agreed to, and Tom, in the detective's estimation, "was just kind of clueless about Belinda's life."

As Tracy Shipley prepared to leave, Tom peered down at her and frowned, his forehead furrowed, and said, "My daughter and son-in-law were happily married. I want you to catch the man who killed our daughter, but when you make an arrest, you need to make sure it's the *right* man. I don't want you to put an innocent man in jail."

"Yes, sir," Shipley said, bristling. "I can assure you that when we arrest somebody, it will be the right person."

Meanwhile that Thursday, Leithner and Schmidt were back at Hastings. They hadn't been able to interview David's closest friend, Quinton Harlan, who'd stayed home from work the previous day. Tension was building in the Harlan home. While Tammey thought David was guilty, Quinton couldn't come to grips with even the possibility that his good friend could murder his pregnant wife. That day, Quinton didn't describe Shaka to the detectives as a vicious animal, but said that at times the children rode on his back. David, he said, loved Belinda and was looking forward to Erin's birth. Not yet ready to admit any doubts to himself, Harlan admitted none to Leithner and Schmidt.

After the interviews, Quinton stopped to talk to Heather in her classroom. He was thinking a lot about what would happen when the school district found out about the relationship between David and Heather. "I guess you'll probably have to leave, go to another school," Quinton said.

"Why would I have to do that?" she asked, appearing startled. "I haven't done anything wrong."

About that time, the two lead detectives on the case were sitting down with Hastings' head football coach, Bobby Stuart. He talked about David's role as an assistant coach at the school. Leithner and Schmidt were both mindful of what Wilson had told them, that to press charges they needed to put a .12-gauge shotgun in David's hands. When asked if he'd ever seen David with a weapon or heard him talk about hunting, Stuart raised their hopes, answering that yes he had. David, in fact, had gone hunting with a group of coaches at Stuart's ranch. But hope faded when the head coach said he couldn't remember if David had actually hunted, and if he did, what type of weapon he had.

After the interview, the detectives went to Hastings' security office and inquired about video surveillance tapes from the Ninth Grade Center for the day of Belinda's murder, in hopes that they would be able to monitor David's comings and goings and determine what he'd worn that day. If they knew what to look for, the clothes could be tested for blood and GSR, gunshot residue. In the end investigators watched hours of videotape but never found David. They knew he was at school that morning because others saw him, but somehow the cameras had missed him.

Across Houston at his office at the sheriff's department, David Rossi processed evidence, sending it to labs for analysis. They'd come away with less than hoped for at the Round Valley house. Most disappointing was that he and Holtke never discovered the murder weapon. What Rossi sent to the lab that day included the "rules of golf" shirt, found in the laundry room; a pair of David's tennis shoes, found outside the back door; the damp towels and drain and P-trap from the master bath; the shelf brackets and Home Depot bag from the Isuzu; Belinda's cell phone and charger; and the man's jogging suit, collected from the master bedroom.

Once everything was catalogued and transferred to the labs, all Rossi and Holtke could do was wait for results.

Early that afternoon, detectives fanned out to the Home Depot on I-10 and Brookshire Brothers grocery store on Franz Road, the two places, along with the park, that David Temple said he'd gone when he and Evan left Belinda at home. At both stores, detectives presented subpoenas for surveillance tapes from three days earlier, January 11, the day of Belinda's murder, and during the time period David said he was in the stores. Both stores had multiple cameras placed at entrances and exits.

With the manager at Brookshire Brothers, Schmidt loaded the video from the day of the murder into a viewer. First they determined that the time stamp on the video was off by sixty-two minutes, much of the discrepancy due to not setting the timer back when daylight savings time ended the previous fall. The tapes from both stores were collected and brought to Lockwood for viewing.

While Schmidt was at Brookshire Brothers, he walked up to a mechanical horse outside the store. David had said that on the day of the murder, he'd put Evan on the horse but it wasn't working. Schmidt inserted a quarter, and as Temple had said, the toy was broken.

Belinda had been dead for nearly three days, and her twin could think of nothing else. Who had murdered Belinda? Houston was such a big city, and big cities could be dangerous. But who would break into a pregnant woman's house and gun her down, execute her and her unborn child? Brenda never considered the prospect that it could have been David. That seemed impossible.

When she listened to Detective Shipley interviewing her parents, Brenda kept silent, but she was glad she'd been able to pull the detective aside to say she wanted to talk to her. She didn't consider David a suspect, but she did want the investigators to understand that all wasn't well at the house on Round Valley when she visited over the holidays.

That afternoon, at a Houston hotel, Brian and Jill, too, wondered about the murder. Although no one else in his family had started to even think about David as a suspect, Brian couldn't get the possibility out of his mind. "I'd never really trusted David," he says. "Something about him always bothered me."

The hours ticked away, and Brian thought about seeing David that evening at the visitation. How could he be in the same room with a man he suspected had murdered his sister? "We didn't want to go any more than the man in the moon," says Jill.

Although the Temples never called to ask for input from Belinda's family, they did call to tell Tom and Carol where and when the wake would be. That evening, Belinda's friends and both families congregated at the Schmidt funeral home in Katy, an old-line establishment housed in a redbrick and white-trim building not far from the cemetery. As guests entered, they saw a closed casket, and beside it Belinda's school picture, one taken just months earlier of her beaming for the camera in front of a blue background. David sat surrounded by his family. Many felt as if they were protecting him from questions. That didn't stop the crowd from whispering about Belinda's death, debating who had killed her. The coffin that held Belinda and little Erin remained tightly closed, but many imagined what they looked like inside, their cold bodies, Belinda's wounded face.

Circulating through the crowd, Ken Temple talked to many, often inserting in the conversation that David didn't own a shotgun. According to Ken, David hadn't owned one in years. One of David's cousins, a young man, stood up and talked, recounting to others his view of Belinda and David's marriage, describing how much David loved Belinda and how he, the cousin, looked up to him. As they sat silently and listened, Brian and Jill judged that what was supposed to be an evening held in remembrance of Belinda and Erin had turned into a support rally for David.

As they walked in, Evan's Tiger Land teachers offered David their condolences, and one after the other, they told stories of Belinda. "She was such a good woman," one said. "An amazing mother."

Instead of acknowledging what they said, David repeated to each, in an almost robotic manner, "Thank you for taking care of Evan."

"He acted like he didn't care," says one of the women. "It was like he was there because he had to be there."

When Carol talked to her daughter's widower, she put her arms around David and hugged him. "What are we going to do without her, David?" she asked, sobbing.

"Well, I know the first thing I'm going to do," he said calmly. "I'm going to sell the house. It took both of our salaries to keep it up."

Looking at her son-in-law, Carol considered how cold that was and wondered why David didn't say how much he loved and missed Belinda. "Well, I'm sure going to miss her," Carol said.

David said nothing, simply walking away.

Finding the Temples in the crowd of teachers, students, friends and family, Staci Rios, Belinda's college roommate, approached David's parents to offer her condolences. As they talked, David walked up to her, saying he knew that she and Belinda had talked on the telephone the day before her death. "I'm glad you got that chance," David said.

Staci cried, looked at David and thought, *I'm sure you did this.*

As the visitation drew to a close, Brian heard that Tom, Carol and Brenda were going to the Temples' house. At first, he and Jill hesitated, but then decided they would go, too. When they arrived, they sat in their car, tears in their eyes, trying to marshal their forces to withstand more time with the man they believed had murdered Brian's sister, when suddenly a Porsche pulled into the driveway, its exhaust system rumbling. While the driver sat in his car, Jill and Brian rang the bell and joined the rest of Belinda's family.

In the living room, the Temples had arranged chairs for their guests, and Brian and Jill chose two near the fireplace. Moments later, the man from the Porsche, wearing a suit and carrying a briefcase, walked in. Ken introduced him to the Lucas family as Paul Looney, David's attorney. Minutes later, Brian and Jill watched as David, his brothers and father gathered around the lawyer and talked, whispering among themselves.

There were many tears that night. In the kitchen, Maureen showed Carol photos of Belinda in the collection covering the refrigerator, and Carol broke down when Becky Temple, Kevin's wife, sobbed while recounting how she'd gone to Old Navy to buy Belinda a new skirt and top to be buried in. She'd also brought a soft blanket for Erin.

Yet what the Lucases would remember most, perhaps, was David's attorney. One of David's uncles announced that Looney had something to say and he stood in the living room, center stage, addressing the group. "We believe that in the next few days, David is going to be arrested," he said. "You all need to support him."

The detectives, the attorney charged, were unfairly targeting David, and Looney described the treatment of David and his parents at Clay Road the night of the murder as disgraceful and uncalled for. Then he announced that investigators were trying to get a judge to sign a warrant that would allow them to interrogate Evan, asking the young toddler painful questions about his mother's death. As Looney described it, the investigation sounded out of control. Looking at the Lucas family, especially Belinda's parents, Looney said, "I want you to go to the courthouse and tell the district attorney's office that you don't want Evan interviewed. Tell them you won't stand for it."

Acting as if police had indeed mistreated them, Maureen and Ken sobbed. But David merely sat back and stared at his hands. Throughout the evening, he'd shunned making eye contact with any of Belinda's family, and Jill looked at him and thought that perhaps Looney didn't want Evan to talk to prosecutors because there was the possibility the boy had overheard or seen something. "I thought the writing was on the wall," says Jill. "Brian was right and David had murdered Belinda, and the police knew it."

"When was the last time you went hunting?" Looney asked David in front of both families.

"More than a year ago," he answered, looking across the room at Brenda.

Her family looked at her, too, wondering. Brenda had told them all about New Year's Eve, just two weeks earlier, when David left the house saying he was spending the weekend hunting with friends. Brenda wondered why David was lying.

"There are things being said about David being involved in the murder," Looney said. "It's all hearsay. David may be arrested tomorrow after the funeral, but he didn't do it."

Later, in a more private conversation, Looney talked to

Carol and Tom, telling them that he feared investigators might have tainted the evidence to frame David. "He said the police officers could have kicked the glass to make it look like the back door was open when the glass broke," says Tom.

As the evening went on, David's father circulated through the Lucas family repeating what he'd told others at the wake, that David didn't own a shotgun. The one he'd had, Ken said, had blown up in his son's hands years earlier, and he'd never owned one again. To Brian he described that last afternoon, when Belinda picked up soup at the house. "She thought that might be the night she'd have little Erin," Ken said, over and over. "It might be the night she had the baby."

As the others talked, David pulled Brenda to his parents' bedroom, segregating her from the family. "I didn't go hunting on New Year's," he confessed. "I was at a party. I got really drunk, and I kissed a girl."

Her chest aching with the sadness of her sister's death, Brenda didn't know what to say, so she said nothing.

"I wouldn't do anything to hurt Belinda," David insisted. "You know that."

"Who was the girl?" Brenda asked, thinking of Belinda's sadness as David walked out the door that day, leaving her alone with their daughter's birth approaching.

"Nobody you know," he said. "I know it was wrong, but I'd never hurt Belinda."

When she arrived, Brenda didn't think anything could have made the evening any more painful. She'd already lost her sister and her baby niece, but David's confession made the horror of Belinda's death cut even deeper.

As she turned to leave, Brenda heard David say, "I hope you don't hate me."

At 9:25 that evening, the third day of the investigation, Chuck Leithner, Mark Schmidt, and Dean Holtke drove to the Temple house on Katy Hockley Road. The investigators rang the bell, and David's brothers answered. Leithner handed Darren a court order signed by a judge. They were to bring Evan to the office of a psychiatrist, Dr. Bruce Perry, the following Saturday morning, to be interviewed.

"This poor boy just lost his mother and the funeral is tomorrow," Darren said, shaking his head. But he took the paperwork and closed the door.

Not ready to call it a night, Schmidt decided to complete one more task, to measure the distance from David's parents' house to the house on Round Valley. The drive took sixteen minutes. In his statement, David said Belinda called him at 3:30, saying she was on her way home. Cell phone records that had come in showed the call was actually at 3:32. It seemed probable that Belinda had arrived home, as David said in his statement, around 3:45. Schmidt recorded the information, making a note to add it to the timeline of events from January 11 investigators were constructing at the Lockwood office.

19

At Hastings Ninth Grade Center on Friday, an unknown student posted a sign near the gym that read: "Killer Coach!" Meanwhile, twenty miles away at Katy High, students erected a hand-drawn sign of their mascot, the tiger, with a tear in its eye. Underneath it someone wrote, "The Day the Tiger Cried." In the corridor where Belinda always stood urging students along to their classes, one student remarked to another that the hallways seemed empty without her. At 11:30 that morning, Katy High closed early to allow students and staff to attend Belinda and Erin's funeral.

Before the service started, Brenda met Detective Tracy Shipley at Tom's sister's house. As the detective listened, Brenda told a different story from the one Tom and Carol had just two days earlier. Her account of the time she'd spent with Belinda and David over the holidays didn't make them sound like a happily married couple. Instead, Brenda repeated her sister's words to David, "You don't want this baby girl."

Belinda's twin talked of David's frequent absences, her sister's sadness and the troubles in her marriage. Then she told of New Year's Eve, when David left Belinda home and said he was going hunting with friends for two days, not even leaving the names of those he was with and phone numbers. "I don't know if David murdered Belinda," Brenda said, "but I knew that they weren't getting along. He wasn't home much, and he didn't want the baby. Something was going on."

She then told the detective about David's confession the night before after the visitation, when he pulled Brenda into his parents' bedroom and admitted that he'd been at a party, not hunting, over the holiday, and that he'd kissed another woman.

When hunting came up, Shipley asked Brenda if she'd ever seen David with a shotgun. That was the one bit of evidence it seemed they were all hoping for, someone who could put a .12-gauge shotgun in David Temple's hands.

"No," she said. "I never saw him with the gear. I assumed he had it out in the truck."

While they talked, Tom walked in, and the detective knew immediately he was fuming. He'd spent the morning thinking about what Paul Looney had said the night before, that the detectives were planning to question his grandson. "I don't approve of you doing this. I hope you don't scare that boy," Tom said. "You better not hurt him."

Shipley explained that a psychiatrist who specialized in pediatric trauma would conduct the interview, but Tom still appeared angry. After she finished talking to Brenda, Shipley sought Tom out again, explaining further that no one from the sheriff's department would even be in the interview room, only the psychologist David's lawyer had hired and the psychiatrist the D.A.'s office had arranged.

"Where did you hear that the sheriff's department was going to interview your grandson?" Shipley asked.

"From Mr. Looney," Tom said. "He told us that two or three detectives would take Evan in a room and question him about the day of Belinda's murder. He said that you're going to make Evan tell you that his father murdered his mother."

"That's not happening," Shipley tried to reassure him.

As he had the day before, Tom then told the detective, "I want to hang the man who did this to Belinda. But I want to be sure we've got the right guy and not convict David because of a dog."

As Tracy listened, Tom Lucas then said that Paul Looney had told him that deputies might have tampered with evidence, to make it appear that David was guilty.

"What do you mean?" she asked.

"Mr. Looney said your men could have kicked the glass around from the back door," Tom told her. "To make it look like the door was open when it was actually closed."

"That's not true," Tracy Shipley insisted.

The pallbearers were coaches, friends of David's, and they made an impressive sight, large, strong, athletic men, there to accompany the coffin of the young mother and her baby. Quinton was among them, physically standing beside Belinda's coffin, and still, despite all he knew about David, figuratively standing beside him as his friend. He couldn't convince himself that David Temple was capable of murdering Belinda.

All First Baptist's 1,200 seats were filled, and the Temples—except for Evan, who stayed at his grandparents' with a babysitter—were in their places in the front row when the Lucas family arrived. Tom, Carol and all their children were crying. Tom looked over at the Temples and saw few tears. Carol had such a hard time even walking that Tom had to put his arm around her and help her. When she looked over and saw David, calm, staring down at his hands, she thought: *He's not even shedding a tear for his wife and baby.* Even then, she never considered the possibility that David could be Belinda's killer.

The handout given by the ushers at the entry included Belinda's school photo and began: "In Loving Memory." Inside was a quote from the Bible: "Grace be unto you and peace, from God our Father."

The Baptist church in Katy, a sprawling building with an entrance under a brick steeple, overflowed. Many who came were from Alief Hastings and Katy High. Debbie and Cindy had made buttons for the faculty and students with Belinda's picture, and they watched David, thinking about Belinda's great sadness the last year of her life, her fear that her marriage was over. The two women were glad that as he looked out at the crowd that had gathered to grieve over Belinda, everywhere he looked he'd see the buttons with her face.

At school, Debbie had begun compiling memories in a book for Evan, one they'd keep until he was old enough to appreciate it. Students and other teachers had written notes, to tell the toddler what they knew about Belinda, things she wouldn't be around for him to learn firsthand. Even the students tried to comfort him, reassuring Evan that Belinda was in a better place, writing: "Your mommy was special"; "She was a wonderful teacher"; "She cared about us"; "You, Evan, were her favorite"; "She bragged to everyone about you"; "Evan, you were the highlight of each day for your mom."

Students wrote poems pondering the questions so many asked: "Why was she taken from us?" "Was it a selfish creep looking for money or was it God's will?"

In a poem one student titled "A Gathering of Angels," the author assured Evan that if he listened closely, he might hear his mother's voice.

"It's okay to cry," one teenager advised, while another said, "Your mother touched all our lives. She was a teacher everyone wanted."

At the funeral service, Don Clayton, David's high-school football coach who'd helped him and Belinda find their teaching jobs, gave a eulogy. He'd say later that it was one of the hardest things he'd ever have to do. The choir sang hymns, including "Be Strong and Take Courage," and the Klein High School band played.

When he addressed the gathering, the pastor's eulogy talked of Belinda's love of her husband and son. "This virtuous young woman has touched so many hearts," he said. While the rest of the Temple family cried, appearing devastated, David seemed untouched by the sorrow all around him.

For the service, Brenda had written a letter entitled "My

Twin." It talked of their special bond, and of Belinda, not only her sister but also her best friend, their years as girls playing sports and raising chickens for FFA, how beautiful Belinda looked on her wedding day, and that having been with her to share their birthday two weeks earlier was "the best gift I could ever ask for."

"You will always be with me," Brenda wrote. "I love you so much and our bond will always exist. . . . Love you, Sis. Brenda (Shrimpie)."

On the back of the handout was a testament from Ken Temple, entitled Fondly Remembering Belinda. "Today Belinda and Erin are side-by-side in the loving arms of Jesus. . . . We will no longer look upon [Belinda's] face, but we will see her and feel her every time we look into the sparkling eyes of her beloved son, Evan Brett Temple."

At the back of the church throughout the funeral sat Tracy Shipley, and outside, deputies watched from their squad cars. They followed the procession of mourners the short distance to Katy Magnolia Cemetery. Its flat, grassed grounds dotted with trees, statues of praying angels and austere crosses, the cemetery held graves dating back to the early 1900s. Four rows back, a grave from 1911 bore the plaintive verse: "While the body slumbers here, the soul is safe in heaven." In summer, birds sang and dragonflies buzzed about the headstones. On this January day, the grass was burned out from the winter cold, and Belinda and Erin's casket rested on braces over the gaping hole of the open grave.

At the gravesite, Tracy watched David and thought he looked like he was trying to "squeeze a tear." Debbie, Tammey, Brian and Jill, Brenda and others saw something else. As they waited for the pastor to begin speaking, David whispered something to one of his brothers and laughed, ever so slightly. Rather than overcome with emotion, it appeared that David was repeating something he found funny.

As family and friends crushed about him, the pastor said, "I am remiss in not mentioning that there are two deaths here. We've also lost baby Erin."

20

After the funeral, Brenda told the rest of her family about David's confession the night of the visitation. "We didn't know how to take it," Carol says, shaking her head in sadness. "We believed that he loved Belinda, but now we wondered."

Tom's father was still in the hospital, and Tom and Carol left for Nacogdoches right after the funeral. They felt confused and angry, but most of all sad. "We never told Dad about Belinda," says Tom. "A while later, he was transferred into a nursing home, but he didn't improve and a couple of months passed and he died."

After the funeral ended, Lenius, the embalmer from the nursing home, filled his truck with the flowers and plants from the church and brought them to David's parents' house. He began unloading, when Shaka charged at him. Frightened, Lenius dropped the plants off the truck bed and left.

By the time Kevin and Becky Temple arrived at Dr. Mark Hatfield's office the following morning, Saturday, January 16, Mark Schmidt and Tracy Shipley had the video equipment in place, and the psychiatrist hired by the prosecutor, Dr. Bruce Perry, was preparing for the session. TV news crews had the building staked out, hoping to catch Evan on tape as he walked toward the psychologist's office, where he'd be questioned about what he'd heard and seen the afternoon of his mother's death.

Shipley saw the car pull up and went out to warn Kevin about the news crews. "You may want to cover Evan's face," she cautioned.

"We're not going to cover Evan with anything," he snapped at her.

But then, after seeing the cameras, Kevin and Becky did just that.

In Hatfield's office, Evan played with toys. He'd been there before, the day after the murder, when David brought him. While the video camera taped the session with the youngster and the two therapists, Shipley and Schmidt waited in a separate room.

After the session finished, Kevin and Becky left with Evan. While Schmidt and Shipley took down the cameras, Dr. Perry told them he'd seen no indication Evan saw or experienced anything traumatic. In his opinion, the toddler hadn't been a witness to his mother's murder. "We went into this without any expectations," says Ted Wilson. "Let it suffice to say that the interview was of no help to us."

The psychiatrist told investigators that it was possible Evan, on Motrin and ill, slept through his mother's murder, unaware of what transpired in his parents' closet. But the week following Evan's interview with the therapists, Looney told television stations and newspaper reporters that the fact that the toddler hadn't experienced any trauma associated with his mother's death cleared David. "This whole cruel episode should be closed," the defense attorney charged. "There's just nothing to indicate that this man murdered his wife, and everything to indicate that he did not."

"All week, Heather's friends were kind of buzzing around her," remembers Hall. "She seemed worried and anxious. She kept saying that David couldn't have done it."

In the days after the murder, Heather's twin, Shannon,

talked to their mother, handing her a newspaper article on Belinda's murder and waiting while Sandy read it. "How horrible," Sandy said.

"The problem is that Heather was having an affair with this woman's husband," Shannon told her mother.

"That's horrible, but what does that have to do with this woman's murder?" Sandy asked.

"They've already started questioning Heather," Shannon explained. "The police think David did it."

Years later, Sandy would say, "That's when it hit us."

That same Saturday, five days after the murder, while Evan was being questioned by the therapists, Shannon, Sandy, and Sandy's husband, Jeff, drove to Houston and to Heather's town house. When they arrived, girlfriends, who'd come to lend support, surrounded her. "We quizzed all of them, asking if they thought David was capable of this," said Sandy. "We didn't know David at all, and it scared us to death."

That day, not only Heather but also her cadre of supporters insisted that David would never have hurt his wife. "They were like, 'No way,' " said Sandy.

Upset, Heather described her meeting with police, claiming they treated her badly and screamed at her, "Tell us the truth. He did it and he did it for you!"

"I kept telling them I didn't know anything," Heather told her family.

When it came to the affair, Heather described it as only one weekend with David. "They both knew it was wrong and said this can't be," said Sandy.

"Momma, the sad thing is that David loved Belinda so much he'd still be married to her," Heather told her mother. "I mean, what's the deal? All we did was have an affair."

A week after the funeral, the phone rang at the Harlans' house. Tammey answered and talked to David briefly, calling her husband to pick up. Her suspicions mounting about David's involvement in Belinda's murder, Tammey listened in as the men talked.

"I'm sorry for dragging you into the whole thing," David said. "How's Heather?"

"She's okay," Quinton said.

"Please tell Heather for me that I'm sorry she had to go through this," David said. "I'm sorry I got her in the middle of this."

Quinton agreed to pass on the message, and the call ended. When Tammey came at him, he knew she was furious. "Why is he asking about another woman when his wife and child are dead?" Tammey screamed. "And why are you the one going back and forth with the messages?"

When Quinton didn't answer, Tammey called another coach's wife and asked if she knew why David had asked about Heather Scott. "What's going on?" she demanded.

"Heather's that teacher, the 'Barbie bitch,'" the woman said. "And people are saying that David's having an affair with her."

The more people Tracy Shipley talked to, the more the detective heard about the Temple family dog. Teachers at school and neighbors were afraid of Shaka. Belinda warned many to be careful around him. "It was becoming evident that no burglar just walked into that house," says Shipley.

Around that time, Leithner released the Isuzu to David's father. When they talked, Ken asked the detective if any other possibilities were being investigated. Leithner said they were. Ken then told the detective about a house similar to David and Belinda's just blocks away, also on a corner. Leithner followed up, wondering if it could be possible that mistaken identity was behind the murder. But when he arrived, the house wasn't the same, with a two-story garage and landscaping that didn't look anything like the Round Valley house. The detective rang the doorbell and talked to a woman. She was friendly and cooperative, but said she didn't know anything about the murder.

As the days wore on without an arrest, gossip drifted through Katy like hopes and fears on the afternoons before a big football game. Some talked of David's high-school years, recounting his victories on the field, saying that a hometown hero could never have murdered his wife and baby. But others remembered David Temple's reputation as a bully. It didn't seem much of a stretch when there were rumors of David trying to run down an elderly couple along the side of the road.

Cindi Thompson heard the talk about David being responsible for the murder. She didn't like to think badly of David, but she thought about that evening years earlier, when Darren came to her home crying and shaking, saying that David had held a shotgun on him, pointing it directly at his head. "David had done this before," says Cindi.

Later, Paul Looney would say that the Temples told him about that same incident, but not as if it were fact. "It was like, there were rumors out there about this having happened, started by some vindictive old girlfriend," says Looney. Another thing he heard from the family soon after the murder was that Becky, Kevin's wife, who'd been close to Belinda, believed David was the murderer. "We all knew Becky had those thoughts. We all knew she had doubts that David was innocent."

The week after the murder, Belinda's photos were taken down off the walls at Katy High. "The kids were upset," says Cindy O'Brien. "They cried when they saw them. They missed her. We all did. And some of them were afraid, thinking that it could happen to their mothers or to them. The children didn't know who murdered Belinda or why."

Mourning but needing to move on, Debbie and Cindy called the Temple house. They'd heard that David was staying with his parents, instead of moving back in at Round Valley. They left messages saying that they had possessions of Belinda's in their classroom, things that David might cherish, including family photos. But David didn't call back. Finally, one afternoon, David and his father walked into the content mastery department, where Belinda had worked.

"We're so sorry about Belinda," Debbie said.

His father cried, but David showed no emotion.

The two teachers had Belinda's possessions carefully gathered, handling them as if they held great value, but David didn't appear to want any of them. "He didn't even look interested," says Debbie. "He only took a few things. I figured the few things he did take, he probably threw out as soon as he left."

When David returned to work, his mother brought Evan to Tiger Land in the mornings. Many on the staff worried about the boy, hoping the other children wouldn't say painful things. They didn't, but Evan, a quiet child, became even more withdrawn. When playing with the other children, he'd always been docile and easy to get along with, but after his mother's murder, something strange happened.

One day, Evan and a little girl played dollhouse. The two children had played together often, just as they did that day, the girl holding the mommy doll and Evan the daddy doll. But this was different. Suddenly, Evan appeared angry. Wielding the daddy doll, he pushed at the mommy doll in the little girl's hand, shouting, "No! I don't like you anymore. You don't come back here!"

"Stop!" the little girl cried. "You're hurting me!"

But Evan kept pushing at the little girl and the mommy doll, visibly angry.

Startled at his odd behavior, Evan's teacher rushed over and took the daddy doll from him. Quickly, she distracted the children, turning their attention to another game.

At Hastings, the first week David returned, many saw an unmarked police car parked on the campus near the Ninth Grade Center. A special surveillance unit at the sheriff's department, nicknamed the "spy squad," was watching David, wondering if he'd do something, anything that could further the investigation.

While the deputies waited outside, some of the staff saw things within the building that made them wonder. On one of David's first days back, a teacher saw him hold Heather's hand and talk gently to her in her empty classroom. By then, rumors were circulating as quickly through Hastings as they were through Katy. "Some of David's friends floated the idea that the killer was a student David had in class, someone mad at him, or that it was part of a gang initiation," said one teacher.

If many were suffering after Belinda's murder, David didn't appear, at least to outsiders, to be among them. Just weeks later, he sold the blue pickup truck, the one he so hated, the one he'd repeatedly tried to get Belinda to agree to trade in, and bought himself a brand-new Silverado. Then, he put the house up for sale. One afternoon, after the sign went up, he and his brothers were outside. On the front lawn of the house where Belinda had died, David threw around a football with his brothers and laughed.

In Kansas City, Brenda struggled with all that had happened, the chasm that losing Belinda had cut through her life, wondering if David was the murderer and telling herself he couldn't be. "I didn't want to believe it," she said.

"Some people were saying that the baby Belinda carried wasn't David's," Debbie said, recounting how angry she and Cindy were when they heard the rumors. They never doubted Belinda. Yet the legal system isn't built on trust, and Ted Wilson had requested that David supply hair and blood samples. When the results came in, addenda were added to the autopsy. Belinda's body showed no traces of any kinds of drugs, and the DNA results concluded that David Temple was Erin's father.

Days passed and the investigation continued, as the focus for the detectives remained finding the murder weapon. Mark Schmidt called Brian Lucas and asked if he'd ever heard David talk about owning a shotgun. Brian recalled the dove-hunting conversations he'd had with David, in which

David bragged about bagging his limit. But he'd never discussed what type of shotgun he'd used.

Meanwhile, David's friends and family helped him move his possessions into storage. Among those who volunteered were Clint Stockdick, Kevin's childhood friend, and his wife, Jenifer. Another was Quinton Harlan. Much of what was in the house was boxed when they got there, and they began carrying David's possessions to pickup trucks to move to the Uncle Bob's storage facility, where David had rented a unit. Since he planned to stay with his parents for the near future, it only made sense for him to leave his furniture and other possessions in storage.

That afternoon, Jenifer Stockdick was in the master bedroom gathering boxes. Just being in the room where Belinda died made her uncomfortable. "It was a little eerie," she'd say. Fingerprint dust covered the walls, and police tape hung across the closet door. Ken Temple had been telling many in Katy that David didn't own a shotgun, but when Jenifer glanced into an open cardboard box, she saw a box of shotgun shells and a tan hunting vest. The box was orange and green, and Jenifer heard it rattle, as if not quite full. In the truck, on the way to the storage unit, she told her husband about the discovery. "I felt uncomfortable that I saw that," she'd say.

Her husband, however, didn't find it surprising, telling her, "David hunts."

Quinton Harlan saw that same box with the shotgun shells in the dining room, as he loaded boxes into the trucks. He recognized the box of shells as one he'd seen in the garage a year earlier, when he'd cared for Shaka and needed to get food for the dog. Momentarily taken aback, thinking about David's denials that he had a shotgun, Quinton quickly buried any misgivings. David, after all, was his friend. Yet Harlan did wonder: if David didn't own a shotgun, hadn't in years, the way he was telling everyone who'd listen, why did he still have a box of shotgun shells?

Neither Quinton nor Jenifer Stockdick called detectives to tell them what they'd seen.

21

Eleven days after her daughter's murder, Carol called Chuck Leithner. She'd been thinking about all she'd heard and wondered, for the first time, about David's involvement. "I want to believe it couldn't be him, but now I'm not so sure," Carol said. She'd read the newspapers, including details about the physical evidence that raised questions about David's story. "Things aren't right," she said, confiding in the detective something she'd never told anyone before. "Belinda told me that David didn't want kids. He didn't want Evan at first when she got pregnant. When David found out the new baby was a girl, it only added fuel to the fire."

In the days that followed, the investigation throttled up. Time was passing, and many felt the Temple murder investigation had cooled, so detectives started a second surge, another attempt to find the evidence they needed to make an arrest.

Since the day of the murder, David had changed parts of his original statement. At first David said that he'd taken Evan to the park in the subdivision that afternoon, but he'd later said they'd gone instead to Peckham Park, a sprawling Katy recreation area with a pond, an indoor swimming pool, and gym equipment. One afternoon, a squad of detectives and deputies descended on the park with pictures of David and his 1991 blue Chevy pickup, the one he'd driven that day. They stopped moms pushing children in strollers, joggers, walkers, children on bicycles, and lifeguards who'd left the pool at four on the eleventh, about the time David said he'd been at the park with Evan. None remembered seeing either the blue pickup truck or David Temple.

The following day, about the time of the murder, the detectives turned their attention back to the crime scene, arriving on Round Valley en masse. They stopped every car, asking drivers if they'd passed the house on the eleventh. If a driver said yes, the deputies asked if they noticed anything unusual in the neighborhood that afternoon. What they learned was that Creekstone was busy in the late afternoons. School buses circulated and mothers and fathers rushed home, many driving or walking past the Temple house to get to the communal mailbox across the street. Yet no one said they saw anything odd. They saw no unusual cars and no strangers, especially none carrying a shotgun.

Tammey Harlan called Tracy Shipley one afternoon, wanting to talk. The detective saw the petite brunette walk into the Lockwood station with Quinton towering next to her. While her husband, who steadfastly defended David, waited in a hallway, Tammey met privately with Shipley, telling her about the problems in Belinda's marriage, including the times David called his wife and her family ugly names. Throughout the interview, Tammey appeared visibly upset. "The problems in Belinda and David's marriage spilled over into ours," she confessed. "I made a decision not to spend as much time with Belinda. I had to."

"Was David physically abusive to Belinda?" Shipley asked.

"I think once he threw her against a wall during an argument," Tammey said. But she wasn't positive about whether she'd heard that or seen it, and when Shipley wrote up Tammey's statement, since Tammey was so uncertain, it wasn't included.

"David was emotionally abusive to Belinda, but in front of most people he was completely different, loving," said Tammey.

Somehow that afternoon, Shipley revealed in the conversation that Quinton, too, had been carrying on a flirtation with Heather Scott. That disclosure quaked the Harlans' already shaky relationship. "It was horrible," Tammey would say later. "It almost ended our marriage."

Along with the pain of her best friend's murder, Tammey now had reason to question her husband's honesty and his love. Although the flirtation had never been more than that, it was a betrayal the Harlan marriage would be lucky to survive.

More time passed without progress toward finding the murder weapon, but as they focused on David Temple, other possibilities opened up, making some people question—despite the mounting circumstantial evidence—if investigators were too focused on David Temple and not looking for other suspects.

The talk of the Creekstone neighborhood, of course, as well as much of the Katy area was Belinda Temple's murder. Not only adults but also the children seemed consumed by it. Within days of the killing, information reached detectives that the young boys who lived directly behind the Temples might have heard something that could help establish a time of death, a fact the medical examiner had not been able to determine from Belinda's remains. The children in question, ages six, eight and nine, were Herman, Brian, and Edward Roberts, the sons of a minister and his wife, a teacher.

The Roberts family was well liked in the neighborhood, thought of as good people. As the boys told police, they arrived home on the school bus at approximately four o'clock that Monday afternoon, after which they did a little homework. They popped a Dr. Doolittle movie rented from Hollywood Video into the den VCR and sat down to enjoy it, while their father, who'd taken pain medication, napped. During the movie they heard what all three boys described as a "boom."

"At first I thought it was a firecracker," Brian said. "Then a gunshot."

When had it occurred? Only the oldest of the boys thought he remembered when in the movie he'd heard the shot, at a point where Eddie Murphy, playing the title role, walked down the street talking to a dog. That scene was twenty-seven minutes into the movie, which put the "boom" at 4:30 or later that afternoon. If that were true, David Temple was en route to or at Brookshire Brothers, and couldn't have murdered Belinda.

Still, there were questions about the boys' accounts. It seemed likely that all the boys had heard something, but what? And were their memories reliable enough to determine a time? They were so young.

Another factor made their accounts even more questionable, the report of a neighbor who heard and saw a truck backfire around the time the Roberts boys heard the noise. He'd even given a description of the truck to police. Instead of a gunshot, could that have been what they heard?

Other neighbors on Round Valley and the surrounding streets wondered about the time of the shot, too, speculating on why no one else heard anything. Some decided that if the shotgun blast happened between 3:55 and 4:25, when school buses travel down the street, stopping every few blocks and setting their brakes with a loud bang, no one would have paid attention. "We would all have assumed it was just a bus," says one neighbor. "We wouldn't even have remembered hearing anything."

The more interesting alternate theory for detectives involved another of the Temples' next-door neighbors.

Using information funneled to him from the Temple family, Paul Looney faxed Ted Wilson, offering up ideas for the sheriff's department to pursue in their investigation of Belinda's murder, not surprisingly, none of which focused on David. Later, Looney would suggest that at least some of the information came from David's younger brother, Kevin, who worked as an investigator for an insurance company. "Someone was out there trying to be Dick Tracy," said Looney.

The most interesting lead was that perhaps the teenager who lived directly next door to the Temples could be angry enough to have resorted to violence. The student was Joe Sanders, a thin, wiry young man who had a reputation on Katy High's campus of being a pot smoker and a compulsive truant. There were some reasons the detectives were already looking at Sanders. The first was that Belinda had been at his house a couple of times, first to ask him to turn down loud music and the second time to let his parents know he'd cut classes so often he was in danger of being sent to an alternative school. "Belinda liked Joe Sanders. He was kind of this laid-back kid," said Berger. "She was trying to make sure his parents knew what he was up to."

On Round Valley, Sanders wasn't the most popular teenager. When his parents were out of town, he'd had a party that prompted complaints. "But he was a good kid," said a neighbor who lived a few houses away. "He watched out for the little kids, retrieved balls from the street so the little ones wouldn't get hurt. He was never a real problem."

When the Temples brought Sanders up with Looney, they, too, failed to describe the teenager as a serious threat, but as a student Belinda was interested in, one she was holding a mirror up to, saying that if he didn't change, he wouldn't succeed in life. "It was in the line of, Joe Sanders didn't have reason to be this upset with Belinda, but we didn't know how troubled he was," said the attorney. "If he was troubled enough, he might have retaliated against her."

The detectives were interested primarily because they discovered Sanders had lied about where he was during the time of the murder. When questioned by Shipley with his parents beside him, the teenager insisted he'd been in school on January 11. When the detectives checked his attendance record, however, they discovered he cut nearly all his afternoon classes. Then something else happened to shine a light on Joe Sanders.

While Belinda and Erin were being laid to rest that Friday, a report came in from the Katy Police Department about a .12-gauge shotgun found in a culvert across from Katy's VFW hall on George Bush Drive. Leithner and his lieutenant drove to Katy P. D. and arrived at 5:50 that afternoon. The weapon was an L. C. Smith double-barreled shotgun. It was rusty, as if it had been outside in the rain, and it was recovered with a brown jewelry box. On the lid were the initials HRG. Inside, the detectives found men's cuff links.

Since none of the jewelry matched the description of anything David reported as stolen from the house, Leithner never took custody of the jewelry box. But he did sign for the shotgun and took it for testing for the presence of glass, either from Belinda's broken glasses or the shattered back door, and blood and brain matter.

The .12-gauge, it was soon discovered, was registered to a Howard Robert Gullet, and after further investigation, detectives learned that Gullet was the boyfriend of Corey Reed's mother. Reed, in turn, was one of a group of teenagers who attended Katy High School and ran around with Belinda and David Temple's next-door neighbor, Joe Sanders. "It all looked pretty interesting," said one of the detectives. "Like maybe David Temple wasn't our guy and there were possibilities there."

When interviewed, Gullet said Reed had stolen the shotgun along with the jewelry box. When Leithner learned that Gullet had a second shotgun, another .12-gauge like the first, he took that in to evidence and submitted it to the lab. Meanwhile, Leithner and Schmidt returned their focus to Sanders, and in the coming days the sixteen-year-old high-school student had questions to answer, principally: why he was lying, where he really was on January 11 and whether or not he was involved in Belinda Temple's murder.

On the twentieth, nine days after Belinda's murder, Mark Schmidt went to talk to Joe Sanders, at the home where he lived directly next door to the Temples on Round Valley. The detectives now knew that Sanders's whereabouts were in question the afternoon Belinda died and that his friend Corey Reed had access to a stolen .12-gauge shotgun. By then, the detectives also knew that both of the shotguns Leithner processed from Gullet had tested negative for blood and glass, but the detectives still wondered about the boys, especially Sanders.

Schmidt sat with Sanders in his unmarked car, questioning what the teen had done and where he'd been the afternoon of Belinda's murder. Sanders answered, but didn't appear forthcoming. He admitted having skipped most of his afternoon classes, and said he'd spent much of the day driving around with friends. Schmidt wasn't satisfied, and the name Joe Sanders began to be mentioned more often in connection with the Temple murder case.

On January 28, detectives sat down with the teenager again, this time writing up an official statement detailing his whereabouts on the day of Belinda's murder. In it, Sanders said he left school at seventh period, at about two that afternoon, when Sanders said his friend Corey Reed drove him home. They picked up Sanders's stash of pot and took off in Reed's car smoking it, only to return about 3:30. After a snack, they called a friend named Ed, who drove over with another teenager, this one named John.

Searching for pot, they drove to yet another teenager's house, but when Sanders and his cronies didn't have the money to buy it, they left disappointed. On the street, Sanders argued with the other teenagers when they wouldn't let him "ride shotgun." Angry, Sanders walked home alone, and the other boys met him there about 4:20 to 4:30. They made up and drove to a Quick Mart to buy Ed cigarettes, and then, about 4:40 that afternoon, Sanders said his friends dropped him off at his house, where he laid down on the couch and fell asleep.

"At six my dad woke me up and said something happened at the Temples'," Sanders said. The teenager and his father walked outside and saw the squad cars and crime-scene tape.

The boy's statement ended: "I knew that Mrs. Temple once came to my house and told my parents that I had 131 unexplained absences [classes cut]. I didn't appreciate Mrs. Temple telling my parents about my absences, but I was not angry about it, nor did I hold a grudge against her. I have no knowledge of anyone who would want to hurt Mrs. Temple, nor have I heard anyone talk bad about Mrs. Temple. Mrs. Temple was liked by everyone, including me."

Yet the statement opened up as many questions as it answered. In it, Sanders also admitted that a week before the murder he'd taken one of his father's shotguns, a .12-gauge Remington single shot, without permission, to go shooting with Reed and his other friends in the woods.

From the beginning, Sanders and his parents were cooperative. They agreed to have their home searched and turned over to Leithner two .12-gauge shotguns and shells. The detectives logged them in and submitted them for testing. At the request of the detectives, Sanders also willingly submitted to a polygraph. When the test showed signs of deception, the teenager took another, and then another. So did Sanders's friends, including the boy who'd allegedly stolen the shotgun, Corey Reed. Over the coming weeks, Leithner brought more of Sanders's friends in to give statements and take polygraphs. All the tests showed the boys weren't being completely truthful. The examiner thought it might be because the boys had smoked pot or taken LSD. Since the teenagers were in special classes at Katy High School, Leithner asked one of Sanders's teachers for help in formulating the questions. The woman broke them down, making them simpler. This time, when he retook the test, Reed passed, backing up what Sanders had told deputies about what he and his friends had done that day.

When Leithner wanted Sanders to take a fourth poly-graph, his parents refused, saying the boy had been through enough, and that he was emotionally distraught over Belinda Temple's murder.

When they talked to the prosecutors, the detectives had little to show to elevate Sanders to the status of a suspect. They had no evidence tying any of the teenagers to the murder scene, not a speck of forensic evidence showing that any of them, including Sanders, had ever even been inside the Temple house. One of the prosecutors, Donna Goode, voiced doubts that if teenagers were involved they'd all be able to keep silent, and she speculated that kids on drugs would have trashed the house, not looked neatly through drawers. When detectives asked teachers and other students, they found no one who'd heard Joe Sanders, Corey Reed, or any of the other boys in their clique ever say an angry word about Belinda Temple.

Days later, the two .12-gauge shotguns collected from Sanders's father came back clean for glass, blood and brain matter. Still, the shotgun shells were interesting. The ones found in the Sanders home were double-ought reloads, like the one used to murder Belinda. But then a ballistics expert examined the shells and ruled them out, determining that nothing about them, from the lead buckshot to the wadding, matched.

The detectives continued to wonder about the boys, not able to eliminate them, unable to understand why Sanders had failed the polygraphs. Finally, after one of the tests, the polygraph examiner talked to one of Joe Sanders's friends, one who had been with him that day and who corroborated what Sanders said about his whereabouts. The question that boy was recorded as answering deceptively was: "Do you have knowledge of who murdered Belinda Temple?"

When the boy answered no, the polygraph suggested he was being deceptive. Yet the examiner didn't interpret the test as if the boy had been involved in the murder, more as if he might have known something he wasn't divulging. None of it made sense until the examiner asked a few more questions, and the teenager explained that he did believe he knew who killed Belinda.

"My mom told me David Temple did it," the boy answered.

From that point on, Leithner, Schmidt and the others found little reason to focus on Joe Sanders and his band of teenage friends. "It wasn't that there was something that said definitively that Sanders hadn't done it," said Wilson. "It was that there was no evidence that made me think he was ever in that house. No DNA, fingerprints, no one saw him there, and the other teenagers, the ones he was with that day, all told the same story, all backed up where Sanders had been."

Goode, too, was convinced. "Teenagers don't usually make very good criminals," she said. "They tend to be impulsive, to leave evidence, and they get caught. The way the evidence laid out, Belinda Temple's murder wasn't like that. It was a calculated crime."

The day of the final polygraph of the teenagers, Leithner was in his office when an inquiry came in from the Texas Teachers Retirement System. Belinda had $60,000 in life insurance. As might be expected, David, as her husband, was the beneficiary. Although he hadn't yet proven it, Leithner checked a box on a form that indicated the beneficiary was implicated in the death.

22

On the forensic front, results continued to dribble in. Gunshot residue tests on David's hands came in as inconclusive. GSR was present but in low levels, so small that it could have resulted simply from David touching Belinda's clothes. The blood in the P-trap was too minute and diluted a sample to type, and the blood on the shirt found in the laundry room came back as David's, not Belinda's. Could he have cut himself breaking the door glass? It was possible, but he had been examined, and it was just as likely that the blood came from cutting himself while shaving.

The more Tammey heard about the investigation, the more certain she was that David was the killer, especially when someone mentioned that Evan's car seat was found in the Isuzu, not in the pickup truck, the vehicle David claimed he'd used to take Evan to the park and the stores that afternoon. Tammey had seen David be so protective of the boy that he sat in the backseat of the Isuzu with him while Belinda drove. "There was no way David would ever have put Evan in a car or truck without a car seat," Tammey said. "It wasn't an option. Unless he was absolutely frantic."

But why would David have been upset or even in a hurry? As he told the story, he was simply leaving the house to take his son to the park while Belinda rested.

Something else needled Tammey in the weeks following the murder. She heard more from people at Hastings about David's relationship with Heather. "I heard about the happy hours, that they were a couple," said Tammey. "I was furious."

Officially, the Alief School District stood behind David. The Hastings High School newspaper even ran an article in which Looney complained that police were harassing the school's assistant football coach. Adding his voice to the chorus of the school's coaches, who backed David, the district's superintendent was quoted as saying: "I sure do hate to see things in the paper that have any mention whatsoever of [David Temple] being a suspect. It really bothers me to see the news media do what they're doing. . . . If there isn't an arrest made then David Temple is going to come back as a coach. . . . If the sheriff's department had any reason to arrest David Temple they would have already. . . . We as a School District want to give [Coach Temple] all the support we can give him. . . . In my mind, I still believe he's innocent."

Just days before the article ran, Leithner and Schmidt dropped in at the Ninth Grade Center to talk to Heather again, to ask her to come to Lockwood to give a second statement. While Tara Hall had already voluntarily given a second interview to police, Heather hadn't called offering any more information. Leithner and Schmidt thought there was more there to know, and kept thinking about the lie detector test Heather had taken, the one where the examiner said Scott wasn't being entirely forthcoming.

At Lockwood, in the maze of detectives' offices, Leithner talked to Shipley. Heather waited in one of the cubicles, and the lead detective on the case wanted to know if Shipley would conduct the questioning. "You're a girl. She's a girl. See if she'll talk to you," Leithner suggested.

The men she worked with had described Scott as "hot," but when Shipley saw her, she thought she had a good figure but an average face. "Have you looked above her neck?" Shipley asked one of the male detectives, who shrugged.

To set up the interview, someone had to make Heather

aware of their suspicions that she'd held back during her first interview. That honor fell to Chuck Leithner, who went into the room with Shipley and Scott. "You lied to me," he began. "Didn't you?"

"No," Scott said, but then admitted, "I just didn't tell you everything."

"That's the same as lying," Leithner said. Acting angry, he left the room, turning the interview over to Shipley.

The detective sat down across from Heather, who although it was January wore a sundress, and asked her if there were things she wanted to clear up about her prior statement. "Why's he being so mean to me?" Scott asked.

"Maybe because Detective Leithner thinks you're not telling him everything," Shipley answered.

"I answered the questions he asked me," she insisted.

"In our business, if you don't tell us everything you know, it's the same as lying," Shipley said, staring hard at her. "What do you want to tell us?"

At first, Heather recounted what she'd already said, that she and David had a casual flirtation, but this time she added other information, including that the relationship with David had turned more serious.

"David made me feel good about myself," Heather told Shipley.

"Have you had sex?"

"Yeah," Heather admitted, " . . . about three times."

"If I went and talked to your roommate, what would your roommate say?" Shipley asked.

"She'd say we had sex all the time because we were in my bedroom," Scott said.

As Shipley asked questions, Heather paused before answering, hesitant as if measuring her response. Finally, she talked about New Year's Eve, saying that she'd tried not to advertise at the party the fact that she and David were a couple. They'd had sex that weekend, once, maybe twice. "To me, David was not dating me for the sex. He didn't push the relationship on me."

When Shipley asked Heather if David had ever said that he loved her, the young blond teacher said that he had. On Friday, January 8, David told her, "You know I think I have fallen totally in love with you."

"What did you tell him?" Shipley asked.

"That I felt the same way," she said.

Shipley thought about the timing of David Temple's pledge of love, the fact that three days later, Belinda Temple was murdered. Could it have been a coincidence?

"You know," Shipley said. "One of the things we use to evaluate a suspect is motive. Belinda and David weren't fighting and it doesn't seem to have been over money, but if he was in love with someone else, that could be a motive for someone to kill his wife."

For a moment, Heather Scott looked at Tracy Shipley and said nothing. Then the blond teacher's face bowed up into a small smile, and she said, "You mean you think he killed his wife for me?"

To Shipley, Heather sounded flattered that David might love her enough to kill Belinda and their unborn child to be with her. Shipley felt disgusted, but tried not to reveal what she was thinking: *Do you think he might kill his next wife if he gets tired of her?*

The detective still had the job of finalizing what Heather had told her, but when Shipley finished typing the new statement, Heather balked at parts of what she'd said, not wanting to include her own pledge of love in response to David's, "You know I think I have fallen totally in love with you."

"It didn't mean anything," Heather protested. The detective suggested that if David had said it, if it were true, it needed to be included, and Scott finally agreed, signing the statement and leaving, still appearing to Shipley as if she were holding back information. Later, Shipley noted Scott's objections and labeled Heather's protest as an example of how Scott tried to pick and choose what she told detectives. In her report, Shipley concluded: "It is obvious to this detective that Heather Scott has been evasive and not completely forthcoming in this investigation."

January was drawing to an end, and the detectives still didn't have what prosecutors needed: they hadn't found a murder weapon or been able to put a .12-gauge shotgun in David Temple's hands. They had motive and opportunity, but no hard evidence.

At the sheriff's department, the detectives had constructed a timeline of Belinda's and David's activities on January 11, the day of the murder. For approximately three hours after Belinda returned to work, David was alone in the house: time he could have used to plan the murder and stage the burglary scene.

Then Schmidt considered Temple's account of the rest of the afternoon: the detectives had no evidence that David went to either of the parks with Evan that day. If they relied on the times David gave in his statement, Belinda arrived home at 3:45. The next time they were certain of was from the surveillance video at Brookshire Brothers grocery store, where David arrived at 4:32. That left a forty-seven-minute gap. Schmidt had driven the route from the Round Valley house to the grocery store and estimated that it took ten to twelve minutes. Subtracting the ten or twelve minutes from the forty-seven minutes left more than half an hour unaccounted for, time David could have spent cleaning up before leaving the house.

The second unexplained period was the span between when David left Brookshire Brothers and arrived at the Home Depot. Based on surveillance tapes from the two stores, the trip had taken him thirty-four minutes. That was excessive for a six-and-a-half-mile drive that Schmidt made in less than twelve minutes. What happened during that additional twenty-two minutes? Where was Temple? Disposing of the murder weapon? If so, where?

The police had one clue, a man named Buck Bindeman. A Katy High grad two years behind David, Bindeman said he saw David at five o'clock on the afternoon of Belinda's murder. A truck aficionado, Bindeman seemed credible, describing Temple's truck down to the shade of blue and the type of wheels. What made Bindeman's information tantalizing was that the sighting was north of where David said he'd been, at an intersection near his parents' house, a place where rice fields fanned out under the big Texas sky.

Since they'd begun looking for the .12-gauge shotgun, Leithner and Schmidt had talked often about the possibility that if David were guilty, he could have hidden it somewhere in the rice fields, ponds, culverts or creeks near the Temple house. David had grown up hunting in the area and knew it well. Yet that left an expansive area, much of it flooded by rice farmers off and on during the year, irrigating their crops. How could they even begin to look?

23

Heather didn't want to talk about the murder. She got mad at me one day when she overheard me talking to someone about it on the phone. She told me I had no right, that it didn't have anything to do with me," said Tara Hall. Yet Hall was involved, with a ringside seat to the drama unfolding, including the continuing relationship between Heather and David. "He didn't call the house for a few weeks, but it didn't seem that long that David wasn't around."

On Valentine's Day, Brenda sent a teddy bear with a balloon to Evan at Tiger Land. David was still living with his parents, and Maureen often dropped the toddler off in the morning and Ken picked him up in the afternoons. On that day, his teacher made sure she gave Evan's grandfather the gift.

"You shouldn't have done that," Ken admonished, with a smile.

"It's from his Aunt Brenda," the woman said.

"Ken Temple looked angry," the teacher would remember. "He took the bag and said, 'Come on, Evan. Let's go.'"

The Tiger Land staff saw as little of David as they had before the murder. On Friday mornings, however, Maureen often brought a suitcase with the toddler, leaving it at Tiger

Land. Around 2 P.M., David showed up to pick up his son, taking the bag with him. The teachers who looked outside saw a woman with long blond hair sitting in David Temple's new truck, a woman they'd later identify as Heather Scott.

Soon Tara began arriving home at the town house and noticing David's new truck pulled off to the side, hidden from the main road. When Valentine's Day arrived, she found a beautiful, expensive-looking bouquet with roses in a vase. The flowers were for Heather, a gift from David Temple. "I thought it was really odd," says Tara. "His wife had just been dead for a little over a month, and it seemed really inappropriate. But I didn't say anything to Heather. I knew she wouldn't like it."

"Are they together?" Tammey asked the other coaches' wives, weeks after the murder.

"Yeah, he's with her," one of the women told her. "He sees her all the time."

"That sent me into a rage," Tammey would say later. "I was bad, really bad."

Infuriated with David, Tammey began following him, putting her younger daughters in the car, watching as he left Hastings after class ended for the day. "I thought, *What am I doing?*" she'd say later. "But I couldn't stop. It was like I had to do it, to make it up to Belinda for not being a good friend."

Hanging a few cars back, she shadowed David in his truck as he drove from school to Heather's town house. Once there, he parked next to a wall that backed up to a small shopping center, and Heather pulled her car in behind him, as if to block the truck from view. Tammey staked out the town house, watching David come and go, once even picking up Heather and Tara's trash from the curb and combing through it looking for clues.

One day she heard Heather and David had both called in sick, and Tammey returned to the town house and saw his truck and her car. "I couldn't believe the audacity," she said. "I wanted him caught." It only made her angrier that she saw the coaches, including her own husband, forming a shield around David, protecting him.

"No one wanted to believe it," says Quinton. "I didn't want to believe it."

Furious, Tammey pounded on the town house door, screaming for David to come out. She felt certain he was inside with Heather, but no one answered.

Before she left, Tammey put a note on David's truck, tucked into the window: "I saw you. I know what you're doing."

At the Harris County District Attorney's building, a plain brown brick nine-story structure near the web of courthouses, Leithner and Schmidt talked to Ted Wilson about the possibility of obtaining search warrants for the school computers to get David's and Heather's e-mails. Wilson, who'd written the definitive book on Texas law and search warrants, began work on the document.

By then, David and Heather had been at it again, e-mailing back and forth at school. On January 26, at 8:57 A.M., two weeks after Belinda's murder, David had e-mailed Heather: "I hope your days are going well."

"It is going great . . . I hope yours is too . . . it is better now that I have heard from you," Heather responded, five minutes later.

"It made me feel better just to see you yesterday and today," David responded.

"[Another male teacher] thanked me for wearing this dress. . . . I guess I made his day also. ☺ Just trying to make you smile."

"That is a job few people can do right now, and you do it very well. Thanks again," he replied.

"Things will get better. . . . It just takes time . . . ☺," Heather assured him.

"You are always right," he concluded.

The next morning, at 10:32, Heather had e-mailed Quinton: "Please make it be 3:00 already. . . . I want to go home and hug my bear you gave me. . . . I guess it is safe to talk to him ☹"

Why was Heather afraid to talk to others? What was she worried about?

That same morning, Heather had also e-mailed David. It would appear later that somehow she'd learned that the detectives were in the process of zeroing in on their e-mails. On the same day that Ted Wilson wrote up a subpoena for Alief ISD asking for all David's and Heather's correspondence, Heather e-mailed David: "Please make sure you delete everything in your deleted folder and your sent box."

Had someone tipped Heather off?

Two days later, the subpoena was served. What the investigators came away with were only those e-mails backed up on the school's main computer system. If there were others, they were gone.

Meanwhile, the search for the murder weapon continued.

Photos on the front page of the *Katy Times* showed searchers combing culverts and fields, standing only a few feet apart, walking through ankle-high water at times, scanning the ground for the shotgun used to kill Belinda. The hunt went on for three days, as deputies, detectives, even inmate trustees from the county jail, walked ten miles a day through field after field, ditches and low-lying areas infested with poisonous snakes, hoping to spot a glimmer of steel that could signal a hidden weapon.

The sheriff's department brought in dogs and helicopters to search the fields. While the others explored on land, a dive team began at Peckham Park, in the small lake where Belinda used to take Evan to feed the ducks. From one body of water, they moved to the next. In one retention pond, a deputy dove into the murky water, only to see a baby alligator swimming toward him. The man swam away, lurching quickly onto the shore, worried that the presence of a baby alligator meant a ten-foot, 300-pound mother gator might not be far away.

Much of the area searched was immediately north and east of Maureen and Ken Temple's house. At one point on foot, Mark Schmidt was so close that he could see their back-yard. But there were stretches impossible to explore, including the muddy bottom of the nearby Brazos River. After so much effort without results, the searches were abandoned, and Chuck Leithner noted in the murder book devoted to the Temple case: *The investigation continues.*

24

In February, Debbie and Cindy ran a full-page remembrance of Belinda in the Katy High *Tiger Teacher Times.* They were still grieving, thinking of Belinda every day when they walked into their suite of classrooms. The students continued to be upset, some talking often of Mrs. Temple, wondering what if anything was being done to catch her killer. Others still thought of Belinda, too. In Nacogdoches, Carol and Tom were becoming consumed by the murder. "They didn't talk of anything else," says Tom's brother, Chuck. "It was horrible for them and for the kids."

David's family, too, seemed to be in turmoil. Ken Temple suffered a heart attack, he'd later say, when he walked into the closet of the master bedroom on Round Valley, where his daughter-in-law died. "I loved her," he'd say. "A heart attack from grief."

Yet detectives increasingly had the feeling that the Temple family was on the defensive, circling the wagons around David, much as they had in his tumultuous school years. "The Temples were playing it like they were the regal rulers of Katy, Texas," says Shipley. "They weren't helping, and they weren't pushing for anyone else to help us solve Belinda's murder."

That month, Quinton and David went out to lunch at a

hole-in-the-wall Mexican restaurant not far from Hastings. After they sat down, David laughed about an unmarked squad he'd noticed following him there. It was nearly six weeks after Belinda's murder, and the sheriff's office still had him staked out, waiting to catch him making a slip.

"Why aren't you talking to the police?" Quinton asked. "Don't you want to know who killed Belinda?"

To his friend's astonishment, David answered, "What good is it going to do?"

Quinton looked at the man who for the past three years had been his close friend. They'd had disagreements, and at times David badgered him. But now Quinton wondered, *Did David murder Belinda?*

Then David again explained his alibi, claiming police had him on video at Brookshire Brothers, buying cat food, when Belinda was murdered. Quinton thought about that and reassured himself that David couldn't be guilty. If what he said was the truth, David hadn't even been in the neighborhood when Belinda was murdered. Still, there were those unanswered questions. "But wouldn't you like to know who did it?" Quinton asked. "I'd want to know who murdered my wife and my unborn child. I'd want them caught."

"It isn't going to bring Belinda back," David replied, as if not even considering the possibility that solving the murders could bring his family and the Lucases closure and some helping of justice.

Not long after, Tammey called Becky Temple. This time Belinda's friend came right out and said what she was thinking, telling Becky, "I think David did this."

"Everything he said was a lie. I'm deathly afraid of David," Becky confided. "I'm beginning to think he did it. Kevin's family is so mad at me." Then, Becky suddenly sounded worried, begging Tammey: "Please don't tape record this. What will David do to me? What will he do to my family?"

"I'm not," Tammey assured her.

* * *

Winter ended, and spring began, and the house on Round Valley sold. At Hastings, David bragged that he made money off the sale.

Meanwhile, at the Harris County Sheriff's Office homicide division, Chuck Leithner moved on to other cases. Mark Schmidt did, too, but he couldn't completely let go of the Temple homicide. It needled at him, bothered him, and the other detectives thought they saw the case changing him. "Mark became nervous, more anxious. He talked about the case all the time," said Shipley. "He wasn't the same old Mark, with a smile on his face."

"I thought about Belinda Temple's murder before I closed my eyes at night and first thing in the morning," said Schmidt. "It was my first big homicide, and it looked like the killer might get away with murder."

Forensics had little to offer, and it seemed that there was no concrete evidence tying David to the murder. Hoping to find more, to prove David lied when he said he didn't own a .12-gauge shotgun, Schmidt canvassed stores in the area that sold guns, from Walmarts to sporting-goods stores that featured display cases and wall racks of weapons. None had a record of anyone in the Temple family buying a .12-gauge shotgun.

When Leithner and Schmidt met with prosecutors, Wilson and Goode agreed that there was circumstantial evidence and more than a little suspicion, yet, they argued, not enough to pin a murder charge on. "We had one chance at David Temple. If he was guilty and we tried him unsuccessfully, we'd never be able to try him again," says Wilson. "We didn't see that there was a hurry. There's no statute of limitations on murder."

Goode agreed, saying what she always believed: "David Temple would confess to someone, or someone who knew something would come forward, or the murder weapon would be found, something that made the case more solid."

Yet, the prosecutors decided there was one action they could take, one way to safeguard testimony until they brought the case into a courtroom: presenting the case to a grand jury would result in an official record of what each witness remembered about the murder, before time intervened and memories faded.

In a secret proceeding in early March 1999, one after another, the main witnesses in the murder case answered questions before a grand jury, including Mark Schmidt; Katy High teachers Stacy Nissley, Debbie Berger, and Cindy O'Brien; neighbors like Mike Ruggiero; Tara Hall and Heather Scott; and the Temple family: Ken, Maureen, Darren, and Kevin. Even Joe Sanders and his friends agreed to testify.

Tammey Harlan wasn't scheduled to appear, but she went with Quinton. As she talked to the prosecutors and detectives in the hallway, they decided to put her, too, before the jurors. Quinton still had a hard time believing David could be guilty, and his answers that day were protective. He described David's grief over Belinda's death as sincere. When it came to Shaka, he said that the dog was all right, once it knew someone. Tammey told a different story, including describing the problems in the Temple marriage, telling the jurors about the weeks of silence between David and Belinda.

In the hallway at the courthouse, Tammey saw Heather leave the grand jury room. Following her instincts, Tammey attacked. "Look what you've done to Belinda," she said, seething.

To prevent more, Mark Schmidt slipped between the two women, advising, "She's not worth it, Tammey."

When the grand jury ended, the members were polled, and they described the case against David Temple as weak. Yet Wilson had accomplished his goal. He now had an official record of the testimony of many of the main witnesses. Everyone, that was, except the only suspect. David Temple appeared as required, but brought Paul Looney with him. In a move not unusual for the focus of a criminal investigation, David pleaded the Fifth Amendment, refusing to testify.

Afterward, the prosecutors again told the detectives that

they didn't have enough evidence. "Did I believe David Temple murdered his wife? Yes," said Wilson. "Did I believe I could prove it in a courtroom beyond a reasonable doubt? No. I didn't know that we were even close to closure on the case."

Days later, after her testimony was given, David called the Harlan house, and Tammey answered. "What did you tell the grand jury?" he demanded.

"We're not supposed to talk about that," she said.

David asked for Quinton, and demanded again, "What did *you* tell them?"

"We told the truth," Quinton said.

"You need to keep your mouth shut," David ordered.

For Evan's fourth birthday, Maureen and Ken brought a cake to Tiger Land, but David didn't come. That month, Schepps, a Houston dairy that had helped the sheriff's department in the past, offered a $10,000 reward for information leading to the conviction of the person who murdered Belinda. Schmidt and Holtke made up flyers with the reward information and a photo of Belinda and spread them through Katy, in store windows, on bulletin boards, at the post office, at restaurants and in grocery stores. They even put them beside Heather's mailbox at the town-house complex.

Not long after, Tom, Carol, Brian and Jill met with the prosecutors and detectives again. This time the detectives detailed the evidence for Belinda's parents, including the broken glass pattern not matching a closed door and the fact that David had been having an affair. "It was the affair that did it," says Tom. "Once I heard that, for Carol and me, it all started to fall into place. We weren't defending David anymore."

That day, Wilson and Goode explained that David was their only suspect but that they didn't have enough to charge him with the murder. "We left there angry and hurt," said Carol. "We were mad that David did it, and there was nothing the police could do."

Feeling guilty, as if somehow he was supposed to have prevented the murder, Tom Lucas considered going after David himself, with a gun. "Fathers are supposed to protect their little girls," he said, shaking his head sadly. "But Carol and my family convinced me not to. They said having me in jail wouldn't help anyone."

At the Harlan home, Tammey began getting odd telephone calls. At times the caller hung up, and at other times someone laughed in the background. It happened only when Quinton was on the road with the basketball team. Without caller I.D., she had no way to track them, but she suspected it had something to do with David Temple. "He knew when Quinton wouldn't be home," said Tammey. "I figured he was trying to frighten me, to make me shut up."

Then one weekend afternoon, Tammey drove into their driveway with their oldest girl, Sydnee, and a McDonald's lunch she was bringing home for the family. Quinton was behind her in his truck with the two younger girls. Just before he arrived, Sydnee ran from Tammey's car into the house. Seconds later, she fled the house screaming, "There's a man inside!"

Instantly, Tammey saw a man run from their home. When Quinton pulled into the driveway, she hurriedly explained, and he ran to search. He found no one, but the sliding glass door that led to the master bedroom, which had been locked, stood wide open. When they investigated why the house alarm hadn't gone off, they discovered that all the sensors had been broken. "I thought it was odd that all of a sudden something like this happened. Maybe David was behind it," said Quinton. "I started thinking maybe it was all true, that Tammey had been right. I knew David was mad at us for talking to the grand jury. It started to make sense that David had murdered Belinda."

Frightened, Tammey bought a gun and began carrying it with her. "We were in fear for our lives," she said.

Quinton and Tammey were so frightened that they left the

house that night, moving in with friends. They even went to Sydnee's school and talked with the principal and counselors, to warn them to be on the lookout, in case David showed up on the school grounds. They went so far as to hand out photos of David to the staff, so he'd be recognized. And Tammey and Quinton had a careful talk with their oldest, telling Sydnee, "Don't go to Mr. David, if you see him and he calls your name."

It was a difficult thing for Tammey and Quinton to do. The girls had grown up knowing Belinda and David so well that they viewed them as extended family. "Sydnee loved David," said Tammey. "She really did."

Still, they worried that if David wanted to find them, he could. And the fear didn't end.

As if proving that point, early that summer, on a Friday evening, Tammey drove to her Storybook Cottage, the quaint teahouse she ran, to open it up and turn the air-conditioning on for a little girl's birthday party the next day. On the way there, Tammey saw David trailing her in his new truck. He pulled up beside her, and then fell back behind her and followed. Tammey sped up.

When she reached her Storybook Cottage, Tammey ran inside, her hands shaking as she held her gun. Moments later, David pulled up and slowed down, not stopping but driving by at a snail's pace, as if to taunt her. Then he laid on the gas and drove away.

That July, the *Katy Times* ran a series on the case, headlined with the question on so many minds: "Who killed Belinda Temple?" Over the coming weeks, the newspaper reexamined the evidence, from Shaka's ferocious defense of the backyard to the broken glass. The series revealed that the burglary appeared to have been staged, and recounted the continuing effect of the murder on the Katy community. And the reporter asked questions, including: If the back door had been left open by the burglar that afternoon, as David Temple told police, wouldn't Shaka have gone inside the house and found the body, leaving bloody paw prints behind?

In the *Times* article, Paul Looney vigorously defended David and attacked the detectives, saying they'd jumped to judgment and that callous behavior on their part had done "emotional damage" to the Temple family. In a strange statement, since the murder resulted in the death of a young mother and her unborn child, the defense attorney said: "Sometimes I think the damage done [to the Temple family] in those first few hours might exceed the damage done by the loss of Belinda Temple."

The series ended: "Detectives are little closer now to charging a suspect or even naming a suspect than they were when they began on the day of the murder," a sergeant in homicide was quoted as saying. "Until we solve this, it will never go away."

In their own defense, Ken and Maureen Temple wrote a letter to the newspaper's editor. In it, they complained that they'd been mistreated by law enforcement and hadn't been granted the sympathy usually given to a victim's family: "Since the tragic deaths of our daughter-in-law and granddaughter on January 11, no level of the media has identified the Temple family as victims . . . Without respect for [David] being the spouse, father, and first discoverer of his wife's body."

That fall, on the surface, life went back into a more normal rhythm, but always with the undercurrent of fear, doubt and anger left by Belinda's murder. Her brother Brian and her father, Tom, called Schmidt often, asking what was being done to solve the case. He had few answers for them. There was still evidence analysis Schmidt waited to get back, from the FBI lab. The agency had what at the time was considered the premier forensic lab in the nation, and Schmidt had submitted some of David's clothing and a pair of his shoes collected the night of the murder, for processing. But the agency was slow, with thousands of other cases in the queue, so the wait would be formidable.

At Maureen and Ken's house, photos of Belinda remained on the refrigerator, and they talked of her often, say family and friends. Perhaps from the unrelenting stress of the murder and investigation, both suffered setbacks with their health. If they had any doubts about their son's involvement, whenever the subject came up, they continued to assert David's innocence. "They steadfastly defended David," said a friend. "They were adamant that he was being falsely accused."

Meanwhile, in Nacogdoches, Tom compiled his own outline of the evidence on his home computer. Waiting for a break in the case, he felt understandably frustrated and angry, as did Carol. "Belinda's death had torn the whole family apart," said his brother, Chuck. "Tom was struggling, trying to get someone to run with the case. It was there every day, in everything they did."

When all appeared to have quieted down, Tammey and Quinton moved back into their home in Katy, and beginning in August, Quinton was back at Hastings working alongside David on the football field, coaching the defense. "We tolerated each other, but interacted very little," said Quinton. "It was strange considering we worked with the same players."

Brenda sent chimes and flowers to Belinda's gravesite, and cards, including one with a verse that read: "To my best friend." When Brian was in Houston on business, he visited Belinda's grave, and then spent hours walking Katy creek beds, looking for the shotgun. Later he'd call Mark Schmidt. "What are you doing?" he'd ask.

"We're trying," Schmidt answered.

A few times, David allowed Belinda's family to visit with Evan, but never alone. Once Jill, Brenda and Brian went to the Temples' house. The entire time they sat outside with Evan and David's parents, Shaka thrashed at the garage door. "If that dog could have gotten out, we would have been mincemeat," says Jill.

* * *

The Temple case was turning into an embarrassment. The Harris County sheriff, Tommy Thompson, had a ranch in Katy, and was regularly approached by neighbors who wanted to know when an arrest would be made. Dean Holtke lived there, too, and people often cornered him, asking why no one had been arrested for murdering that nice teacher from Katy High School. On Sundays, when Dean went to First Baptist Church, he looked over and saw Ken and Maureen Temple.

Although nearly everyone who approached Holtke and voiced an opinion held that David was the murderer, when detectives talked to people who knew the Temple family, they nearly always came away with little. "It was like hitting a wall out there," Shipley said. "There was this attitude that they didn't want to be the one to disparage a hometown football hero. It was frustrating."

There was one person, however, who would talk with them, if, at first, reluctantly: Cindi Thompson, who'd been Darren Temple's girlfriend so many years earlier in high school. Cindi just happened to know Dean Holtke's wife, so well that Cindi had sung at their wedding. When Dean heard rumors that Cindi knew something about David threatening someone else with a shotgun, he called her. After some convincing, Cindi agreed to talk to Holtke. When she did, she recounted that night when Darren shook, terrified, telling her how David had held a shotgun on him.

Since the murder, Tom and Carol had tried repeatedly to see their grandson alone, hoping to have him for a weekend, to spend time with the only tie they had left to Belinda. Evan looked so much like their family. He had Belinda's eyes and her smile, and Brenda's thick, dark brown hair. Although he did meet with them, David wouldn't allow the Lucases to be alone with Evan. Instead, David offered to meet them at McDonald's or a shopping center, where they walked together. At every moment, David stayed protectively at his son's side, and the rift between the two families grew wider.

One afternoon, David agreed to bring Evan and meet Belinda's parents at the cemetery. Perhaps to open their son-in-law up to talking to law enforcement, Tom and Carol agreed to have Mark Schmidt drive them there. When David saw the detective, he scooped up Evan and ran to the car. At the Temple house, Ken came out and told the Lucases, "If you want to see Evan, you'll have to come by later."

When they returned without Schmidt, no one answered the door.

That fall Carol and Tom gave a television interview to a Houston station. "David is a suspect in the case. Do you think he did it?" a reporter asked.

Rather than defending her son-in-law, Carol said, "I would hate to find out that someone my daughter married would do this."

The next time they called asking to visit Evan, David told them, "I don't think I can ever forgive you for saying that."

The animosity built as the Lucases heard, all the way in Nacogdoches, that their son-in-law was dating the woman he'd been seeing when Belinda was murdered. It never seemed as if David was hiding the relationship. That fall, David and Belinda's Round Valley neighbor, Natalie Scott, went out for dinner with her husband, Robert, to the C&H Steakhouse, a plush restaurant that served thick slabs of beef with sides of baked potatoes and asparagus. After they were seated, Natalie noticed David across the dining room, sitting with a blonde in a red dress, a woman she'd later identify as Heather Scott.

"Isn't that David?" Robert asked Natalie.

"Yes it is," she said. Although she repeatedly looked over at him, David never acknowledged that he knew her.

25

Fall came and the football season began. To the surprise of many, Heather showed up in the stands where the coaches' families sat for Hastings' first home game. "You've got to be kidding," Tammey said, confronting her. "How dare you?"

Instantly, Heather shot up out of her seat and left, moving to another area. That wasn't enough to placate Tammey, who stood and glared at the woman who, along with David, she blamed for Belinda's murder. The Temples sat nearby with Evan, but when Tammey went to talk to the toddler, his grandparents slid in closer to him, as if protecting him. They did the same when Kay Stuart, the head coach's wife, stopped to say hello. "Maureen and Ken Temple shut it down real quick," said Stuart.

Few knew that Tammey wrestled with her own situation, that her husband had indulged in a flirtation with David's girlfriend. "Tammey told me that she loved Quinton and that she understood he'd made a mistake," said Shipley. "She said they were struggling, trying to work it out."

In early September, Brenda called Mark Schmidt to ask if she could help with the investigation. He declined the offer, but Brenda couldn't accept that. Her sister was dead and after hearing the evidence against him, Belinda's twin believed her brother-in-law was responsible. Despite Schmidt's refusal, Brenda tried to think of some way to help. One day, she came up with an idea and bought a tape recorder with a mechanism that allowed it to be inserted into a telephone line.

On September 14, at 8 P.M., Brenda dialed the Temple house and David answered. "Hey, what have y'all been doing?" she asked, with the recorder on.

The call was congenial, as Brenda asked about Evan. David said that the four-year-old was doing well, and talked a bit about his son's life, much of it involving David's family. Evan was a regular at the Hastings football games with Ken and Maureen, and David had made plans for his son to go on his first airplane ride, taking a trip to California with Kevin and Becky. As the conversation progressed, David talked of football, but Brenda turned the subject to her dead sister, asking if Belinda's headstone had arrived.

"Just got it . . . it's out there now," David said, bragging, "It's the nicest one out there."

"I still can't believe this happened, David," Brenda said.

"I've cried every day of the past two weeks nonstop at the games," David said. While others saw his girlfriend cheering at the games, David, sounding tearful, insisted he yearned to see Belinda in the stands.

When Brenda asked if he'd heard anything about the investigation, David said he didn't know "if they're even doing anything. There's no way to know."

"Have you ever asked?"

"Yeah," he claimed.

"Is there anything you can do to move along the investigation?" she prodded.

"They aren't going to do anything for me. Not for anybody," David said. In truth, David hadn't called to inquire about the progress or to try to spur along the investigation, nor had anyone in his family. Instead, David said his lawyer told him that the case would be solved one day when someone talked or got "caught doing something else, speeding with the gun in the car."

"How could anyone just go in there and do that to a pregnant woman?" Brenda said, angry.

Sounding heartbroken, David told his dead wife's twin that he was filled with sadness at not being able to go home to the house on Round Valley and have Belinda waiting for him. When it came to the murder weapon, he said it could have been a sawed-off shotgun someone hid in a baggy pants leg. Despite so much found in the home and on Belinda, he claimed that Belinda's jewelry was gone. Yet how was it that the thieves had taken nothing of his, not one item? "I wear my watch, my wedding ring I had on. . . ."

Brenda didn't know until much later that she'd caught David in a lie. Pictures from the scene that night clearly showed that he wasn't wearing either his wedding ring or his watch that night. Both were in the bedroom, with his heavy gold championship ring on a plate next to the television.

"It's one sick individual, whoever did this . . ." Brenda said, talking to the man she believed to be the murderer. "Eight months pregnant, just insane whoever did it. It tears me up every day."

On a Sunday afternoon, Brenda called the Temples' house again. This time Maureen answered, and they discussed Evan. Maureen tried to coax him to the telephone to talk to Aunt Brenda, but the toddler, who didn't like talking into telephones, refused.

"Does he ask about Belinda a lot?" Brenda asked.

"Just this morning, we were folding towels, and he started rolling one. I asked why he's doing that, and he says, 'My mommy says it's prettier that way.' "

When Brenda said she missed her twin sister, Maureen could be heard crying. "I know you do," David's mother said. "Every day, every time Evan says something about his mommy . . . this has been so hard for him."

"Those two were so close," Brenda observed.

"He won't forget her," Maureen assured her. "We talk about her all the time."

When Brenda asked if she thought the police would ever solve Belinda's murder, Maureen said that she wished it would be solved. "I hope you know that David would never have hurt her in any way. If you have any common sense, Brenda, you know your sister was not afraid of him."

"Yeah," Brenda said, swallowing what she truly thought to keep the older woman talking. "I can't imagine someone could do that to a pregnant woman . . . I see babies, and I wonder what Erin looks like."

With that, Maureen Temple cried again. She advised Brenda, "Close your eyes and think of [Belinda] and she's there."

The next day, Brenda called again, and this time David answered the phone. He told her that he went to the cemetery often. When Brenda said she worried about Evan, David responded, "He's doing good."

Quickly, David turned the subject around to football and Hastings' latest team. But Brenda brought it back to Evan, asking if her nephew should have counseling, to help him through the loss of his mother. As he had in the past, David reassured her that Evan was well. Then David mentioned that he'd received a letter from an attorney Tom and Carol hired, asking for visitation with Evan. "None of y'all are supporting me. I don't know what you expect me to do," he said. But then, as if that weren't a suggestion that he'd punish them by withholding visits with Evan, he said. "You know, you can see him at any time."

"Well, you said a while back that you didn't want [my parents] seeing him," Brenda said.

"Well, I told them that," David admitted, but then maintained, "It was ridiculous [for them to get a lawyer]." He paused, as if considering what he'd just said, and then charged, "You haven't supported me, Brenda." As if explaining his building anger, he claimed unidentified people called to tell him things about Brenda and her parents. "I know what you've said and what you've done." The conversation continued and he chastised her for not taking his side against the investigators, and insisted he had "totally nothing" to do with Belinda's murder.

"Why haven't you taken a polygraph? What are we supposed to believe?" Brenda countered.

"You have never asked me or anything else. You only believe the sheriff's department and they've lied to everybody . . . my family and everybody else. . . . You don't support me," he charged. Then, after attacking the newspapers, saying they, too, spread lies about him, he insisted that her family had hired a private investigator. Brenda said that wasn't true, and once again asked why he wasn't helping police find the murderer.

"You have no idea what my family went through," he said again, never answering her question.

On the telephone, David repeated what he'd told Quinton Harlan months earlier. When Brenda asked if he wanted the crime solved, David responded, "What difference would it make? It won't bring Belinda back." Then he said something even more shocking, "Belinda wouldn't want all this. She'd want us to leave it alone."

Again, Brenda asked about the polygraph, saying that if he took it and passed, perhaps the police and her family would accept his innocence. "Polygraphs don't work," David said. " . . . Belinda would roll over in the grave if she knew what was going on with you and your parents, that you would think that."

At times David's answers made no sense, as when Brenda again pointed out that David had told her parents he wanted them to have nothing to do with Evan. And then again, she asked about a polygraph. "Why don't you just go and do whatever to clear your name?"

"Questions have been answered," David said. "Every single one of them."

He implied that his family had wanted to give a reward, but had been turned down by police, another lie, since the

Temples had never contacted the sheriff's department offering to put up a reward.

"The newspapers keep pointing at you, David," Brenda said.

David responded that he'd sent facts that backed him up to the newspapers, but they'd refused to run them. "You all assume the worst," he said.

"I don't know, David," Brenda said, crying.

"You should know. Belinda would want you to know. And you damn well know. We were happier than anyone in your family who's married. You don't know that?" he asked. "Your brothers or your parents. You know that."

Although she knew that David and Belinda were anything but happy the last time she saw them together, it made no sense for Brenda to alienate him by disagreeing, and she said, "I know."

"What the hell do you think happened in the days, ten days you were gone?" David asked.

"I have no idea," she answered.

"[Belinda] was the best thing that ever happened to me, Brenda, ever," David insisted.

"So why'd you have that affair with that girl?" Brenda asked, pushing him to talk.

"It wasn't an affair . . . why do you think nothing came out about it in the paper? It was nothing. I told you that. I wasn't having an affair and sleeping with her."

"Who was this girl?" Brenda asked.

"It's not anybody you know," David said, again insisting, "You know how happy your sister was."

But Brenda recounted how he'd lied to Belinda and his parents that New Year's Eve, when he told them he was going hunting. "Next thing, all this happens, and you tell me you were with a girl. What am I supposed to believe?"

"It's blown out of proportion," David insisted.

"I don't know what to believe. This just drives me crazy, David," Brenda said.

"So what would you want me to do, Brenda? Call you and support you and let you see Evan . . . ?" he challenged.

"When he grows up and figures out how you treated his dad, what do you think he'll think then?"

"I just want you to go to that detective and talk to them, get your name cleared. Why are there so many questions up in the air?" she prodded.

"There aren't any questions. Why don't you call and ask [the detectives], Brenda? And they're going to give you the total fuck runaround. . . . The D.A. called me and said they had nothing. Those are his words. The D.A. is the one who called me and said there was a private detective."

It was another lie. Ted Wilson had never called David Temple, about either the status of the case or a private investigator. Finally, David insisted that when the case was solved, implying he wouldn't be found to be the murderer, "Y'all are going to feel like shit. I want you to remember that."

At a playoff game late in 1999, Tammey was carrying one of her daughters to the restroom when she saw Heather approaching her. "Look at her," Tammey challenged. "Look at this child. Belinda had a baby girl."

"You need to calm down," Heather said, walking away.

"I know what you are," Tammey shouted.

The following game, when Ken and Maureen walked in, they shot Tammey an angry look. Not long after, Heather walked in wearing a football jersey, jeans and a baseball cap. She sat with the Temples and, after the game, left with David's parents and Evan.

"David's parents know," Tammey told Kay.

That December, a month before the first anniversary of Belinda's murder, Cherica Adams, the girlfriend of Rae Carruth, an All-American wide receiver picked up on a $3.7-million first-round draft choice by the Carolina Panthers, was ambushed in her car. Carruth blocked Adams in while three men pulled up beside her and fired guns. Adams was conscious long enough to call 911 and describe what had happened to the operator.

Adams, like Belinda Temple, was eight months pregnant. The ambulance arrived quickly, and the child survived. Carruth was later convicted of conspiring to commit murder and sentenced to nineteen years in prison.

Around that same time, the Center for Disease Control issued a report: homicide was the third leading cause of injury-related deaths for all women ages fifteen to forty-four. But for pregnant women, murder ranked number one.

Determined to help the case along, Brenda called David again that winter, with little result. Then, on December 12, she called and Maureen answered. The conversation started out friendly, as they discussed what Brenda planned to send Evan for Christmas. Maureen said that they'd been out to Belinda and Erin's gravesite, and that they didn't talk to Evan about his mother being buried there, because he wouldn't understand. "We just call it Momma's marker," she said. "We told him she's in heaven. It's too hard."

"Maureen, I want to ask you something. Did you know about the affair David had?" Brenda asked.

"The what?" the older woman said.

"The affair," Brenda pushed.

"He did not have one, Brenda," his mother answered, sounding upset that Belinda's sister would make such a claim.

"Ahhh. Are you sure about that?" Brenda asked.

"I know there was something that happened, but I'm not going to discuss that, Brenda," David's mother said. "If you want to discuss that, you can discuss it with David."

"I mean, I just didn't think he could ever do that to Belinda," Brenda said. "And that really hurt me."

"Yeah," Maureen said.

"I mean, I don't know what's what, but he did tell me that night before the funeral that he did go out with a woman and kissed her and stuff. I don't know what's up with that."

"I don't think there was anything to it at all or Belinda would have tiddle-taddled to us, because she tiddle-taddled to us whenever he wouldn't do certain things," Maureen said, dismissing her son's infidelity as nothing to be concerned about. "[If it were true] we would have had an indication, but I'm not going to discuss that with you, Brenda."

"I'm not going to say who I talked to, but I heard that he is still seeing somebody down there, and that just tears me up," Brenda said.

"Yeah," Maureen agreed, again.

"A teacher at the same high school he's at. She's going to the football games. I mean. I mean, I don't know if y'all know about it or not. . . . I've heard she's been up in the stands."

"Who are you talking to, Brenda?" Maureen asked, sounding peeved.

"I'm not going to say," Brenda said.

"Then I'm not going to answer you. . . . People need to mind their own business," David's mother said, sounding angry. "Answer me right now, Brenda. Do you think David murdered Belinda?"

Having had enough of the charade, Brenda said, "I really don't know, Maureen. He plays all these games."

Maureen Temple hung up, and the telephone went dead.

26

On the first day of January 2000, Belinda Temple's murder was erased off the homicide division's open-case board. A new year was starting, one that would bring new murders to solve. On January 11, Debbie Berger and Cindy O'Brien met with Tom and Carol at Belinda and Erin's grave to mark a sad event, the first anniversary of the murder. They banded together, beside Belinda and Erin's monument with the phrase: WE FEEL THE TOUCH OF ANGEL WINGS.

That same afternoon, Schmidt sat in his county-issued car outside a suburban Houston home. A car pulled up and two women got out, one carrying a baby. Once the women were inside the house, Schmidt walked up to the front door and rang the bell. Pam Engelkirk, David Temple's college girlfriend, answered the door. The woman she'd arrived home with was her mother. The irony was that just that day, Pam had mentioned to her mother that it was the first anniversary of Belinda Temple's murder.

As the detective listened, Pam recounted her years with David, including the day her football-star boyfriend pushed her into a wall. It was another piece in the puzzle, further evidence that David had been prone to violence even before he'd met Belinda, but it wasn't enough.

"I can't sleep at night because of this case," Schmidt confided. "And I won't until justice is done."

That winter, a friend in Katy saw David get out of his car in a parking lot and walk up to a restaurant. He went inside and grabbed one of the fliers asking for help solving Belinda's murder out of the window. He tore it up, stuffed it in a garbage can and then walked back to his car. He got his son out and brought him inside the restaurant to eat dinner.

In Nacogdoches, Tom was losing patience. He pored over his own timeline of the events of the murder day, everything he could glean from reports on the murder and what he'd heard from detectives. At times he wondered if someone in David's family had stashed the murder weapon. Were Ken and Maureen covering for their son?

That winter, still struggling with all he knew, Quinton called Schmidt and offered to give a new statement. This time, Quinton supported what Tammey had told detectives, that the Temples' marriage had been troubled. Schmidt took notes and asked questions, his ears pricking up when Quinton mentioned something he hadn't told police before: that when he'd helped David move out of the Round Valley house and in with his parents, Quinton had seen an open box of shotgun shells.

It would seem strange how David would so quickly learn what was going on within the investigation. On an evening not long after Quinton gave that statement, he saw David following him in Katy proper. David pulled into a parking lot, and Quinton pulled in behind him. David got out of his truck and stormed up to Quinton's truck door.

"What are you telling police?" David barked.

"The truth," Quinton said.

"Keep your damn mouth shut," David ordered. He glared at Quinton, furious, then turned and walked away.

Afterward, Quinton called Schmidt, asking for not the first time: "What's the holdup? Why don't you arrest David?"

"We're not going to have another O. J.," Schmidt responded. "When we arrest him, we're going to have everything we need. It'll be a done deal."

While he didn't disagree, having David free to follow him, to confront him, gave Quinton Harlan no comfort.

That February, Ted Wilson drew up another search warrant, this one for the unit David had rented at an Uncle Bob's facility. Schmidt wanted to see if the shotgun shells Quinton told him about were still in storage. A copy of the warrant was served to Looney, as David's attorney, and Schmidt and Holtke, who'd been promoted to a detective in homicide, descended on Uncle Bob's, with its row after row of garage doors off a maze of corridors. The manager cut off the lock to the unit, and Schmidt and Holtke sifted through their prime suspect's possessions. The shotgun shells had disappeared.

Hoping for a break in the case, Schmidt drove to Kevin Temple's house to talk to David's younger brother and his wife, in case they might be willing to tell him something that could help. "They wouldn't talk to me," the detective wrote in his report.

After a second grand jury that didn't indict David Temple, Ted Wilson and Donna Goode had little involvement. "There wasn't anything new, no new evidence," says Wilson. "There wasn't anything for us to look at."

The Temple murder book stayed on Mark Schmidt's desk, but for many, the case went cold. "Mark kept beating himself up about the case, saying I should have done this or that. But if the evidence isn't there, you can't make it," says Shipley. "Mark wouldn't let the investigation die."

Early that year, Heather told her mother that she was seeing David Temple. At first, Sandy Munson admits, she worried. "We were very concerned," she says. "We were wondering if Heather could be in danger. We didn't know David."

In Franklin, Sandy would say that she and Heather's twin, Shannon, spent hours discussing the relationship, whether or not David could be the killer. At Easter, Heather brought David to visit for the first time. Over the coming year, the family would get to know him. "We were very cautious, and were up one side and down the other wondering about him, talking about if he could have done it. We really ran him through the mill," says Sandy. After a while, she and Shannon came to the conclusion that David couldn't be guilty. Why? "David just seemed like a big teddy bear. That's the way he always was with us. And we trusted Heather's judgment," says her mother. "If she loved David, he must have been a good man."

When Heather told her mother about how she'd ended up dating David, she'd maintained that they hadn't reignited their relationship until a year after Belinda's murder. "Heather said that they were just friends, and it was quite a while before anything romantic happened," says Sandy. "Heather said David couldn't have murdered Belinda, that he loved Belinda, and if she were still alive, he'd be with her."

In Houston, Heather's roommate, Tara, had a very different impression. She'd seen the Valentine flowers David sent Heather just weeks after his wife's murder, and then saw David showing up at their town house. One day, a few months after the murder, Tara arrived home and found David helping Heather plant flowers outside the town house's front door. But it often seemed all wasn't well. At times, Heather told Tara that the relationship was over. Afterward, David called and left angry messages on their machine: "Sorry I let you get close to my son," he said in one, sounding as if he were livid.

Minutes later, he called back and said: "I'm the best thing that ever happened to you."

Not long after, Heather and David made up. "They always did," says Tara.

When Heather moved out of the town house, Tara had the impression it was because her friend and David wanted more privacy.

* * *

That spring, 2000, the *Katy Times* discovered the search warrant for David Temple's storage unit. Tammey didn't know anything was wrong until someone at the school where she worked brought it to her. In the article, the reporter quoted the warrant, which read that someone David worked with had given a statement to police saying that he'd seen shotgun shells in the Round Valley house. That same coworker's wife, according to the *Times*, told detectives that Belinda and David weren't getting along and that Belinda had confided that they'd gone for long periods of time without speaking. Included in the article was also the first news account of David's affair with Heather.

Frightened, Tammey called Quinton at work to warn him. "It didn't say Quinton and Tammey Harlan, but it might as well have had a picture of us blown up above it," she says. Tammey knew David would have no problem figuring out they had been the source, and that David would be enraged and looking for her husband.

While they were talking, Bobby Stuart, the head coach, walked into Quinton's office and said, "Come with me, *now*."

As ordered, Quinton followed Stuart and they went to talk to the school's principal.

"David was pissed off and looking for Quinton," says Tammey. "They were worried about what he might do to him."

While Quinton waited, the principal called the district's main office, and the personnel director rushed to the Ninth Grade Center. As the morning developed, Quinton soon realized that he wasn't the one the district would back. Instead, with the school year's end only weeks away, the personnel director suggested Quinton take his sick days and find a new position.

"He said it was for my own safety. I couldn't understand why I was the one being forced out," says Quinton. "They all knew that David was guilty. Why was I the only one standing up saying the truth? This guy killed his wife. They all knew he did it."

Meanwhile, detectives showed up at Tammey's school and took her to collect their oldest, Sydnee, from her grade school, then to the day care to pick up the Harlans' two younger daughters. Quinton rushed home and for the second time since Belinda's murder, the Harlans threw clothes into suitcases. The detectives escorted the family to Quinton's parents' house.

"That fall, we took jobs in Fort Worth," says Tammey. "It was like we vanished. We didn't know if David found us, what he'd do."

In truth, Quinton wasn't alone. One of the other coaches, Bill Norwood, left Hastings that spring. Rather than being forced out, he left because he couldn't bear looking at David, suspecting what he'd done. "I couldn't stand seeing David every day," he says. "I couldn't stay. I left and moved away to East Texas, because I figured David had murdered Belinda, and he was going to get away with it."

In May, Dean Holtke sent another batch of specimens from the Temple murder case to the FBI. While in Houston, Brian Lucas met with Schmidt at a coffee shop. They'd gotten to know each other well, and the two men talked about the case, but also about their lives. Although he was sympathetic with Tom Lucas, the detective didn't deny that the constant phone calls from Belinda's father were taking a toll. "Your father is driving me crazy," he told Brian.

"Why can't you get the FBI in on this thing?" Tom Lucas demanded in his booming voice one day on the phone with Mark Schmidt. "Seems to me that they might be able to help. Aren't there more tests that could be done?"

Explaining that it wasn't the federal government's jurisdiction and that he was continuing to investigate, the detective tried to defuse Tom Lucas's anger, but as the case dragged, Belinda's father was becoming increasingly dissatisfied. Despite the pressure it put on him, Schmidt didn't blame

Tom. With two daughters of his own, the detective understood how frustrated Tom must have been.

When Schmidt didn't offer any good news, Lucas wrote to the governor and asked to have the Texas Rangers assigned to the case. The letter from Austin he received in return explained that the Lone Star State's legendary investigators don't intercede in a case unless a law enforcement agency requests help. Then another disappointment, when a producer from *America's Most Wanted* responded to one of Tom's letters and rebuffed an invitation to investigate. The TV show only looked at unsolved cases, the producer explained, not those where police believed they knew the murderer but were unable to prove it.

More than a year after their daughter's murder, Tom and Carol were increasingly distressed by what they saw as a lack of action on the part of the police. Belinda's death seemed to be tearing the family apart. "My parents were obsessed with the murder to the extent that we felt they weren't involved with any of us," says Brian. Although the family hadn't been close, they drifted further apart.

The Lucases had found another source of support from Parents of Murdered Children, an organization founded by victims' families that held monthly meetings in a Houston church. "It was an opportunity to talk to folks who walked in our shoes," says Tom.

Over the years, at times, Mark Schmidt went with the Lucases. "We're working hard," the detective told those gathered. "Someday we'll come through."

At the meetings, Tom and Carol met a tall, lanky man named Andy Kahan, who worked for the Houston mayor's office as an ombudsman, aiding the families of crime victims as they interacted with police. It was the only post of its kind in the nation, and Kahan had carved out his own niche, becoming a go-between for families dealing with law enforcement and one of the nation's leading advocates against murderabilia, possessions of convicted murderers sold as souvenirs, such as John Wayne Gacy's clown paintings.

At one meeting, Tom confessed his desire to take justice into his own hands, to stake out David's house or school with a gun. By then, both of Belinda's parents were relying on antidepressants to help them survive their daughter's death. "Am I the only dad who thought about retaliation?" he inquired. When he asked who else in the room had considered such an action, the room filled with raised hands.

At times, Tom and Carol talked to Kahan, hoping for help. Being from the mayor's office, the victims' advocate could often get answers when parents couldn't. But when Kahan talked to the detectives, he came away able to do little for the Lucases. "It was one of those times when I couldn't help," says Kahan. "Some families can lose themselves in a murder. Brothers and sisters lose not only a sister but their mother and father. It causes incredible strain. The Lucases were in a terrible Twilight Zone. They were lost, trying to find a light at the end of the tunnel."

What Kahan found out from detectives is that the Temples weren't showing any interest in closing the case. They hadn't called or talked with law enforcement about Belinda's death since the first week. "I work with families all the time, and they want the murderers of loved ones found," says Kahan, who became a sounding board for Tom and Carol. "That the Temples weren't pushing law enforcement spoke volumes."

On August 13 of that year, 2000, Brenda called Becky Temple, Kevin's wife, who'd been so close to Belinda. The two women talked about the murder, and Brenda admitted that she still felt torn apart by the loss and the lack of closure on the case.

"I have bad dreams," Becky confided. Until recently she hadn't even been able to look at a photo of Belinda, and she hadn't talked to David in seven months.

"We all know about Heather. It's no surprise, come on," Brenda said, when saying that Maureen had hung up on her after she'd mentioned David's girlfriend.

"Kevin and I made a decision that we wouldn't have anything to do with David and Heather," Becky said. When it came to David's mother, Maureen dealt with unsettling issues "by just ignoring" them.

As the two women talked, Becky asked Brenda questions about Belinda and how she'd been during Brenda's final visit, just days before the murder. "I didn't see David much while he was there. He was running around," Brenda said.

"Jerk," Becky said, and Brenda agreed.

Life was so unsettled after her sister-in-law's death that Becky said she and Kevin were considering moving to London, to get away from the Temples. When Brenda said the presents and notes she sent Evan probably annoyed David's parents, Becky answered, "I don't know that he even gets them."

Twelve days later, Belinda Temple's face stared down on commuters who took I-10, the Katy Freeway, from Katy to Houston each day. A billboard was raised along the highway, paid for by Schepps Dairy. Like the fliers, it featured Belinda's picture and information about the $11,000 reward, $10,000 from the dairy and another $1,000 from Crime Stoppers. At a news conference announcing it, Tom said, "to the person who put the shotgun to the back of my daughter's head and killed her and my granddaughter, all I want to say is, 'We will get you.'"

Although it was there for three months, it would generate no leads.

What the billboard did do, however, was unnerve Becky Temple. In September, when she and Brenda talked, Becky said, "I know it's a good thing, but I really don't want to see it." By then, there'd been a truce in the Temple family. Partly it was because Becky and Kevin had stopped asking questions about David and Heather. "It works better that way," she said.

Tests results came in from the FBI that October. Items including David's tennis shoes came back without traces of window glass. That didn't dissuade Holtke and Schmidt, who took the unusual step of hand delivering more evidence to the FBI lab in Washington, D.C. This time they included metal fragments and wadding from the shotgun shell. The detectives also brought the shoes Belinda wore that final day, her eyeglasses, the cordless phone found in the closet next to her body, and David's warm-up suit and tennis shoes. The FBI had a new test for gunshot residue, and the detectives were hoping for new results.

Meanwhile, in Franklin, Texas, Heather's mother prepared for a wedding. "Heather and David visited and told us they were going to get married," said Sandy. "I told David, 'I just want to know that you're going to love her with all your heart and take care of her.'"

David assured her that he would, but Sandy didn't say what was truly on her mind. "I wondered, *Oh, Lord, is this the right thing?*"

Brenda drove to Katy to see Evan before Christmas that December. When she returned home, she sent him a framed photo of the two of them together, and then wondered if David or his parents had given it to the boy.

Weeks later, on the anniversary of Belinda's murder, Tom and Carol again met Debbie Berger and Cindy O'Brien at Belinda's grave. Two years had passed, and little seemed to be happening in the investigation. David gave the newspaper a short interview for an article on the case: "Everybody who knows me knows I had nothing to do with it," he said. "My extended family prays every day for [Belinda] and that this will get solved."

27

One day, in his living room in Nacogdoches, Tom watched a video of Belinda playing high-school basketball. Suddenly, he shouted at the image on the television, like he used to what seemed like a lifetime ago at her games, "Go Belinda! Good shot!" Then he stared at the television, thinking about his youngest child, wondering if her murderer would ever be prosecuted. To Tom's disappointment, the sheriff's department hadn't used a profiler he'd recommended, instead asking an FBI profiler to review the case and the crime-scene photos. What that expert told Schmidt and Holtke was that the manner in which Belinda's head was covered was significant. That the killer took the time to reposition the slacks hanging on the rod above her, that he covered the damage to her head, suggested the killer was connected to Belinda in some way. In a sense, the murderer was attempting to cover up what he had done, perhaps out of guilt.

By then, Tom Lucas's dissatisfaction with the detectives in Houston was boiling over. He'd e-mailed and called Mark Schmidt frequently, often frustrated, once going so far as to suggest that the case hadn't been solved because of a cover-up at the sheriff's department. With the detective feeling increasingly badgered, Schmidt's sergeant e-mailed Tom:

"Detective Schmidt is one of the hardest working and dedicated detectives I have had the pleasure to work with. . . . I assure you that everything is being done that can be done within state and federal laws. There is no cover-up taking place. . . . The FBI is looking at evidence that we have and that takes time. . . . Furthermore, please communicate with me in the future."

Miffed that he'd been told not to communicate with the detective on the case, Tom complained to a higher-up at the sheriff's department, and the restriction was lifted. A few days later, Tom e-mailed Mark Schmidt again: "I have to have closure. . . . I'm 60 years old, and I do not want to take this to my grave."

That winter a Maryland study was published in JAMA, the Journal of the American Medical Association. The authors concluded that homicide was the leading cause of death in pregnant women. Pregnant women and new mothers were two times more likely to die of homicide than women who had not recently been pregnant. The study's conclusion: "A pregnant or recently pregnant woman is more likely to be a victim of homicide than to die of any other cause."

The study caused little notice, despite its surprising assessment. It was the first far-reaching study of its type, but made little impact in the media and didn't funnel down to the general public.

Meanwhile, at Hastings, rumors floated that Heather Scott was marrying David Temple. "No one seemed surprised," says a coworker. "We all knew they'd been together since right after the murder."

Four months later, Brenda called Becky Temple for the final time. By then, Becky and Kevin had moved to Austin, as much as anything, Becky said, to get away from Katy, Kevin's family and all the bad memories. She brought Brenda up to date, saying Evan loved basketball and that he had a bowling party for his birthday.

"I hear David is getting married," Brenda said.

"Yeah," Becky said.

"That's quite sickening," Brenda said. "I just hate it for Evan. . . . She'll never be the mother Belinda was."

Becky agreed, saying Evan was a good boy, and that he had "a lot of his mother in him."

What Becky said next hurt Brenda deeply. Becky and Belinda had been close, and Brenda never thought that Becky would fall into line with the Temples' unwavering support of David. "Are you going to the wedding?" Brenda asked.

"Probably, you know, for Evan," Becky said.

On May 25, 2001, David purchased a house in Richmond, Texas, adjacent to Katy, a one-story on a cul de sac called Magnolia Circle, in the West Oaks Crossing subdivision. There were palm trees around the swimming pool and a thickly built front door capped with a glass arch. Although newer, the neighborhood looked little different from Creekstone, where he'd lived on Round Valley with Belinda.

Two weeks later, David and Heather married. The reception was in a country club, attended mainly by family and close friends, and Heather wore a stunning white wedding gown. "To have your daughter married to someone you think might have murdered someone, no mother would allow that," says Sandy Munson. "But there's never been anything that we believe points to David committing the murder."

Yet others disagreed. Only two of David's fellow coaches attended. "There weren't many of us who believed David didn't kill Belinda," says one. "Most of the coaches didn't want anything to do with it."

At the wedding, an old high-school friend of David's was shocked at how thin Heather was. He'd always known David to prefer athletic girls. "The wedding was eerie," says Mike Fleener, whose wife was eight months pregnant at the time. "We knew from friends who were Katy cops that police would be watching the wedding, which made everything feel even stranger. The whole time, we were wondering if David murdered Belinda."

Months later, Tara visited her old roommate at Heather and David's new home. The house was beautifully decorated and immaculate. "It looked like Heather, very stylish," says Tara. "She had candles all around, and everything looked like a magazine." Heather seemed happy, and she doted on Evan, who called her Mom.

At the Harris County D.A.'s office, Donna Goode heard about the wedding. She and Ted Wilson talked of the case often, lamenting that they hadn't been able to prosecute David. "Every time I would think about the Temple case or Tom Lucas would call, or we'd hear from Mark Schmidt, I'd think, I wish there were somebody who could work on this full time, really go after it, try to solve it," she says. "But the caseloads in homicide and at the D.A.'s office are heavy, and that wasn't something Ted or I could do."

Whenever he could, Mark Schmidt kept the case alive. That fall, he went to Nacogdoches and interviewed college friends of David and Belinda's, coming away with more stories that painted David as a bully and tales of his explosive violence on the football field, but little else to help.

Back in Houston, Schmidt waited for the test results from the FBI to come in. It seemed at times that only the lab experts had the potential to finally break the logjam the Temple case had become.

Then, that September 11, the World Trade Center and the Pentagon were attacked by hijacked commercial jetliners used as missiles. As the nation wept, the Twin Towers burst into flames, crumbled and fell. The United States was at war with a frightening enemy, and its citizens demanded their government pursue the evil behind the attack. At the FBI lab, resources were reallocated to help in the fight. For domestic crimes, the repercussions were staggering. The specimens awaiting analysis from the Belinda Temple case, along with those from thousands of other crimes across the country, were pushed back in the FBI lab's queue to make room for evidence collected to help fight the war on terror.

Two months later, Tom e-mailed his son-in-law, now married to the woman he'd been having an affair with at the time Belinda was murdered. Although he'd been turned down in the past, Tom asked to see Evan for the holidays. "If Evan could come and spend some time with us during the Christmas break, we sure would like to spend some time with him. He is all we have left of Belinda."

The response from David was a resounding, "No."

"I am hoping you will reconsider," Tom e-mailed back, saying that he'd sent out a card with a gift certificate for his grandson for Christmas. As with Brenda, Tom and Carol would never know if Evan received any of their gifts. There were never any notes or phone calls to say thank you.

On the third anniversary of Belinda and Erin's deaths, Tom wrote a poem lamenting the lack of attention to the case and recounting how Belinda called him and Carol. "Number Five checking in, Mops and Pops!" she'd say. In the poem, Tom called Erin and Belinda "bundles of joy," and talked of Belinda's beauty and enthusiasm. He labeled her murderer "a lowly coward."

While the Lucas family waited, little happened to give them comfort throughout 2002. It would prove a quiet year for the investigation, although Schmidt and Holtke continued to work in the background, conducting an occasional interview or reevaluating evidence. Another study came out on pregnancy and homicide that year, this one conducted in Massachusetts. Again, murder was found to be the leading cause of maternal death, followed by cancer.

As 2002 drew to a close, on Christmas Eve, a woman named Laci Peterson disappeared in Modesto, California. She was seven and a half months pregnant, a pretty brunette whose photo dominated the evening news and sent shock waves around the world. Her husband, Scott, was a good-looking young man who told police he'd been fishing when his wife vanished. Law enforcement mounted an extensive search, but Laci's body and that of her unborn son, Conner, weren't discovered until the following April, when they washed ashore in San Francisco Bay.

The parallels between the Temple and Peterson murders were remarkable, including that at the time of his wife's disappearance, Scott Peterson was having an affair. His girlfriend, a massage therapist named Amber Frey, was a thin blonde who bore a slight resemblance to Heather. Dark humor's not unusual in homicide departments, where detectives deal almost daily with tragedy. Many see it as a way of relieving tension. As the Harris County homicide division watched the Peterson case unfold, they didn't miss the similarities with the one that had haunted many of them for more than four years. "The joke that went around was that Scott Peterson called David Temple and found out how to act. David told him, 'Scott, whatever you do, don't let them find her in the house,'" says one detective.

The Peterson case dominated the news, making headlines of the studies that had been quietly issued over the previous years linking homicide and pregnancy. Suddenly, they were included in front-page articles on the case and in lead segments on television news magazines. For the first time, Americans became aware of the silent epidemic of domestic violence killing young mothers and their infants.

As the Peterson case progressed, in Houston, it renewed interest in the Temple case. The *Chronicle* ran an article listing the similarities in the two cases, and when Holtke saw friends in Katy, they again began asking about the Belinda Temple case, marveling that no one had been charged with the shocking crime. Holtke agreed, but could give them little comfort.

Frustrated and angry, Tom Lucas complained to the sheriff's department, asking for Schmidt to be taken off the case. Brian, who believed that the detective cared about Belinda and was doing all that could be done, argued with his father. "I told my dad to leave Mark alone," says Brian. "Mark knew the case front to back, better than anyone else."

* * *

In spring of 2003, Heather Scott Temple was named Teacher of the Year at the Hastings Ninth Grade Center. She told her mother that she and David were attending church, working hard to raise Evan. In Franklin, Sandy Munson believed she understood why her daughter didn't get pregnant. "Heather wanted to have children, but how could they, with the murder hanging over them?" Munson asked.

Still, even with the uncanny similarities of the Peterson case as a backdrop, at times Munson thought they worried for nothing. As the years passed, the murder had come up less often. "We didn't talk about it. We didn't think about it," she says. "Nothing happened. David wasn't charged. We didn't think there was anything to worry about."

Then, something remarkable happened.

In Washington, D.C., at the FBI lab, on April 23, 2003, a report was typed on official stationery, listing individual pieces of evidence Holtke and Schmidt had submitted from the Belinda Temple murder case, including a warm-up jacket and pants of David's found in the master bedroom and a pair of his tennis shoes recovered from outside the back door. On page two it read: "Results of Examinations: During the discharge of a firearm particles are produced. These particles are from the primer mixture of most cartridges and can be deposited on surfaces in the vicinity of a discharging firearm, including clothing worn by the suspect and shooting victim.

" . . . Gunshot primer residue particles were detected on the shirt from the victim, pants from the victim, the jacket from the victim's husband, the shirt from the victim's husband, the tennis shoe from the victim's husband . . .

"Tin was also detected in a number of gunshot residue particles from the victim's clothing and the victim's husband's clothing. Therefore, the gunshot primer residue on the victim's clothing was found to be consistent with the gunshot primer residue on the husband's clothing."

In Houston, when he received the report, it felt as if the seas had parted for Mark Schmidt. All the years of working the Temple case, of submitting and resubmitting evidence, had finally paid off. The GSR results "were the smoking gun," he said. "We were celebrating."

Yet there were more tests that could be done, the FBI lab suggested. Metallurgy studies had the potential to further analyze the GSR, breaking the elements down to such specificity that the results could not only determine if the GSR on all the items was consistent but perhaps more precisely link the residue on Belinda's clothes to that found on David's clothes and shoes, proving that he was with Belinda when the fatal shot was fired.

Excited about the potential evidentiary value of the test results, Schmidt resubmitted the Temple evidence to the FBI lab yet again and waited. Throughout 2003, Schmidt, Holtke, Shipley and others who'd worked the Temple case hoped that at last they were reaching the end of the road that led to a murder charge and a trial.

In January 2004, the fifth anniversary of his daughter's murder, Tom Lucas told the *Katy Times* that he believed there was enough evidence "pointing toward a particular suspect." Yet Belinda's father didn't name the man on everyone's mind for the murder, his son-in-law, David Temple. Both Tom and Carol were studiously watching the news from California revolving around the Peterson case. When the trial began late that same year, they monitored the testimony, struck repeatedly by the similarities with Belinda's death. Then, on November 13, the Peterson jury came in with a verdict. Guilty.

In Nacogdoches, Tom and Carol fumed. Why was it that California had been able to successfully prosecute Scott Peterson, when David remained free, living his life, married to his former mistress who was now raising their grandson? Why had David been able to avoid paying the consequences for Belinda's murder?

For not the first time, Tom Lucas wrote an e-mail, this one to Harris County District Attorney Chuck Rosenthal. In it, Tom argued that his daughter's murder had been mishandled and ignored, and that if Rosenthal's office didn't prosecute, "I told them I was going to get on the World Wide Web and tell everyone about Belinda's murder and how they'd botched it," says Tom.

Not long after, Rosenthal e-mailed Kelly Siegler, his star prosecutor, a petite woman with dark reddish-brown hair and a fiery resolve. Often described as a pit bull in designer suits, Siegler was considered one of the toughest prosecutors in the nation. She'd handled high-profile murder cases, often using controversial but highly effective tactics. Defense lawyers described her as a great lawyer but also someone who "pushed the limits," and her methods as "over the top." *People* was so impressed, it featured her in the magazine, and a Hollywood producer had once pushed an ABC TV pilot for a series based on her life.

What Siegler said she worked for in the courtroom was "that oh-my-God moment, when the jury finally realizes that's how it really happened."

When Donna Goode and Ted Wilson heard Siegler had been handed the Temple case files to review, they'd later say that they felt relieved. "I was glad for a fresh set of eyes," says Wilson.

Some things had changed over the years. First, Siegler now had the FBI lab results not only finding gunshot residue on David's clothes but GSR that was consistent with that on the clothes Belinda wore the night of her murder. Secondly, "the Peterson case had changed perceptions," says Siegler. "It made the public more aware that these types of murders *do* happen; husbands and fathers do murder their pregnant wives and their unborn babies."

Called by some a "drama queen" in the courtroom, Siegler, who'd taken over from Ted Wilson as the head of the D.A.'s special crimes unit, was known for her ability to mesmerize jurors by demonstrating her theories on a case. For one, she brought in a pickle bucket and sat on it while she told jurors that the defendant sat on one like it after he killed a four-year-old girl. Perhaps her most controversial ploy was used in the Susan Wright trial, when Siegler tied down and straddled her co-prosecutor on a bloody mattress, then demonstrated with a nine-inch blade her theory on how Wright stabbed her husband 193 times.

Siegler's vigor and determination, she'd say, came from her childhood, growing up in the small town of Blessing, Texas, where her father died when she was young. Her mother, who worked in restaurants, married again, this time to a man Siegler described as abusive. When her mother told police, Siegler said an officer responded: "If I were you, I'd learn to keep your mouth shut, so these things wouldn't happen to you."

Perhaps that explained her view of her job as a prosecutor, to relentlessly go after those she believed guilty, and a folder filled with cold cases she kept in her desk, one she called her "Waiting on God" file.

After Rosenthal, her boss, asked her to look at the Temple case, Siegler called Schmidt. When they were face-to-face, she said, "We're going to take a look at the Temple case." After living with disappointment for nearly six years, the homicide detective was almost afraid to hope.

Over the Thanksgiving holiday, Siegler read the Temple files. When she finished, she asked another prosecutor in the office, Craig Goodhart, to do the same. With salt-and-pepper hair and a brusque manner, Goodhart had a photo of Arnold Schwarzenegger holding a machine gun in a scene from *The Terminator* as the wallpaper on his laptop. In a courtroom, Goodhart was focused and intense, much like Siegler, and he was someone she'd come to trust, both to help her decide if a case was winnable and to second chair on a big case in the courtroom. "Craig and I both tell it like it is," says Siegler. "If I get out of hand, he'll tell me to ease up, that I'm being a bitch, and I listen."

After reviewing the evidence, Goodhart told her, "I think it's sixty/forty that we can win this. I'd file it."

Siegler had been thinking the odds were eighty/twenty. "But I know I can get overconfident. I worry that I'll get too big for my britches and think I can win a case no one else can," she says. "But even at sixty/forty, we had a good shot.

"That was all I needed," she says. "I took the case."

Goodhart and Siegler met with Mark Schmidt to deliver the good news. "We're going to proceed with the Temple case, and get a warrant for David Temple's arrest," she said. Siegler explained that it wouldn't be easy, that the evidence was largely circumstantial. They had no eyewitnesses, no DNA, very little forensic evidence, only the GSR test results that could potentially tie David Temple to the murder, yet Schmidt smiled. "Knowing Kelly's talents, I was guardedly optimistic," Schmidt would say later.

Before going any further, Siegler invited Brenda and her parents to the D.A.'s office to discuss the case. Once they sat down with her, she explained, "We're going to proceed and charge David. But don't think that it means that this case is a slam dunk. It's not. We're going to give it a shot, but it's not a sure thing."

All three of the Lucases cried, relieved and anxious, grateful and worried.

Days later, on November 29, 2004, two weeks after the Peterson verdict, Siegler wrote the arrest warrant, including facts from the case, everything from Temple's professions of love to Heather just days before the murder to the staged burglary scene and the jewelry not taken in plain view. For the first time, the warrant disclosed the FBI gunshot residue evidence that tied David's clothes to those Belinda wore on the night of her murder. Yet Siegler left some evidence out, including the account of Buck Bindeman, that he'd seen David near his parents' house at five the evening of the murder. That evidence went directly against David's alibi, and Siegler had no intention of tipping her hand too soon to David's defense attorney.

By the time she took on the Temple case, Siegler had successfully prosecuted nineteen death-penalty cases. Those stakes wouldn't be on the table in the Temple case. Belinda's murder had taken place in 1999 and it was only in September of 2003 that the Texas State legislature passed a law mandating that the killing of an unborn, viable infant was murder. Since in Texas a capital offense required a murder with special circumstances, of a police officer or during the commission of a second felony, David wouldn't be eligible for the death penalty.

The next morning, David dropped Evan off at school. Holtke and Schmidt tailed in an unmarked car, when two squads moved into place, boxing David's truck in at a traffic light. Then the deputies turned on their lights. Schmidt and Holtke got out of their car and walked over to David, ordering him out of the truck. As the handcuffs clamped around his massive wrists, David complained that they hurt. "They weren't built for a man that big," Holtke would say later.

In Schmidt's unmarked car on the way to the jail for booking, David didn't ask any questions. Finding it odd that David didn't ask what was happening, Holtke read him his Miranda warning, and then decided to ask a question of his own: "Do you know what this is about?"

In the backseat, David said, "No."

"Belinda," Dean said.

David shook his head, as if stunned.

"You've got to be shitting me," he said dismissively. "That was like six years ago."

28

While Schmidt and Holtke drove David to the jail for processing, Tracy Shipley waited for Heather at the Ninth Grade Center. Once she arrived, the detective told David's wife that he had been arrested on a murder charge. Shipley then asked Heather to talk to her downtown.

At her office on Lockwood, Shipley questioned Heather about what had happened in the years since she'd married David Temple. While offering little insight regarding David, Heather seemed to want to talk about Evan, proudly telling Shipley how the by then nine-year-old called her "Mommy."

"I didn't ask him to. He did that on his own," she said.

"Did you and David ever talk about Belinda?" Shipley asked. "About who murdered her?"

"No, never," Heather insisted.

She seemed guarded in her responses, and Shipley didn't believe the woman, who looked thinner and remarkably older than the last time she'd seen her. "You never asked David who he thought murdered his wife?" Shipley said, incredulous. "You're living with the man, and the conversation never comes up? You expect us to believe that?"

"We just never talked about it," Heather insisted.

At the jail, David invoked his right to an attorney and refused to answer questions. Later that same day, Paul Looney walked David through the system, and by late afternoon, he was out on a $30,000 bond.

In the *Houston Chronicle*, Tom was quoted as saying about the arrest: "It's been hell. You start to feel like maybe Belinda didn't matter to anyone. Like maybe nobody but us cared."

The following week, the *National Enquirer* ran photos of David, Heather and Belinda under a headline that shouted: THE NEW LACI PETERSON. Heather was the "new Amber Frey," and David, according to sources, "an outrageous liar whose deceitful tricks seem ripped directly from Scott Peterson's game plan."

When David and his family gathered in Looney's office, the attorney would later say that he laid out the case as he saw it, giving his thoughts on how he would present the case in a courtroom. "I told the Temples that we were going to go with the truth. We had to proceed with the case as it was. We needed to understand that the folks on a jury weren't going to like David. He had a reputation as a bully. The shotgun incident with Darren was bound to come up. David was unfaithful to Belinda. At the time of the murder, he was having an affair. He'd later married the woman he had the affair with. None of it made him a model citizen," says Looney. "We'd lay that out to the jury, but then explain that the jurors weren't going to like what they heard from the prosecutors either. Because they were prosecuting a man with no evidence that he committed a murder."

Later, Looney would wonder if that speech lost him a client.

The next thing Kelly Siegler heard was that Looney wouldn't be the attorney she'd face in the courtroom. David Temple and his family had hired the man considered the top gun in Texas defense attorneys, Dick DeGuerin, a man in his sixties who'd been a commanding presence in Lone

Star courtrooms for decades, representing defendants in some of the most sensational cases in the state, from Senator Kay Bailey Hutchison and Congressman Tom DeLay to Branch Davidian leader David Koresh. In November 2003, DeGuerin and a Texas dream team of lawyers—including Mike Ramsey, Chip Lewis and Brian Benken—represented New York multimillionaire Robert Durst, on charges that he murdered a neighbor while living as a cross-dresser in Galveston. The jury's verdict in the Durst case, where the victim had been dismembered, stuffed in garbage bags and thrown into the bay, was a surprising not guilty.

Known for his trademark Stetson and cowboy boots, DeGuerin got his start working for Percy Foreman, the legendary Texas lawyer who defended Jack Ruby when he was charged with the murder of President John F. Kennedy's assassin, Lee Harvey Oswald. In Texas, DeGuerin ranks at the top of every top lawyer list. In courtrooms, he's famous for withering cross-examinations, exhaustive in length. "The thing with Dick DeGuerin is that he'll pound and pound away at a witness until he gets what he wants," says one prosecutor. "He'll ask the same question over and over, changing it a little, until he gets the answer he needs. Then he'll point to that bit of testimony in his closing and say, 'See, that proves my client isn't guilty.'"

"It made me sick," Siegler said about the moment she first heard that DeGuerin had taken on the Temple case. What she also heard throughout the courthouse and floating around the district attorney's office was that many in Houston's legal community believed this was a case DeGuerin would win.

Knowing the stakes and the little physical evidence she had, Siegler understood why. There was no DNA evidence, no eyewitness, no fingerprint evidence, no ballistic evidence, and the sheriff's department hadn't been able to find the murder weapon. The only scientific evidence she did have, the gunshot residue tests from the FBI, DeGuerin filed a motion to keep out of the courtroom not long after taking on the case, charging evidence hadn't been carefully preserved and could have been contaminated, along with reports that the FBI science was questionable at best. In the background, rumors flew that there was more at stake than a hefty fee for the defense attorney. DeGuerin, some said, was after revenge. The Temple case was his opportunity to hand Siegler a loss in a high-profile case, after she'd repeatedly beat him in the courtroom.

The first match between Siegler and DeGuerin had been in 2000, in Houston's infamous "Wig Shop Murder," the case of Dror Goldberg, an Israeli American charged with the stabbing death of store clerk Manuela Silverio. Before the case came to court, Goldberg fled, and was later found in Germany. At the trial, a school police officer testified that in high school, Goldberg had a notebook where he'd drawn a woman covered in blood and described how to commit a murder with a knife.

As Siegler saw it, that case was a learning experience. "I had never gone up against a warrior as good, as prepared, as aggressive as Dick was," she remembered. "Dick's an excellent lawyer. I totally respected him."

Watching DeGuerin, Siegler thought she saw a pattern: DeGuerin, she judged, asked witnesses not involved in certain areas of the investigation questions about evidence they hadn't handled. "Dick asks the wrong witness his questions perfectly," she said. "People try to be helpful and answer, they make mistakes and then he uses that."

What Siegler did was alert her witnesses not to answer any questions that fell outside their personal spheres of knowledge. In the end, Goldberg was convicted and sentenced to 48 years, and Siegler had won.

Four years later, Siegler and DeGuerin battled head-to-head in a courtroom a second time, in the case of James Tucker, an ex-pastor charged with the sexual assault of a church employee. During that trial, while the victim described what happened from the stand, Siegler reenacted the alleged assault with a male colleague. After the demonstration, Tucker pleaded no contest to an unlawful restraint charge, and Siegler won again.

DeGuerin made similar charges against Siegler. In the beginning, he insisted he was "a big supporter of Kelly." But over the course of those two trials, in which he suffered two well-publicized losses, his opinion changed. Instead, he charged that she "inserted testimony in her questions, facts not in evidence," and used tactics usually reserved for defense attorneys, who have more latitude in courtrooms than prosecutors. "For a defense attorney, it's all about giving our client every possible defense," said DeGuerin. "For a prosecutor, it's supposed to be about justice."

Despite the prevailing opinion that the Temple case was one he could win, DeGuerin would say that he felt less confident: "I figured it would be tough because of the long time lapse, that witnesses' memories had faded. That David had married the girlfriend, jurors weren't going to like. And, of course, because I'd be going up against Kelly Siegler."

The *Houston Chronicle* dubbed the Siegler-DeGuerin match-up in the David Temple case "The Clash of the Legal Titans." As the news hit the homicide division, many of those who'd worked on the case worried. "I heard that Dick DeGuerin was on the case. People talk about him like they quake when he enters a courtroom," said Tracy Shipley. "He's high-dollar, and I wondered, *why this case?* Then I heard that it was a grudge match, that DeGuerin had a thing about Kelly. I got mad. This isn't about a grudge between two lawyers. It's about a dead woman and her dead baby."

One might assume that all was falling into line at the end of 2004, that finally David Temple would enter a courtroom and the questions surrounding Belinda's murder might finally be answered. That assumption, however, would prove to be wrong. Over the coming years, Andy Kahan, the victims' advocate who'd befriended the Lucases, would see the David Temple case as "the proverbial Murphy's Law in force. Everything seemed to conspire to delay, delay, delay."

The first court battle between the two bitter opponents took place on February 1 of the following year, 2005, when they met in the 178th District Court, the purview of Judge Bill Harmon, a grandfatherly man who had been sitting on the bench since 1984. That day a motions hearing was scheduled, but DeGuerin quickly rose and chastised Siegler for not yet taking the case to a grand jury and getting an indictment. "This family is living with a cloud over it," said DeGuerin, waving his arm at where David, who looked like a husky banker in a dark gray business suit, sat surrounded by his parents and brothers. "We want to remove it as quickly as possible."

Siegler bristled, telling the judge that she would soon take the case to a grand jury to get the indictment, but DeGuerin pushed, asking for an evidentiary hearing, one where all the evidence would be laid out, so he'd be able to see firsthand what prosecutors had against David Temple.

Some would see that approach as a mistake.

In the Harris County District Attorney's office, there was a long-standing open file policy, where a defense attorney was able to inspect everything that prosecutors had against their clients before trial. "It worked well for us," said another prosecutor. "A lot of times, once they see what's out there against them, the defendants will plead out."

There was a wrinkle, however. The open file policy wasn't mandatory, but rather at the discretion of the prosecutor. When a defense attorney asked for an evidentiary hearing, the D.A.'s office strategy was to automatically close the file. From that point forward, the defense was given only what the law required. On that afternoon, in Harmon's courtroom, Siegler eyed the defense attorney and asked, "Are you sure you want that, Dick? You know that will close the file."

DeGuerin's firm had a long history of asking for the hearings if they entered a case pre-indictment, and DeGuerin frowned at Siegler and insisted that was precisely what he wanted. Judge Harmon set the evidentiary hearing for March 2, but in the end, it would prove a fruitless exercise.

Weeks later, Siegler went to a grand jury and got the indictment. Once she had it, under Texas law, DeGuerin was no longer entitled to the hearing. Dick DeGuerin, one of Texas's best defense attorneys, had lost the opportunity to see the evidence against his client and achieved nothing in return.

"I was trying to get it off dead center," DeGuerin would say later. "I was pushing the case along. Kelly used that as an excuse to close the file. I knew I wouldn't get the exam trial. You never get them in murder cases."

"Dick was a prosecutor before a defense attorney. He should have known," Siegler would counter. "Asking for the exam trial was a dumb move. How do you prepare for a circumstantial evidence case without seeing the evidence?"

As he awaited trial, David Temple was suspended with pay from Hastings. Later, as the time dragged on, he'd be sent to work at an alternative school in the Alief district, teaching physical education. "It's a place where they have the toughest kids," said one of his colleagues. "A really hard place to teach."

Meanwhile at his desk on Lockwood, Dean Holtke organized the Temple evidence, cataloguing each item with a master number, to avoid confusion between different lab and evidence numbers that had accumulated over the years. When the trial began, he didn't want any potential for misunderstanding. Whenever they talked about the Temple case, he and Mark Schmidt pondered what would happen in the courtroom, how tough DeGuerin could be. "We were stressing out about it," said Holtke. "We believed David Temple was guilty, and we had one shot at him, and that was it."

Siegler was doing her own methodical trial preparation. First she assessed the overriding issues. One was whether or not she could put Heather Temple on the stand. In most states, including Texas, a marital privilege prevents prosecutors from forcing spouses to testify against each other. It's considered a way to keep the institution of marriage sacred. But Siegler determined that didn't apply in the Temple case, because the privilege wasn't retroactive; David and Heather weren't married at the time of Belinda's murder.

That August, the attorneys were back in the courtroom. Kelly Siegler, true to her warning, had closed the file, and Dick DeGuerin wanted the judge to release evidence, including any videos, scientific reports and alibis. The judge took it under advisement, and then scheduled another hearing for the following day to announce his decision, but this time, when DeGuerin arrived, Siegler handed Judge Harmon a motion asking for his recusal from the case. Siegler wanted the judge to step down, and DeGuerin was furious.

The rift had begun a month earlier, over a prison informant. After seeing an article in the *Houston Chronicle*, the man, with a long record, wrote to David at the address in the article, the one on Round Valley. The new owners turned the letter over to the district attorney's office, and it was given to Siegler. In the letter, the inmate said that in 1999, he'd shared a cell with a man who bragged about "getting away with murder" and said his motive had been revenge against David, who had "done him wrong in the past."

In the days that followed, Siegler brought the inmate to Houston to interview him on a bench warrant, but using a different case number so as not to alert the media. "It's something that's done relatively often," says another prosecutor. "Not everyone does it, but it's not unusual."

DeGuerin charged that Siegler had taken the step to hide the inmate's existence from the defense, and to frighten the inmate, who was afraid of his fate if the word got out, because "snitches get killed in prison."

Eventually, the truthfulness of the inmate came into question by Siegler, while DeGuerin asserted that the witness had been terrorized. Whatever the reason, the inmate later refused to testify. In the meantime, however, DeGuerin had asked one of his former law students to represent the man. That lawyer filed a complaint with the Texas State Bar against Siegler, charging that she had falsified a court document by substituting an unrelated case number. The lawyer wanted Siegler's law license revoked. "It was a chicken-shit thing to do," said Siegler, who was notified on a Friday night while she was home with her family.

If there remained any congeniality between Siegler and DeGuerin, the filing replaced it with more bad blood. It was as if this were truly the proverbial final straw. Judge Harmon was caught in the middle when he wrote a letter to the state bar backing Siegler, saying that what she'd done wasn't unusual in Harris County and showed no ill will. The complaint against Siegler was denied, and the threat to take away her license evaporated. But the repercussions weren't over.

While Siegler liked Harmon and considered him a good judge, she had some fear that DeGuerin could overpower him. "Dick's such a good lawyer, some of the judges are intimidated by him," she said. "I thought maybe that could happen. Judge Harmon is laid-back, and I thought he'd give Dick a lot of latitude."

"Kelly saw it as an opportunity to get rid of Bill Harmon," says DeGuerin. "She filed to have him removed because she wanted a judge who'd be more favorable to the prosecution."

Siegler would say it was a matter of fairness, since Harmon had backed her in the complaint, and that DeGuerin had brought it on himself. DeGuerin fought Siegler's motion, and the battle was on again. Eventually, Siegler prevailed, but in a roundabout way. As the case languished on the court calendar, Judge Harmon left the 178th, replaced on the case by a visiting judge, Douglas Shaver, a retired, balding man with a stern frown and a monk's fringe of pure white hair, whose judicial attitude was markedly stricter.

Dick DeGuerin was furious, and Kelly Siegler delighted.

That February, the Temples attempted to show up Tom Lucas where he'd become something of an expert, on television pleading his case. Nancy Grace was airing her first show on CNN, and Andy Kahan had introduced her years earlier to Tom and Carol. The TV personality had listened as they detailed Belinda's murder and been touched by their sadness and frustration. Having never forgotten Tom and Carol, Grace invited the Lucases as her first guests to tell their story.

That afternoon, in a preemptive strike, the Temple family, sans David, Heather, and Evan, stood at Belinda and Erin's grave and read a statement vehemently defending David. "This district attorney's office has decided to choreograph an ill-fated prosecution against David," Darren said. "It is not coincidence that David's arrest was a few days after the Laci Peterson verdict."

That night on the show, Nancy Grace pointed out that the Temples' graveside statement was the first they'd issued in the six years since Belinda's death, and that they'd chosen to do it on the day the Lucases were flying to New York to be on her television show. After showing a clip of Darren declaring his brother "completely innocent," Grace introduced Tom.

"Do you think David Temple murdered your daughter?" Grace asked.

"After looking at all the facts . . . I believe David Temple killed Belinda," Tom said.

When David's father got on the camera via a Houston hookup, he defended the press conference, saying that he couldn't think "of a better place to do it. . . . That little piece of real estate is very precious to us. We are the ones who care for it."

On the interview that night, Ken Temple appeared frustrated, pushing Grace, with her famously acerbic approach, to let him depict the case the way he saw it, as if he and his family were the primary victims. "We've remained quiet a long time," David's father said. "We've suffered and we've grieved silently."

On the roller coaster that propelled the Temple case toward trial, the prosecution hit a high point that April, when Mark

Schmidt, who had continued to investigate, finally received a report from the ATF that showed David's father had, indeed, as David had told so many, purchased shotguns. On the government paperwork faxed to his office, Schmidt saw that on December 11, 1985, Ken Temple purchased a .12-gauge. By then, Darren was off in college, and the only two Temple sons living at home were Kevin and David. Was that shotgun a Christmas gift for David?

Then, from the view of the prosecution, the roller coaster plummeted over the top of a cliff.

On September 1, 2005, while Holtke and Schmidt awaited the metallurgy results, the FBI sent David Rossi, the lead crime-scene investigator on the case, a letter. In it, an FBI lab spokesman said that the agency was abandoning all metallurgy studies. "We no longer do these tests," it said, without explanation.

Days later, a story broke in the *Washington Post* discrediting the testing. For decades the FBI had been contending that they could break down what they described as the chemical signature of bullets and shotgun shells from gunshot residue and tie the GSR back to a specific source, even a specific box of shells or bullets. The technique had even been used in the investigation of John F. Kennedy's assassination, when the FBI maintained they'd been able to match all the recovered fragments from the fatal bullets to a single source, suggesting Lee Harvey Oswald was the lone gunman.

The problem was that, in an independent review, the National Academy of Sciences found the testing "deeply flawed" and concluded that it gave misleading results. Within days, a letter was faxed to police departments across the country, advising them that the FBI would no longer do metallurgy testing. "It was junk science," DeGuerin would say. "And it brought into question a lot of the gunshot residue testing the FBI lab was doing."

The FBI lab's result was the only forensic evidence in the Temple case, and not long after, Craig Goodhart stood before Judge Shaver explaining that prosecutors needed an extension. The FBI expert who had done the work on the Temple evidence had been decertified. He was no longer licensed to do GSR testing. The FBI had assigned a new expert, Diana Wright, but she wouldn't use the prior results. The bottom line was that the Temple evidence was again in the queue to be retested. Shaver granted the request, giving the prosecutors more time.

Months later, when the results finally came in, they weren't as beneficial for the prosecution. Unlike the first examiner, who found GSR on David's clothes and shoes, Wright only found it on one item, the warm-up jacket recovered from the bed in the master bedroom. Wright also wouldn't go so far as to say that she could positively link the GSR on the jacket to that found on the clothes Belinda wore.

"We were disappointed," says Siegler. She and Goodhart talked over the effect on the case and what they still had to show the jury. They'd just lost most of their only forensic evidence. "But we decided we could live with it, and we decided to go ahead with the case."

Still, that didn't settle the matter of the gunshot residue. Although prosecutors only had one remaining item of David's clothing to point to, DeGuerin filed a motion that argued that, too, should be barred from evidence. The FBI lab was so contaminated, he insisted, no tests conducted there could be considered reliable. A storm was brewing over the gunshot evidence, one that would continue to build.

As the months passed, the battlefronts multiplied in the Temple case. While the fight over the GSR evidence raged, Siegler filed another motion, this one to allow extraneous offenses into the trial. Among the prior transgressions of David's charged in the motion were the car robberies committed in high school, the assault of the basketball player in Nacogdoches, that he'd committed criminal mischief against his high-school girlfriend when he'd reportedly killed her pet rabbits, and something that must have added to the Temples' seething anger: that in 1984, David had held a shotgun up to Darren's head.

Anticipating her testimony, Cindi Thompson had talked to her father about whether or not to take the stand. Their families were close, and she felt certain the Temples would chastise hers if she did. She hated to see her family suffer. "If you were involved in something, I wouldn't expect Maureen and Ken to cover for you," Cindi's father advised her. "You've done nothing wrong."

Yet Cindi remained troubled about the testimony. Her angst only worsened when, days later, Darren Temple called. They'd talked at times over the years, like the old friends that they were. "What is this about?" he asked, mentioning that he'd seen her name on a list of witnesses for the prosecution.

Cindi told him it was about the night David held a shotgun on him while Maureen pleaded with David not to shoot. As Cindi described it, the conversation that followed was strained. "I'm not saying I didn't tell you that," Darren responded. "I'm saying it didn't happen."

It seemed clear to Cindi that Darren was telling her not to testify, and they argued, Darren growing increasingly upset. "If asked, I have to tell the truth," Cindi said. She remembered that night well, including the fear on Darren's face. She had no doubt that it was real.

"Yes, you have to tell the truth," Darren agreed. "But I'm not saying I didn't tell you that. I'm saying that it didn't happen."

Upset, Thompson called Siegler, telling her what had happened and explaining that she worried that testifying would hurt her family. "I'm not the wicked witch," Kelly told her. "If you really can't, if your family will suffer because of this for years to come, I understand."

Cindi thought about it for a moment and then said, "No. I have to. I have to do it for Belinda."

It seemed that circumstances continued to plot against the trial. Diana Wright, the FBI analyst who had conducted the second set of GSR testing, was pregnant and wouldn't be available for testimony for months, so Murphy's Law ruled yet again and the trial date was again postponed, this time to October 16, 2007, a full three years after David Temple's indictment.

Meanwhile, Kelly Siegler packed a long red file box with index cards, hundreds of white rectangles, each bearing a question to ask David Temple if and when he took the stand. It was a complicated case covering a long time span and filling eight boxes of evidence, but Siegler believed it formed a web, one that could ensnare David Temple.

As the weeks before the trial dwindled, Siegler interviewed witnesses and pored over reports. There were disappointments. She'd heard that Michael Slater, one of David's fellow coaches, was the last to see him at Hastings on the morning of the murder, and others told her that Slater said David was fuming at Belinda, furious that she'd made him leave work early to care for Evan. Yet Slater, a friend of Heather's and David's, said it wasn't true. "Mr. Slater wouldn't go there," she says. "If it was true, he'd never admit it."

One of the biggest problems for the prosecution was that Siegler still couldn't put a .12-gauge shotgun in David Temple's hands. Although she had documentation showing Ken Temple bought one such weapon in 1985 and plenty of witnesses to testify that David had shotgun shells and talked often of bird hunting, no one could testify they saw a shotgun at the Round Valley house. Would jurors hold that against the prosecution? Would they be willing to convict without a murder weapon?

Making the situation even more complicated, by then, the prosecutors had been dealt another blow. Sergeant Sam Gonsoulin, the first to respond to the scene, had died of cancer. "I had eight pages of questions for him," says Siegler. "He was the best one to talk about the dog, Shaka, and he was the one who'd had the most interaction with David, one of those who saw that he didn't seem the least bit upset about Belinda's murder."

As the trial neared, Siegler worried, but she realized the evidence was what it was. She couldn't change it. All she could do was walk into the courtroom prepared.

One of her main concerns was making sure her witnesses, especially those who'd investigated the case, were ready. They had to understand what she did about DeGuerin, how good he was at cross-examination. "I worried about Chuck Leithner losing his temper, and that Mark Schmidt, who likes to talk, would answer questions he shouldn't," she says. "People are people whether they're witnesses or not. Their personalities can affect how they do on the stand."

To preview the evidence and prepare her witnesses, two weeks before the trial began, a dry run was held, a mock trial in which the evidence was laid out and the witnesses were prepared. Not all the witnesses would be grilled, only the detectives who'd investigated the case. In a locked courtroom, Siegler put one after the other on the witness stand. She questioned them, taking them through their testimony as they recounted their part of the puzzle that made up the case against David Temple.

Needing someone to play Dick DeGuerin, to cross-examine the witnesses, Siegler enlisted the aid of one of homicide's brightest minds, Lieutenant John Denholm, a thirty-year veteran of law enforcement who was in the final months of law school. A husky man with a hoarse voice and an authoritative manner, Denholm prepared by reading the Temple murder book, forming questions for each of the detectives, and introducing tactics he believed DeGuerin would use in the courtroom.

Over the course of a day, Siegler and Denholm grilled the detectives, from Holtke and Schmidt to Leithner. In the courtroom were nearly twenty of Siegler's fellow prosecutors, who made suggestions. In her opening statement, one thought Siegler approached the case too chronologically, and that she needed to put the important facts up front. "It was all an exercise to prepare because of Dick DeGuerin," says Siegler. "He'd be prepared, and we had to be."

For his part, as he reviewed the evidence and questioned the detectives, Denholm saw areas he knew DeGuerin would mine for reasonable doubt, all the defense needed to prove to get a not-guilty verdict.

Along with his concerns over the lack of any physical evidence, Denholm felt certain DeGuerin would, as he often did in a trial, provide the jury with an alternate suspect. In the Temple case, Denholm didn't see that as difficult, not with Joe Sanders living right next door. The teenager had lied to detectives about where he was that night, failed multiple polygraphs, and admitted he'd been out shooting shotguns with friends who'd burglarized a house just weeks before Belinda's murder. Sanders had a potential motive, that Belinda had exposed his truancy to his parents. If De-Guerin needed more, he had it. Two .12-gauge shotguns had been found in the Sanders home along with reloaded double-ought buckshot shells. While not matches, they were of a type similar to those used in Belinda's murder. "This was more than wiggle room," says Denholm. "This was a giant problem for the case."

To Siegler's relief, the detectives performed well on the witness stand. Yet Denholm felt that he'd uncovered holes in the case, and he wondered if Siegler had enough evidence to win over the jury.

With opening arguments approaching, Siegler saw the biggest hurdle as the case itself. "I figured even after the Peterson case it was going to be hard for a jury to believe that a husband could do that to his own wife and unborn child," she says. "Our worst serial killers don't kill babies. And David Temple was an All-American boy from a good family, a football hero. Would they believe he was capable of such an awful crime?"

29

Courtrooms are uncomfortable places, especially during high-stakes trials. On the opening day of David Temple's trial, October 16, 2007, Tom and Carol, Brent, Brian and Brenda sat in the front row on the right side of the courtroom, behind the prosecutors. On the other side of the same bench, behind the defense table, congregated David's parents and brothers, along with aunts and uncles. After nearly nine years of building animosity, the two families were nestled up against each other, yet neither acknowledged the other's presence. At times the atmosphere in the courtroom felt so electric, so charged, it seemed to threaten to snuff out the very air, making it difficult to breathe.

"We were worried," says Brian Lucas, who sat shoulder-to-shoulder with Darren Temple in the center of the bench. "When we found out Dick DeGuerin was David's attorney, we were scared to death."

The trial would be a long one, some estimated up to six weeks, and boxes of files and exhibits ringed the attorneys. Wearing a dark gray suit, David conferred at the defense table with DeGuerin and one of his associates, Neal Davis, a pale, nattily dressed man with carefully combed brown hair.

In a funereal dark blue suit with black trim, Kelly Siegler

rose to address the jury, fourteen men and women, including alternates, picked the day before. Behind Siegler, her second chair, Craig Goodhart, watched from the prosecutors' table.

After reading the indictment, that the state of Texas charged David Temple "knowingly and intentionally" murdered Belinda Temple, Siegler laid out her case for the jury, emphasizing, "The truth is always in the details."

Constructing a portrait of the murder from the fine points would be the core of Siegler's case. Boiling the murder down for the jurors, she outlined what she said testimony would show, beginning by painting a picture of what police found in the closet on Round Valley, Belinda Temple's body "on her tummy, face down, dead of a shotgun wound to the back of the head."

But that wasn't the worst of it, she explained, in her sometimes folksy manner. "The other life that ended that day was a perfectly healthy, six-pound little baby girl, its heart beating inside its mother's womb."

Siegler left no doubt whom she blamed for the cold-blooded execution. Pointing at David Temple, Siegler charged: "The only person in the whole wide world who had a motive is her husband, David Temple."

Appearing fifty pounds heavier than his glory days playing football, David's face was puffy, making his eyes narrow slits. Temple, Siegler said, was a man no one ever said no to. "David Temple has always, his whole life, gotten his own way."

Then Siegler fleshed out Belinda for the jurors. She was the perfect wife, pretty and fun, a wonderful mother. A spunky woman, Belinda acted differently around her husband, who was controlling and overbearing. His motive for the murder? David had fallen in love with another woman, a teacher named Heather Scott. He didn't want Belinda anymore. Two years after Belinda's brutal murder, Heather became David's wife. Why didn't David just get a divorce? He couldn't, Siegler contended, because no one would have understood why he'd divorce Belinda. Even David's parents loved her.

Preparing the jury for the trial ahead, Siegler read David's statement. She then systematically tore it apart, showing inconsistencies with the evidence. She explained staging to the jury, laying out the groundwork that she contended clearly showed that no burglary had taken place on Round Valley that night. David Temple, a man who had a reputation for meticulously planning even backyard barbecues, she said, staged the burglary scene at the house to cover up his wife's murder.

"David Temple was lying, cheating and deceiving," Siegler said. Pointing at him, Siegler told the jurors that by the end of the trial they "would believe that this man, David Temple, is guilty of the murder of his wife, Belinda. . . . The details always tell the truth. . . . Belinda was executed by her husband."

Glad to have completed her opening, Siegler took her seat and DeGuerin replaced her, center stage, in the courtroom. His face flushed, his hands steady, he began, "David Temple did not kill his wife, Belinda Temple, and the evidence will show you he didn't."

He then dropped a bombshell that would leave many in the courtroom wondering why the legendary Texas lawyer was taking such a stand. He had a client who, at the time of his wife's murder, was involved in an affair with another woman. There would be evidence from many who would say that David and Belinda's marriage was troubled. Yet DeGuerin stood before the jurors and an overflowing audience and announced, "David and Belinda Temple were deeply in love with each other. David and Belinda Temple were happy in their marriage. . . . David was eagerly awaiting the birth of a little girl both David and Belinda named Erin."

In his classes at the University of Texas Austin's law school, DeGuerin instructed students to "embrace the ugly baby," the evidence that a lawyer knew waited in the wings that would show his client in a bad light. The ugly baby in the Temple case was the affair and the resulting marriage, a union many would interpret as evidence that David had, indeed, fallen in love with Heather. At the very beginning of the trial, DeGuerin seemed to ignore his own advice, asking jurors to close their eyes to evidence he knew would come, that David had fallen out of love with Belinda and in love with Heather.

It appeared that what DeGuerin believed he had going for the defense in the case was the apple-cheeked, whole-some image of the Temple family. "They called David and Belinda the golden couple," DeGuerin continued. "They called Belinda the sunshine girl, because she always had a smile." He pointed out David's family in the gallery, and said they would testify that David and Belinda were happily married and that David wasn't as the prosecutor pictured him, a controlling husband.

As he displayed photos on the courtroom screen of David and Belinda during happy times, many wondered if DeGuerin would succeed in convincing the jurors that his client had no motive for murder, that despite his affair, David loved Belinda and grieved after her death. When Paul Looney heard about the tack DeGuerin was taking, he feared it would backfire. "You don't tell the jury that you're going to prove something that's going to blow up in your face," he says. Yet Dick DeGuerin had a stellar reputation. Could he be making such a blatant mistake, or was it all part of an overall strategy?

As Denholm predicted during the mock trial and Siegler had no doubt that the defense attorney would, DeGuerin then offered jurors an alternate suspect, Joe Sanders, the teenager who lived next door. "We don't know who murdered Belinda Temple," said DeGuerin. "But we know David Temple didn't."

Opening statements ended when DeGuerin played the 911 tape for the jurors, and they saw David Temple openly weep. The mammoth warrior of a man flushed and tears flowed unabated. He appeared the way his lawyer described him, a grieving husband and father.

"How close is the television show *CSI* to the real world in crime-scene investigation?" Kelly Siegler asked Dean Holtke when the crime-scene investigator turned homicide detective took the stand. Siegler had begun by putting another officer before the jury, the woman who, with Gonsoulin, had first responded to the scene, to talk about Shaka's fierce defense of his yard, so threatening she'd pulled her gun preparing to shoot the chow, before David Temple arrived to intervene.

"Objection," DeGuerin cried out. While Siegler wanted to prepare the jury, let them know that all the fancy forensic flourishes they saw on television didn't exist or weren't available in most labs, DeGuerin didn't want the jury's expectations lowered. He wanted them to demand the prosecutor produce science to prove her claim that David was guilty.

The first time Holtke saw David Temple, he was seated on a bench near the back door. "At that time, in your mind, was he a suspect?" Siegler asked.

"No," said Holtke, who gave jurors their first glimpse of the crime scene, using photos of what detectives saw when they arrived. Much of it was touching, from the family photos on the refrigerator to Evan's backpack draped over a kitchen chair. In the master bedroom closet, they saw Belinda's body, and Holtke explained how the killer pushed the hangers to cover up the mass of blood spatter and brain matter on the wall.

At each turn, from the television still plugged in but off its stand to the dining room drawers partly open but undisturbed, Holtke explained why the scene appeared staged. Perhaps the biggest anomaly for a burglary scene was that out in the open, near the body, photos showed Belinda's jewelry box undisturbed and David's jewelry, including his heavy gold ring, not taken. David Temple had reported to his insurance company that Belinda's jewelry had been stolen, but what did Holtke see inside the box on the dresser?

"Women's jewelry," he said.

Holtke showed photos of the garage with barely enough room to walk between the cars and another of Evan's yellow bike hanging from the ceiling. "Did it appear to you that the bike had been recently ridden?" Siegler asked, after pointing out that David said the toddler had been doing just that in the garage.

"No," Holtke said, and DeGuerin again objected.

The dynamics between the two attorneys were combative. At times, DeGuerin appeared ready to jump out of his seat at Siegler, as if he could barely contain his fury. Most of the time, Siegler maintained an unaffected yet intensely serious manner. When Holtke became too technical, she instructed, "Tell me that in girl talk."

Perhaps the most damaging testimony was the broken window glass that had fallen not straight out from the doorway but off to the side in the den. In his opening statement, DeGuerin argued that the glass scattered into the den because the glass broke when the door hit a wooden hutch with shelves positioned behind it. "Did you see anything consistent with that door being forced up against the hutch?" Siegler asked.

"No," Holtke said. "The glass was consistent with the door being open . . . when the glass was broken."

With so much blood around Belinda, Siegler asked if someone checking her pulse would have gotten it on his or her hands or clothes. Holtke said they would. The jury already knew that David told the 911 operator he'd checked Belinda's pulse, yet no noticeable blood was seen on his clothes or body.

Throughout, Siegler illustrated Holtke's testimony with photos from the scene, each designated with a number. The photo of the inside of David's truck without a car seat for Evan became State's Exhibit 191, and the photo of the hanging bicycle was number 189. Then, as the jury waited, the bailiffs brought the Temples' back door into the courtroom, still soiled with fingerprint dust. Over the years, even more of the glass had fallen out, clearing an entire pane. As Siegler pointed out a dent DeGuerin mentioned in his opening—one he said proved that the door hit the hutch—Holtke disagreed. He and the other detectives on the scene had examined the door and never saw the indentation. Perhaps that dent, like the missing glass, he suggested, could have happened in the sheriff's department property room, where it had been kept for nearly nine years.

As would be expected, DeGuerin wasted no time in attempting to dismantle Siegler's arguments. First, he questioned Holtke's expertise, implying he was far from an expert on staging. The detective had said David didn't appear upset the night of Belinda's murder, but DeGuerin asked, "Don't people react differently to trauma?"

"Yes," Holtke agreed. Yet, although the defense attorney pounded away, on many matters Holtke stood his ground. When DeGuerin speculated that the detectives assumed they weren't walking into a burglary scene because they saw nothing missing, Holtke disagreed. "My conclusion was based on what you would normally see at a burglary and it just didn't look right."

Preparing for the battle that was to come, DeGuerin grilled the detective over the way the crime scene was processed, and Holtke admitted that he hadn't covered his clothes, and had worn his gun. Studies in the past decade, since the murder, had shown that an unclean gun could leave GSR without being fired, transferring it by brushing up against a piece of evidence.

"If Belinda heard burglars and rushed into the closet to hide and call 911, the burglars could have heard her and gone after her," DeGuerin said.

"I can't say if they would have heard," Holtke responded.

Leithner and Schmidt followed Holtke to the stand, backing up much of what their fellow detective testified to, including the glass shards in the den and the position of the body in the closet. Both mentioned David's lack of emotion on the scene. With Leithner, Siegler talked about the statements taken at Clay Road, especially David Temple's. "He never looked me in the eye," Leithner said. There was David's apparent confusion, when he changed his mind about which park he'd been at that night. The following day, Belinda and Erin's bodies were in a suite at the medical examiner's office being autopsied, while David conferred with his lawyer and decided to withdraw his consent to have police search his house.

Throughout, DeGuerin painted the detectives as abusive toward the Temple family. But on the stand, Leithner, despite his reputation for sometimes being confrontational, remained calm.

"Did there come a time when you interviewed Joe Sanders?" Kelly asked, bringing in to evidence the name she knew DeGuerin would banter about in coming weeks.

"Yes," Leithner said he did, but on further questions the detectives said he investigated Sanders but came to the conclusion that the teenager wasn't Belinda's killer.

"Did there come a time when you were satisfied or completely finished in your mind that you had what you needed from Joe Sanders?" Siegler asked.

"Yes," Leithner said, as a spirited conference erupted between the attorneys and the judge. DeGuerin wanted it in the record that Sanders had failed multiple polygraphs.

"That's going to be denied," said Judge Shaver, reminding the defense attorney that polygraph results were inadmissible as evidence.

"One was a reload?" DeGuerin asked Leithner during cross-examination, referring to the shells taken from Joe Sanders's home, double-ought like the shell that killed Belinda.

"Yes," Leithner said.

Leithner targeted David Temple in a rush to judgment and ignored all evidence to the contrary, DeGuerin insisted, but the detective disagreed. "I don't think we concluded he was the only suspect early on," he said, pointing out that they had investigated others, including Joe Sanders. "I don't believe . . . that we had tunnel vision."

"Did you call David names during that interview?" De-Guerin charged.

"I don't believe so," Leithner said, shifting uncomfortably in the witness stand.

DeGuerin then put up photos of the pet-food dishes in the garage, and implied that David would testify Shaka was confined there at the time of the murder. How was that possible, when Angela Vielma would testify that she walked past as David returned home? Vielma didn't see the dog, and Shaka didn't rush out barking at her. Yet, even if the dog wasn't free to attack a burglar, Leithner insisted there were other signs that the crime scene was staged. "That's just one element," he said.

When Mark Schmidt took the stand, he folded his hands on his lap and waited. The day had been a long time coming, and Schmidt had been so anxious about his testimony that he had much of the three binders that made up the Temple murder book memorized. "I've been living with it for almost nine years," he'd say later. "I wasn't going to walk into that courtroom unprepared."

"Are you nervous?" Siegler asked, after Schmidt introduced himself.

"Yes, ma'am," he said with a slight shrug.

Schmidt, too, said he'd looked at the back door with the broken glass that night, inspected it, and didn't see the dent. Siegler asked about the many shotguns the sheriff's department sent in for testing throughout the years, the two from Joe Sanders, the one stolen by his friend, one from a neighbor who called, worried that her dead husband might have committed the murder. All had tested clean for glass, blood and brain matter. They'd searched rice fields and ponds, and had never found the murder weapon.

Then Siegler had Schmidt lay out David's statement about where he'd been that night, locking in entries on a large timeline she'd constructed for jurors, including when David said Belinda arrived home, when he was seen on the videos at Brookshire Brothers and Home Depot. On the screen,

Siegler showed photos from the stores' surveillance videos. The picture that emerged was that if David planned to kill Belinda, he had hours to prepare from the time she returned to school until 3:45, when he said she arrived home. The exhibit showed the two main blocks of time unaccounted for: the first, half an hour after Belinda arrived home and before David showed up at Brookshire Brothers. David said he'd gone to a park, but no one had come forward to corroborate his account. The second unexplained half hour: when the trip from the grocery store to the Home Depot took three times what it should have.

Schmidt testified that Joe Sanders cooperated, as did all of the teenager's friends, voluntarily turning over shotguns for testing and giving statements. Meanwhile, none of the Temple family tried to push the investigation. "Did any member of the Temple family talk to you about offering a reward?" Siegler asked.

"No, ma'am," said Schmidt.

"The grand jury did not indict David Temple in 1999?" DeGuerin asked, when he began questioning Schmidt, implying the jurors decided there wasn't enough evidence.

Siegler jumped up to object, which the judge sustained, but DeGuerin simply asked the same question again, following it by, "There was no [indictment] in the case until 2005?"

"Correct," said Schmidt.

On the stand, Schmidt appeared anxious but resolute. He played with his tie at times, and when he frowned, deep furrows etched his brow. DeGuerin was as determined, and attempted to give the detective little wiggle room. "The house was a mess when you released it, right?" DeGuerin asked, describing fingerprint dust covering walls and doors. It seemed an odd thing to point out, since it suggested that forensics had done a thorough job, yet hadn't uncovered any unexplained fingerprints.

"Yes, sir," Schmidt agreed.

The defense attorney asked if the television stand on the

chest of drawers, the one next to the dish with David's jewelry, could have obstructed the view of the jewelry, perhaps explaining why it wasn't stolen. "Possibly, yes, sir," Schmidt said.

The detective agreed that there was no question that just after 4:30 on the afternoon of the murder, David Temple was shown with Evan at the Brookshire Brothers grocery store. That was about the time the Roberts boys would testify that they heard what they believed to be a gunshot. If David wasn't even in the neighborhood, how could he have murdered his wife?

Of all those who would take the witness stand, Quinton and Tammey Harlan had the most intimate views of David's and Belinda's lives. Quinton took the stand first, talking about everything from how gingerly he handled Shaka to the way David cheated on Belinda. Then, he recounted how David called Belinda names. At times the jurors eyed David, as if wondering about all they were hearing. While Quinton couldn't put a .12-gauge shotgun in David's hands, the two men had talked about bird hunting, David describing the many times he'd gone as a young man, and Quinton had seen a box of shotgun shells in the Round Valley house.

Yes, Quinton admitted, he, too, had flirted with Heather Scott that fall, kissed her and bought her gifts, and when Tammey discovered it, it had nearly destroyed his marriage. But he talked more about David's conduct, how he derided Quinton for not controlling Tammey. Quinton said David had once asked him if he'd leave Tammey for Heather.

"I said no, but asked him if he'd leave Belinda," Quinton said. "David said, 'I don't know.'"

Dick DeGuerin objected, charging Siegler was mounting a character assassination, attempting to prove David was guilty by smearing him in front of the jurors. The judge disagreed, and the testimony went on.

"Did David Temple ever do anything on the spur of the moment?" Siegler asked.

"Not to my knowledge," Harlan answered. The implication was that if David intended to murder Belinda, he'd have a plan, including where to dispose of the murder weapon.

There were so many incidents that contradicted DeGuerin's portrait of David as a loving husband. Before Belinda and Erin were even buried, David asked Quinton, "How's Heather?" And when Quinton asked why David wasn't cooperating with the investigation, he said, "What difference is it going to make?" and "It isn't going to bring Belinda back."

"Did you ever see David drive Evan without a car seat?" Siegler asked.

"No, ma'am," said Harlan.

When he took over, DeGuerin attempted to paint Quinton with the same brush being used to tarnish David Temple. Wasn't it true that while Tammey was at home with their children, Quinton was at school e-mailing Heather and afterward going out with the other teachers drinking? Quinton disagreed, saying he'd only been to one happy hour that year. Yet he admitted, "I did a lot of things I'm not proud of."

When it came to his relationship with Heather, Harlan described it not as flirtation but lust, and said that it came at a time when he was unhappy with his marriage.

"You blame your relationship with Heather on David, don't you?" DeGuerin charged.

"No, I take full responsibility for my stupidity," he said.

David was joking when he insulted Belinda, DeGuerin insisted.

"No, sir," Quinton disagreed.

When it came to Tammey, Quinton said, "My wife is strong willed. You'll see."

"I'm sure we will," DeGuerin said.

While her husband testified, Tammey Harlan sat in the prosecutors' witness room outside the courtroom. At one point, she looked up and saw Darren and Kevin across from her, in the defense conference room. Darren stood up, opened the door and stared at her, and she saw incredible anger in his eyes. He then sat down at the table and continued to watch her with contempt.

Once she took the stand, Tammey looked as Quinton described her, strong willed, yet there was another element: heartbroken. She blamed herself, she confessed, because she'd moved away from Belinda during that final fall and winter. But she said she felt she had to, "if I was going to save my own marriage."

Like Quinton, she described David as verbally abusive and controlling, and added that he disparaged Belinda's family, calling the Lucases "white trash, crazy and fat." At one point after some emotional testimony about their son-in-law's snipes, Tom and Carol got up and left the courtroom, furious.

Yet Tammey went on, describing Belinda as a bright woman, a competitive, forceful individual, except when she was around David. Then Belinda appeared meek, submissive. "I would tell her to stand up to him and tell him how she felt and not allow him to treat her that way," Tammey said. "Belinda was incredible. She was a much better wife than I am. . . . She put up with a lot, and she just always smiled and kept going."

"What did Belinda do with her keys when she entered the house?" Siegler asked. Tammey said her friend kept them on a tray by the kitchen telephone, and that she kicked her shoes off when she walked in the door. On the day of the murder, the keys were found on the staircase, and Belinda's shoes were still on her body. Lastly, Tammey insisted that Belinda would never have allowed David to take Evan out when he was sick or to put him in the truck without a car seat.

"Are you testifying today that all the blame belongs to David Temple?" Siegler asked.

"No, no," Tammey answered. "Quinton is a grown man. He makes his own decisions. He's the one who chose to do what he did."

"You hate David Temple, don't you?" DeGuerin asked.

"I do not like David," Tammey replied.

The defense attorney attacked much of what she'd testified to, but Tammey Harlan refused to back down. Then De-Guerin painted a scenario where Belinda felt threatened and Evan was in the house. He asked Tammy if her friend would have left her son unprotected to hide in a closet. Tammey said Belinda would have protected Evan, but what went unsaid was that Belinda knew David loved the boy and that, if he was the attacker, Belinda would have known that he wouldn't have hurt their son.

"You called Heather 'Barbie bitch,' didn't you!" DeGuerin insisted.

"That's right," Tammey said, looking not at all apologetic.

Thursday of the second week, a stir ran through the courthouse. Word was out that Heather would take the stand. When she walked in, David Temple's wife looked dangerously thin, not at all the attractive blonde she'd been when he first met her. Before the trial, Tara Hall had warned Siegler that Heather didn't like to have her actions questioned and that she would become quarrelsome. "But I still didn't see it coming," says Siegler.

That day from her perch in the witness stand, Heather fought to be in control. She argued, over and over again trying to insert testimony, attacking the detectives and the prosecutors, claiming they'd been unkind to her and kept her for hours on end, an assertion that rang hollow when Siegler pointed out that Heather had arrived at Clay Road with Hall that day to give her statement in their own car. She could have left at any time, and was, in fact, only there for two hours. Although called by the prosecutors, it quickly became clear that Heather was testifying for the defense.

That fall of 1998, Heather said she was unsure of herself and seeking flattery when she flirted with two married men. Yet she minimized the importance of her relationship with David, describing sex with him by saying, "It wasn't memorable."

A titter went through the courtroom that caused the judge to threaten to clear the crowd if they didn't maintain silence. The relationship, she said, was little more than a flirtation, and David was in love with Belinda. Yet Heather wore a wedding ring, one David had given her, and that alone made her statements seem less than honest.

At times Heather became so contentious, refusing to answer questions, that the judge removed the jury to chastise her. "You don't need to be getting in an argument with either of these lawyers. You're not going to win," Judge Shaver warned. "Listen to their questions and answer them, and don't volunteer anything else."

"Did you kiss Quinton Harlan while you were flirting with David Temple?" Siegler asked.

"Yes I did," Heather responded.

After Belinda died, Heather said she saw David as a friend, yet again the marriage appeared to prove otherwise. When Siegler asked Heather if the grand jury in April 1999 was soon after something terrible had happened, Heather looked confused. "Are you talking about the detectives questioning me?" she asked.

"We're kind of here about Belinda's death," Siegler said, not trying to hide the sarcasm. "I'm talking about that."

The moment hit hard to many in the crowd who had seen the photos of the crime scene, with Belinda's head shattered, the right side of her face a hole, her pregnant belly exposed to the world. There were pictures Siegler decided she couldn't show anyone, those she didn't want to see, of Erin's tiny body nestled inside her mother, cold and dead, a perfectly formed baby who would never be born.

Then there were those declarations David made three days before Belinda's murder, when he said he was falling in love with Heather.

"I do not agree to those words in my statement," she charged. Yet Heather had signed or initialed every page.

"Are you saying that Tracy Shipley made those words up?" Siegler asked.

"They were forced upon me," Heather replied. Yet she'd given that same testimony in front of the grand jury, leaving the impression that she was being evasive.

"There were no discussions of a divorce [from Belinda], were there?" Siegler asked.

"No," Heather agreed.

What other option was there that would allow Heather and David to be together? Siegler asked. The implication hung in the courtroom: David didn't talk of divorce because he was already planning to murder Belinda.

When it came to Heather's first statement to police, Siegler said, "You left out the sex, didn't you?"

"I didn't intentionally leave it out," Heather protested.

"Come on, Mrs. Temple," Siegler said, rolling her eyes.

There was a lot of repair work needed when DeGuerin took over Heather's testimony. He asked about David's demeanor the day Belinda's headstone arrived. "He was very upset," the current Mrs. David Temple said, appearing more relaxed.

"Have you ever heard David say a negative word about his marriage with Belinda?"

"Never," she answered. The detectives, she said again, forced her to include David's professions of love in her statement—she hadn't wanted to. Yet what she didn't say was that it wasn't true.

At times, even after the judge ruled she shouldn't, Heather charged ahead with an answer, leading him to clear the courtroom again to chastise her. There seemed little doubt that David's new wife was intent on getting her view in front of the jury. Yet she said the detectives were the ones with "an agenda."

Despite everything, including the shrine of Belinda's photos David's parents kept in their home, she said her marriage to David was strong and their relationship with Evan good. "Would you be his wife, would you be the stepmother of Evan, would you be in the Temple family, if you had questions about [David killing Belinda]?"

"No, sir," Heather said.

Perhaps Heather should have realized that her testimony would be challenged by much of what Tara Hall would say on the stand. Where Heather suggested she was practically held captive when they made their first statements, Hall said they drove their own car and were free to leave. "Were the detectives nice to you?" Siegler asked.

"Yes," Hall answered.

And when it came to the year after the murder, when Heather insisted she and David were merely friends, Hall testified that a month after the murder, David sent Heather Valentine's Day flowers and that spring he planted flowers at their town house.

Throughout Hall's testimony, David, who'd been stoic throughout much of the trial, scribbled on a yellow legal pad, passing it to his attorneys. When DeGuerin took over the questioning, he pressed Hall, insisting that the flowers and the work in the town house courtyard had been a full year after Belinda's murder. But Hall shook her head, saying she was sure she had the date right.

When it came to the relationship with a married man, De-Guerin asked, "Did you give Heather any advice?"

"I didn't think she would welcome my opinion," Hall said.

Yet not all would go so well for the prosecutors.

In contrast to all the sensational testimony and the crowds filling the courtroom, one Monday hearing that followed would be poorly attended, yet it was to decide an important matter: whether or not FBI tests showing gunshot residue on David's warm-up jacket were admissible. Craig Good-hart argued for the prosecution, while one of DeGuerin's partners, Matt Hennessy, challenged the evidence for the defense. Kelly Siegler never thought her side wouldn't prevail. Yet the defense had a lot of ammunition, a wealth of well-documented problems at the FBI, including studies that said the lab was contaminated with GSR. Hennessy was persuasive, and, to the prosecutors' disappointment, Judge Shaver ruled with the defense. With that, prosecutors lost their only piece of forensic evidence.

Late that afternoon, Siegler and Goodhart met in her office to talk about what the ruling had done to the case. "We decided it would have been a wash in the end anyway," says Siegler. "If it had been included, Dick DeGuerin would have just told the jury about all the problems at the lab and called it unreliable. We felt good about the way the trial was going, so we forged ahead."

One reason Siegler wasn't overly upset was that something else had happened over the weekend, something that might finally allow her to put a .12-gauge shotgun in David Temple's hands. Throughout many trials, tips filter in to both sides behind the scenes. For the prosecutors, one was from an old friend of the Temple family who suggested that Siegler contact Clint Stockdick, a high-school friend of Kevin's. When she did, Stockdick seemed reluctant but finally cooperated. That Monday the disappointment of the GSR evidence was lessened when Siegler added Stockdick and his wife, Jenifer, to the witness list.

"What will he say?" DeGuerin asked.

"Ask Kevin," Siegler answered. "He grew up with Clint. He'll know."

That evening, Siegler would later report that Stockdick's phone rang but he didn't pick up. "Kevin left a message," says Siegler. "He told Clint, 'We're all clear on this. David never owned a twelve-gauge, only a twenty-gauge shotgun.'"

On the stand, Clint Stockdick described the Temples as his childhood second family. It appeared evident that he hadn't wanted to testify against David, yet he knowledgeably discussed the Temple-family shotguns. He'd hunted often with the Temple brothers, and said they traded shotguns between them. First, he said that in the past the Temples used to reload shells, like the buckshot used in the murder. Then Stockdick testified that he'd not only never seen David with a .20 gauge, he'd never seen one at the Temple household.

Instead, all three Temple brothers, including David, used .12-gauge shotguns. The family owned four of them, including a sawed-off shotgun, a Mossberg.

"When David Temple went hunting, what did he use? Siegler asked.

"He used a twelve-gauge," said Stockdick.

"Not a twenty-gauge?"

"No, ma'am," Stockdick answered. "I'm positive."

Throughout the testimony, DeGuerin looked uncomfortable, frowning, writing on a legal pad. "Were you aware that they had a twenty-gauge?" DeGuerin asked.

"No, sir," Stockdick said shaking his head. The defense attorney came at the question from different angles, but never shook Stockdick's testimony.

After her husband left the stand, Jenifer testified briefly, backing up what Quinton Harlan had said earlier, that she, too, had seen an opened box of shotgun shells at David Temple's house after Belinda's murder.

In the days that followed, much would be put before the jury, from Debbie Berger's memories on how unhappy Belinda and David's marriage had become to the ever-expanding timeline that filled in the events of January 11, 1999, the day of the murder. When Berger took the stand, she felt nervous, but once there, she settled down. "I had a calm come over me," she'd say later. "It was the last thing I could do for Belinda."

There were those small moments when it appeared the momentum of the case might swing to the defense, as when Mike Ruggiero took the stand and talked of an unidentified car speeding through the neighborhood late that afternoon. But that possibility seemed to implode when other neighbors testified they'd walked by the Temple house or driven by that afternoon and seen nothing. One impression Ruggiero and the other neighbors agreed on was that Shaka was a highly protective animal. "I got stopped dead in my tracks by their dog," he said, explaining that he feared the animal.

At times, Ruggiero appeared to be trying to help his old

neighbor, as when he talked about Creekstone—which others described as quiet—as if it were riddled with crime. Yet, after David pounded on the Ruggieros' door, he didn't wait for Mike, who came out and followed behind him offering help. And instead of taking the dog inside with him, where it might confront a burglar, David left Shaka in the backyard.

On cross-examination, Ruggiero insisted that David appeared frantic that day. He said Evan didn't look ill, as others had described him. And when it came to the door, the one that earlier he'd said he didn't see hit anything, Ruggiero testified that it could have hit the hutch, as DeGuerin had suggested as an explanation for the glass pattern.

That afternoon, while David ran toward the house and Ruggiero followed, Siegler asked if "the word 'Belinda' ever came out of David's mouth."

"No," Ruggiero answered.

"Have you ever asked yourself why not, Mr. Ruggiero?" Siegler asked, implying that David didn't shout out his wife's name because he already knew Belinda was dead.

As the prosecution wound down, witnesses filled holes in the case Siegler and Goodhart had presented. Buck Bindeman proved one of the most important, as he testified that during one of David's unaccounted-for periods that afternoon, at 5 P.M., when David said he was traveling from the grocery store to Home Depot, Bindeman saw him at an intersection in his truck, not far from David's parents' house on Katy Hockley Road, surrounded by the rice fields where he'd so often hunted.

On the stand, Bindeman described David's truck down to the shade of blue.

As the prosecution's last witness, Brenda Lucas had come to speak for her twin sister, to tell of the last time they were together, when Belinda appeared gravely unhappy in her marriage to David Temple.

"Was Shaka ever in the garage?"

"No," Brenda said, saying the pet-food bowls in the photos

that DeGuerin pointed to on the garage floor weren't for Shaka but for Belinda's gray cat, Willie.

Like the Harlans, Brenda described the way David ridiculed Belinda. "The whole day of her birthday, did you see David give Belinda anything?" Siegler asked.

"No," Brenda testified.

By the end of Brenda's testimony, the lies David told that New Year's Eve were before the jurors, along with evidence of David's callous attitude toward his wife. Finally, Siegler played one of the tape-recorded conversations Brenda had with David, the one from September 14, 1999. As Siegler displayed a crime-scene photo of David's jewelry, including his wedding ring and watch, David was heard saying he had his jewelry on at the time of the burglary.

In front of the jurors, Brenda had proven that David Temple was a liar.

"You agreed with David on the tape that they were happy," DeGuerin said.

"They were not happy," Brenda countered.

"It was an effort to get him to say something you could use against him," DeGuerin said.

With that Brenda agreed.

After a short break, DeGuerin took the floor and did what attorneys often do after prosecutors finish presenting their case: He asked for a summary judgment, a not-guilty verdict. As the attorneys argued, Judge Shaver listened. "They haven't proven their case," DeGuerin contended. "It's at least as likely that it was a botched burglary."

"What are the odds that three days after David Temple tells Heather Scott he is falling in love with her a burglar breaks in and murders Belinda?" Siegler scoffed. "This is a case of little bits and pieces. You put the pieces together, and you have a picture."

Judge Doug Shaver looked down, shook his head and said, "Motion denied." The trial would continue.

30

Despite all Siegler's bits and pieces, many in the courtroom wondered if the prosecution had proven David Temple's guilt beyond a reasonable doubt. A group of reporters congregated outside the doorway to the 178th District Court and whispered. "Pretty flimsy," said one who'd covered many cases over many years. "I don't think there's enough. No weapon. No forensics. Not a drop of DNA."

Another nodded. "You may be right," she said. "I don't think I'd be able to convict based on what we know so far."

As they talked, others offered opinions. One was that DeGuerin would quickly rest, without putting on a defense. With only the prosecution's case, jurors, it seemed, would have to acquit. This outcome was what Donna Goode and Ted Wilson had worried about nine years earlier: that the case was too thin. Although it appeared David Temple was the murderer, there wasn't enough evidence to prove it. In fact, since the GSR evidence had been ruled inadmissible, Goode and Wilson had nearly all the evidence Siegler put before the jury within a year of Belinda's death. The exception, and it was an important one, was Clint Stockdick. For the first time, his testimony put a .12-gauge shotgun in David Temple's hands. But was that enough?

Perhaps the only one who didn't consider the possibility

was Kelly Siegler. After battling him in the past, she thought she had DeGuerin figured out. "I knew that he'd prepared his case and that he wouldn't not put it on," she says. "He'd told the jurors during the opening that he would put David and his family on the stand. Dick wasn't the kind of lawyer who'd disappoint them."

So even though she realized the limitations of her case, Siegler was banking that DeGuerin would proceed with his, and that it would work to her advantage.

The following morning, November 6, as Siegler predicted, Dick DeGuerin walked into the courtroom and called his first witness, a custodian of records for the apartment Heather moved into after she moved out of the Perthshire town house. The reason was that on the stand, Tara Hall had maintained that Heather moved into an apartment of her own just months after Belinda's murder, while Heather said she lived with Hall for another full year and moved out in summer 2001.

The custodian produced records that showed Heather was, perhaps, right. The first month she lived in the new apartment was in the summer of 2001. That was also when Heather filed an official change of address with the School District. Still, Hall, who was recalled to the stand, didn't back down about how quickly David renewed his courtship of Heather, even when DeGuerin pushed her. She insisted David sent Heather flowers within weeks of Belinda's murder, and that it was the first spring when he was at their town house planting flowers. "I know because it struck me as so inappropriate at the time," says Hall. "His wife and baby had just died, and he was courting Heather."

As the questioning proceeded, the tension in the courtroom built. At times, DeGuerin slammed his yellow legal pad down with a sharp slap onto the defense desk; his face flushed a bright red. Siegler and Goodhart visibly bristled with energy, appearing to want to lash back, Siegler's eyes burning with anger. To the surprise of many—since she'd been such a difficult witness—DeGuerin put Heather back on the stand. It backfired during cross-examination, when Siegler brought up a three-inch binder of Heather's school e-mails. During her first round of testimony, Heather said that just days after the murder, Quinton sent her a suggestive e-mail. "Find it," Siegler said, dropping the binder on the witness stand, the sound echoing through the courtroom.

"It's not there," DeGuerin said, jumping up. "She knows the e-mails aren't all there."

For not the first time, Judge Shaver shot looks that chastised both attorneys, as if warning them to cool down.

There would be fourteen witnesses that day. Among them were all three of the Roberts boys, now young men, who as young children in 1999 heard a "bang" that sounded like a shotgun blast. It was their testimony DeGuerin counted on to set the time of the murder at approximately 4:30, when David was at Brookshire Brothers. If the Roberts brothers' accounts seemed credible, the jury could have reasonable doubt.

The brothers took the stand and told their stories. Meanwhile, in the witness room waited one of the Temples' former neighbors from Round Valley, a man who'd told police that on the day of the murder he, too, had heard a bang at 4:30 that afternoon. But he had been standing outside at the time, and he said he saw the source: a backfiring pickup truck. The prosecution's problem was that nine years later, the man's recollections were hazy. So Siegler listened to the Roberts boys, watched the jury's reaction, and decided not to call her rebuttal witness. In her judgment, the jurors would see the boys as too young at the time to be sure about what they heard.

Peggy Ruggiero's husband had testified early in the trial, called by the prosecution. A friendly woman with dark hair, she appeared nervous when she took the stand. She described the Temples' marriage as happy and recounted the day of the murder, backing up much of what her husband had said, yet her testimony ultimately hurt the defense. Repeatedly, DeGuerin had suggested that Evan wasn't sick that day. It was an important point in the way he'd structured his case, because if Evan was truly ill, it made little sense for David, a doting father, to have taken the toddler to the park and shopping.

"Do you remember testifying to the grand jury that Evan didn't eat much of his Happy Meal that night?" Siegler asked on cross-examination.

"Correct," Ruggiero said, backing up the day care workers who testified that the usually ravenous toddler was so unwell that day that he had no appetite.

Over the weeks of the defense, it would seem that Dick DeGuerin's case never quite gelled. An expert witness testified on the glass pattern from the broken door window, again suggesting that the door hit the hutch behind it, causing the glass to scatter into the den instead of straight ahead. But the diagram he showed the jury didn't match crime-scene photos.

Recalling Mark Schmidt also proved a disappointment. With an earlier witness, DeGuerin had portrayed the Temples' neighborhood as a dangerous place, one where other murders had occurred in the past. While the defense attorney used Schmidt to again point a finger at Joe Sanders, detailing the .12-gauges and shotgun shells found in his home, Siegler presented the detective with records of all the police reports for the Temples' subdivision for 1998 and the first months of 1999. Schmidt described them as nearly all nuisance calls.

"How many murders?" she asked.

"One," Schmidt said. The victim was Belinda Temple.

In hindsight, however, the most detrimental testimony would come from those who most wanted to help David Temple.

On the stand, David's father appeared like an erect, proud man, a part-time preacher and a family man. He went through a brief history of the family, with its generations in Katy, and then talked about his sons. Yes, he'd bought his boys shotguns, he said. But although he'd bought his other sons .12-gauges, he said he'd bought David a .20-gauge. Why? Because it was cheaper.

"Did you ever buy any other shotgun for David?" De-Guerin asked.

"No," Ken Temple said. What happened to David's shotgun? After saying the barrel had split, he said, "David destroyed it."

Ken talked of his family's love for Belinda, and, as all David's family would when talking of her, sounded sincere. And he insisted he saw none of what others had testified to, that his son ridiculed her or had been controlling. He described Belinda as strong and spirited, a woman who would never have put up with such behavior. That last day, he said Belinda stopped to pick up Maureen's soup, and they talked briefly. Belinda was in a hurry to get home. Yet he insisted Evan wasn't ill. When Ken and Maureen learned that Belinda was dead, "it was like a fog . . . it was like being in a daze that you were hearing words but nothing was ringing true or sounding real."

The police didn't interview but interrogated the family, he said: "They told us, 'You need to prepare yourself that your son is guilty of murder.'"

"Mr. Temple, can you not say that Evan was sick?" Siegler asked, when she took over. If the toddler didn't want to eat or play, what did that mean about the way the youngster felt?

"Not well," Ken said, in a clipped, irritated response.

The prosecutor then asked about the harmonious marriage Ken described between Belinda and David, asking, "Would you agree with me that the affair would disrupt a little bit of that harmony you told us about?"

"At the time, yes," Ken agreed, but then, with an undercurrent of anger, he said, "I have never discussed the affair or its details with David."

When it came to the shotguns, Siegler said, "So you've got three boys. Oldest gets a twelve-gauge. Youngest gets a twelve-gauge. Middle son gets a twenty-gauge?"

"Yes," Ken said. The questions kept coming, the Temple

patriarch forced to repeat his testimony until he turned to the judge and demanded, "Have I not said 'yes' enough?"

The judge looked at the gray-haired man on the stand and frowned. First Heather Temple had been so difficult the judge warned her to cooperate; now David's father displayed little patience with the proceedings, as if he were above it all and the courtroom simply a distraction. "You will listen to her questions and answer her questions," Judge Shaver ordered, leaving no room for argument. "Do you understand that?"

"Yes," Ken said. Yet he continued to argue with Siegler, even over details like the date of his grand jury testimony. During his testimony with the defense attorney, Ken described what would come to be known as the Temple family meeting, when others waited outside while David confessed his infidelity. During it, he asked David if the family needed to know anything. In response, David admitted he'd been with another woman, and that he'd spent New Year's with her.

"How many times did David deny to you all that he needed to tell you anything before he told you about the affair?" Siegler asked.

"Maybe once," he said.

"Did he tell you it had been going on for three months?" Siegler asked.

"He did not," Ken responded.

When asked if any of the women in the family were at the meeting, Temple responded in oddly stilted language: "The females were not present at that time."

"Your sons knew the [rice fields] like the backs of their hands?" Siegler asked, bringing the jury back to her theory about where David had disposed of the shotgun.

"They knew the acreage around our home, yes," David's father agreed.

The Temples' oldest son, Darren, followed his father onto the stand. A middle-aged man with a slight paunch, he vaguely resembled David. When DeGuerin asked Darren if he and David looked alike, the oldest Temple son casually joked, "They say I'm the better-looking one."

But quickly DeGuerin turned the questioning to hunting and guns. Like his father, Darren insisted that David wasn't an avid hunter and that his middle brother had owned a .20-gauge, not a .12-gauge, shotgun. When it came to Clint Stockdick's testimony that David shot a .12-gauge and that Clint had never even seen a .20-gauge at the Temple household, Darren shrugged it off. "Did you ever see anything to indicate to you that Belinda and David's marriage was on the rocks?" DeGuerin asked.

"No, sir," Darren answered, describing their union as a "very loving, healthy relationship."

David, Darren said, was devastated by the murder, sobbing and distraught, and he described the family meeting as "intense, between my father and his three sons."

"Did you learn about the affair?" DeGuerin asked.

"We learned about the affair," Darren said, describing his own reaction to the news as "visibly angered." When Maureen returned from the beauty salon, she was told, and their mother was "incredibly emotional . . . upset . . . disappointed in David."

During cross-examination, Siegler led Darren directly back to that family meeting, two days after Belinda's murder. Earlier, with DeGuerin, Darren had talked of David's "affair," but now Siegler asked, "Do you remember testifying in the grand jury . . . that your brother was not having an *affair* and that you had no knowledge of any *affair*?"

"I don't remember saying that to the grand jury," Darren said.

To refresh his memory, Siegler handed Darren his grand-jury testimony. Immediately, it appeared Darren realized his predicament. "There's a definition of *affair* that I would like to discuss," he hedged.

"Are we doing a Bill Clinton?" Siegler asked with a skeptical frown. "We're going to argue about what *affair* means?"

Suddenly, Darren changed his language, using the word "unfaithful."

"So you didn't lie to the grand jury?" Siegler asked, with a scoff.

More than one juror frowned when Darren said, "No, I did not."

In the end, when he left the stand, the impression left in the room was that Darren Temple and his father had been less than honest: first, about David's shotgun; second, when Darren testified at the grand jury.

The response to Darren deteriorated further when Siegler brought up Cindi Thompson. The defense had filed a motion to prevent her from testifying about the shotgun incident, and to discuss the matter, the judge cleared the jury and then asked to hear what questions Siegler had for Darren about the event.

In slow, dramatic detail, Siegler described what Thompson would testify to, that Darren had told her that David held a shotgun to his oldest brother's head while their mother begged for Darren's life. Throughout, Darren shook his head, denying it ever happened. The judge reserved his ruling on the testimony for a later date, but that evening, Cindi received a text message from Darren, asking her to talk to DeGuerin's investigator. "We need your help," Darren said.

Cindi didn't respond.

The following day three more of the Temples would take the stand: Becky, Kevin and Maureen. Sparks flew with all their testimonies.

An outside salesperson with a software company, Becky looked professional on the stand. She said she'd never felt intimidated by the Temple men, and that Belinda was a strong, independent woman. She described David as a remarkable father, and said that throughout the last year of Belinda's life, the marriage was loving and respectful. But Tammey and Brenda had said Becky voiced very different opinions, including her belief that David was Belinda's murderer. "Do you remember a time, Mrs. Temple, when you had a conversation with Tammey Harlan and you told Tammey that you thought David killed Belinda?" Siegler asked.

"Oh, my Lord," DeGuerin said, standing up and slamming down his legal pad.

Judge Shaver cleared the jurors from the room, and the defense attorney charged Siegler's question was inflammatory. With as much vigor, the prosecutor assured the judge that Harlan had told her just that, and that she'd asked the question in good faith. Furious, DeGuerin spat out his reply: "I don't think anything Tammey Harlan said was in good faith."

The judge ruled for Siegler, the jury returned, and the questions continued. Much of what Brenda had on the tapes contradicted what Becky said on the stand, and Siegler asked to put the tapes in evidence. In the end, a compromise was reached, when Becky agreed to stipulate in front of the jury to nine different statements she'd made to Brenda, including that after the murder she didn't speak to David for months, that Kevin and Maureen had a falling-out over Heather, and that David's parents were the ones who took Evan to visit Belinda and Erin's grave. One of the most damaging statements was when Becky told Brenda that she didn't want to see Heather because, "I don't like to be lied to."

When the judge allowed the statements in, he said to the defense attorney: "So you understand, Mr. DeGuerin, I seem to have a situation here where one side I hear about [the Temple family] being Ozzie and Harriet, and on the other side seems to be information that that isn't true. You painted in one direction. I need to let them show the facts that show it may not be true."

As her testimony continued, Becky Temple cried, saying that she had "a lot of anger, a lot of hurt," after the murder. "We couldn't stand to live [in Katy] anymore . . . couldn't stand to drive down the I-10 freeway and see a billboard with my sister-in-law's picture on it. . . ." No matter where she went, Becky saw posters and fliers with Belinda's picture.

When he took the stand, Becky's husband, Kevin, like his older brother, insisted that David had never owned a .12-gauge shotgun. When it came to his old friend Clint Stockdick, Kevin suggested he must be mistaken when he said the Temples had four .12-gauge shotguns and no .20-gauge. Yet, when Siegler asked, "Is Clint Stockdick a truthful man?" Kevin answered, "Yes."

"Where's the Mossberg?" Siegler asked. Mossberg was the maker of the .12-gauge shotgun Stockdick remembered David shooting, the one Stockdick testified was cut down after the barrel split. "Remember a Mossberg?" Siegler pushed.

"No," Kevin answered, with a frown.

"Anybody in your family have any paperwork on that twenty-gauge?" Siegler prodded, insinuating it didn't exist.

"I don't," Kevin answered.

Like Darren, Kevin had told the grand jury he knew nothing about David's affair. "Was that the truth?" Siegler asked. "What do you call what David was doing?"

Kevin answered, "That he had been unfaithful."

Asking Kevin to step down from the stand, Siegler handed him a shotgun, which hung long and heavy in his arm. Then she stood back and asked, "Mr. Temple, could you show us, sir, how you'd hold that twelve-gauge shotgun and pick up that television in State's Exhibit 220 at the same time?" Exhibit 220 was a photo of the den television off its stand, weighing fifty pounds.

"I could not do it," he answered.

As the last member of the family took the stand, it felt as if the courtroom had turned against the Temples. Yet Maureen, her gray hair cut short, looked like a prim and proper Southern grandmother, a churchwoman and a favorite aunt. Visibly proud, she described David's football career. "He was the best middle linebacker Katy High School ever had," she said. "He was super."

She described a wholesome home life, including a large

extended family and summer vacations on the Comal River. Belinda was a good choice for David and, "I think she loved me like I loved her. . . . She was a mother who played and sang and danced."

David's mother talked on, elaborating in her answers, and Craig Goodhart objected, saying that she was not responsive. DeGuerin asked her to limit her answers, but Maureen looked concerned and said, "Okay, but I do a lot better if y'all just let me visit."

The night of the murder, she said David whispered in her ear, "The girls are gone. . . . I don't remember, but Ken said that I screamed and wailed. . . . David's eyes were funny. I assumed he had been crying."

On the screen were photos from cheerful times, vacations and Christmases that the defense attorney displayed for the jury. David, Belinda and Evan, smiling and happy.

"By any stretch of the imagination, could you ever have expected that David could do anything like [murdering Belinda]?" DeGuerin asked.

"Absolutely not," she answered. But one of the detectives, she said, shook a finger in her face and told her that David was a murderer.

"Had you done anything to justify that?" DeGuerin asked.

"No, sir," she answered, eyes wide. "I was just sitting in the room, waiting for David."

When Craig Goodhart took over, he asked if Maureen really meant to say that David and Belinda's marriage was perfect.

"Did I say perfect?" she asked, looking surprised.

"Yes, ma'am," he said. "Twice. I circled it."

"I'm sure they had fights like every married couple," she said, and she agreed she'd heard the phrase, "No one knows what goes on behind closed doors." In her statement to police the night of the murder, Maureen had said that on the street outside the house, David told her when she asked what happened, "I don't know."

"He never said, 'The girls are gone,'" Goodhart asked softly. "Did he?"

Yet Maureen insisted that her son had said precisely what she'd testified to, whispering it in her ear.

Rather than calling her son's liaison with Heather an *affair*, David's mother described his relationship with Heather as "time with a schoolteacher, a female."

"What did he do with the female schoolteacher?" Goodhart asked.

"Well, that he spent a couple of nights with a female schoolteacher," David's mother said. When asked how she'd describe what David *did* with the woman he cared so much about he later married, Maureen said, "A two-day weekend . . . I do not know about an affair. I know about a two-day weekend."

"Was your son having an affair or not?" Goodhart asked, looking exasperated.

Maureen Temple answered, "No."

Although so many others saw David with Heather, renewing their relationship quickly after the murder, Maureen insisted they were all wrong. Her son lived a monk-like life for two and a half years, she said, and David returned home to her house every evening to sleep.

And when it came to the detectives, she again described them as rude—Tracy Shipley in particular, who Maureen said, "was ugly to me."

"Do you remember telling Detective Shipley, 'I just could not have raised a son that would kill his wife?'" Goodhart asked.

DeGuerin objected, and the jury never heard what Maureen would have answered.

Anticipation spread through the courthouse as David Mark Temple took the stand. Throughout the previous five weeks, he'd appeared unemotional, crying only rarely, as when his mother was on the stand. Sitting behind the prosecutors' desk, Kelly Siegler was disappointed. She didn't want the defendant to testify. "I knew he couldn't do worse than his family, and that he'd probably do better," she said. When a defendant took the stand, Siegler said, juries expected *Perry Mason*, where a guilty party confessed. "That doesn't happen," she said.

"I loved Belinda very much," David began. "As well as she me, and loved my son and my unborn daughter, as I will to the day I die."

"Can you expect the jury to believe a man can love his wife and be unfaithful?"

"I made a mistake. I wish I could go back and change, but I cannot," he said. "But I loved my wife very much, from day one to the day that she died." Belinda, he said, was "beautiful inside and out," and "healthy as a horse," and they'd both planned and looked forward to her second pregnancy.

At the time of the murder, David described his relationship with Heather using the words she did, "flirtatious e-mails, a casual romantic relationship."

"Were you in love with Heather then?" DeGuerin asked.

"Not at all," he insisted.

Although Belinda told many that she'd done it alone, David insisted he'd helped paint the nursery, and that he was "working to get the shelving up, the crib and bassinette."

Although others, including Heather, had testified that he attended happy hours and Quinton explained that they were on Thursday nights, David acted as if they were Fridays instead and said, "It's impossible to have a Friday happy hour during football season."

During his time on the stand, David appeared to have much he wanted to say. He had, he said, given Belinda a purse for Christmas and perfume for her birthday. When Evan woke up from his nap the afternoon of the murder, "he felt his normal, rambunctious self . . . full of energy."

On the stand, David Temple's account of that day differed from the statement he gave police on the day of the murder. Instead of Belinda arriving home at 3:45, he now said that it was closer to four o'clock. "I told her to rest, that I would take Evan to the park and we would be back in time for supper." Although Tammey had testified that dinner was always served at Bunco, David insisted he and Belinda went out to dinner on her Bunco nights, and he'd rushed home that final night to take her to a restaurant. Instead of a nap, Belinda had gone upstairs to lie down and read a magazine, he said, explaining why she was still wearing her glasses when she was shot. Yet, Brenda had testified that Belinda wore the glasses not for reading but for driving.

On the stand, David Temple was a soft-spoken yet intense man with a steely gaze. "I had to buckle Evan into the car seat," he said about their drive in the truck. When the physical evidence contradicted what he was testifying to, such as the photos that showed the car seat was in the Isuzu, not his truck, David didn't try to clear up the matter. Instead, shrugging, he said, "I have no idea."

The reason it took him twenty-five to thirty minutes to drive a distance usually covered in ten to twelve minutes, he said, was because "traffic was heavy that day." And when it came to Buck Bindeman, who said he saw David miles from where he claimed to be that day, David simply said that the man who knew him from high school, who'd described his truck in perfect detail, was mistaken.

When it came to the teenager who lived next door, David said, "I did not trust the Sanders kid," and that they'd had problems with him in the past.

Narrating the discovery of Belinda's body, David talked quickly, his face flushing. Although he had no blood on him, he claimed he'd grabbed and shook her. "Just couldn't imagine what was going on or just the pain that you're feeling until you've seen something like that about somebody you care about," he said.

When it came to his interview that night, David, too, claimed the detectives were rude, and said that, "I was called every name in the book."

"Did you have anything whatsoever to do with the death of Belinda?" DeGuerin asked.

"I did not," David said, his voice firm. "I loved Belinda with all my heart. . . . I wanted [Erin] more than anything."

"Do you have sex with all the women you flirt with?" Siegler asked, sitting behind the long red file box filled with questions she'd prepared. At times, she rifled through, rearranging, as she finished one topic and went on to another.

"No, ma'am," David answered, as politely as Southern mothers teach their sons. "I do not."

When Siegler asked if a taped conversation with Brenda, when David said he didn't sleep with the woman he'd spent New Year's Eve with, was a lie, David said, "Yes." One after another, Siegler asked about David's words preserved on Brenda's tape-recorded conversations, and he over and over again had to admit that he'd lied.

There would be many things David said that didn't ring true, like his insistence that he'd hurried home to take Belinda out for dinner, as he always did on Bunco nights. The women in the league knew the hostesses served dinner, and Belinda had always eaten with them. And why would anyone, as David insisted Belinda did, routinely leave her keys on a step halfway up a staircase?

"Are you telling this jury that you really believe Joe Sanders is the person who put a shotgun in the back of your wife's head and blew her face off?" Siegler asked.

"I have no idea," he responded. "I wouldn't doubt it one bit that he did it."

"So the burglar went through three jewelry boxes and the little stem in the bathroom to get this stolen jewelry?" Siegler asked, referring to the list supplied to the insurance company that included, among other items, three pairs of Belinda's earrings.

So much of what David testified to sounded unbelievable. To prove the point, Siegler again put up the photo of David's jewelry on the dish, and played the tape in which he told Brenda that he was wearing his watch and ring at the time of the murder. "Can we agree to the fact that on the day Belinda was murdered, in your house, the burglar didn't take one single thing that belonged to you?" Siegler asked.

"To the best of my knowledge, yes," Temple agreed.

When it came to his dead wife, David said again, "Belinda was a strong woman."

"But as strong as she was, it didn't compare to you in your relationship, did it, Mr. Temple?" Siegler asked.

As to his relationship with Heather, there were those matters in her statement, including that just three days before the murder, he'd told her that he loved her. "I didn't," David said. "I did not use those words. I did not."

"She made a mistake about all that?" Siegler asked, and Temple said that yes, Heather was mistaken, along with Tara Hall about when he gave Heather flowers and worked in her garden.

Brenda said she hadn't seen David give Belinda a birthday gift, although she was with them the entire day. "Mr. Temple, did Brenda lie?" Siegler asked.

"Yes, ma'am," David said. "She did."

So had Tammey and Quinton Harlan, and Natalie Scott, Debbie Berger, and others who testified that David hadn't helped in the nursery, that the marriage had been troubled, and that Shaka was a fiercely protective watchdog.

"You didn't want a baby daughter, did you, Mr. Temple?" Siegler asked.

"That's a lie," DeGuerin shouted, jumping out of his seat. "I object."

"Explain to us how it could be that you can leave the garage so fast, fast enough for a burglar to get in the house, past the dog, break the glass, get upstairs and find Belinda, shoot her in the back of the head, with her shoes and her glasses still on," Siegler said.

"It's not my job to explain," David said, staring at her. "I don't know."

"You're the one who says it was a burglar, Mr. Temple," Siegler said.

As to Shaka being in the garage, David said, "It wasn't something I dreamed up."

"No," Siegler responded. "It's lied about."

When Siegler asked why he didn't have blood on his clothes from kneeling at his dead wife's side, David claimed that he braced himself with a hand on Belinda's back, and that he'd felt her neck on the right side, to see if he could find a pulse at her carotid artery.

"When you saw her like that, didn't you grab her, hug her, and love her, and say, 'Belinda, what happened?'" Siegler demanded, her voice dramatic and her eyes focused solidly on David. Dick DeGuerin objected, it was sustained, and David never answered.

Siegler looked at Temple skeptically, and asked why he owned shotgun shells: "You didn't own a shotgun?" she asked.

"I don't know exactly where the shotgun shells came from," he said. "They were from previous use is what I said."

David claimed there was no Mossberg .12-gauge, as Clint Stockdick described, and Siegler asked if the real discussion inside the house that day when the Temple men held their meeting was to decide what they would jointly say about David owning a shotgun.

"No," David said.

"Where's the Mossberg? Where is the sawed-off shotgun?" Siegler demanded.

He threw it away, David said, because the gun didn't work, but it wasn't a Mossberg and it wasn't a .12-gauge.

Why was he passing messages through Quinton to Heather two days after Belinda's murder? "Because, Mr. Temple, you were in love with Heather?"

"I've already stated that I was not in love with her, did not pledge my love for her to her at any stretch of the imagination, that I ever loved her, ever."

"Ever?" Siegler asked.

"At that time," he answered.

Siegler smiled. "But you married her?"

During a bench conference before he finished his questions for David, DeGuerin again asked the judge to allow in the information on Joe Sanders's failed polygraphs. Again the judge ruled against him. Then the defense attorney asked his client about the alternate suspect, the teenager who'd lived next door. "What is your conclusion from these things?" De-Guerin asked, referring to Sanders having had access to two .12-gauge shotguns and reloaded double-ought buckshot.

"I would not like anybody to be falsely accused, because I know how that feels," David said. "But that needs to be totally investigated."

Along with David loving Belinda, there were perhaps two other lynchpins of the defense's view on the case, one being that the glass was in the living room because when the door swung open it hit the hutch, spewing shards of glass to the left instead of straight ahead. The other was that a more reasonable suspect in the case was the teenager next door, Joe Sanders.

To testify about Sanders, DeGuerin recalled Detective Dean Holtke, who again testified that yes, two .12-gauges were found in the Sanders household along with the same size shells as the one used in the murder. After DeGuerin turned over the witness to Siegler, she pointed out that no glass or blood was found inside Sanders's shotguns and that the reloaded shells didn't match. She then asked Holtke to help bring two pieces of evidence into the courtroom. Minutes later, Holtke and a bailiff returned with the back door from the Round Valley house and something else, the hutch DeGuerin said had caused the dent in the lower part of the door. The weekend before his testimony, Holtke had traveled to Nacogdoches to claim it from Tom and Carol's home. After the murder, it was one of the few things of Belinda's David had given to her family.

As the jurors watched, with a crime scene photo displayed on the courtroom screen of the hutch in place behind the door, Holtke lined up the door and hutch as they were that day in the house. The door was raised slightly to match the thickness of a standard threshold, and then Holtke swung it open. The dent didn't match anything on the hutch.

Looking disappointed, DeGuerin rose and approached the door, and on re-direct tried to line it up again. "It's not even close to where the dent is," Holtke said, stating what was obvious to everyone in the courtroom.

DeGuerin then said that maybe it was the doorstop at the top of the door that caused the glass pattern. "What scenario are we going with here?" Holtke asked.

"I don't know," DeGuerin snapped. "I wasn't there."

Then, as the detective looked up at the picture of the hutch from the crime scene, with knickknacks carefully arranged, he asked, "If there was something violent that hit this furniture, don't you think the stuff on the shelves would have moved?"

"No, I don't," DeGuerin snapped. "But you're not supposed to ask me questions."

The defense rested, and the prosecutors called one final witness, in rebuttal.

After all that had been said about Joe Sanders, when he walked in the room and got up on the witness stand, he looked like a young, clean-cut man in his twenties, with buzz-cut dark blond hair and a crooked frown. Siegler led him through the events of the day of the murder, how he'd cut classes and spent much of the day hoping to score pot. He'd been grounded after Belinda told his parents that he'd been truant, yet in mounds of school records entered into evidence, there were no mentions of Sanders being aggressive. In fact, it would appear the young man was too laid-back, so much so, he often fell asleep in class. On the stand, he was polite, saying that he'd seen Belinda almost daily at Katy High School, "Whenever I needed help."

When he did see her, he said, Belinda joked with him, urging him through the halls to class. "She was a very nice lady," Sanders said. "A good teacher."

Yet Belinda had inserted herself into his life. She told his parents he'd cut 131 classes and was in danger of being reassigned to an alternative school. Sanders's parents took away his truck. Sanders insisted he wasn't angry, instead he simply returned home from school over lunch, when his parents were at work, and took the truck.

As Siegler asked questions, Sanders described cooperating with detectives, repeatedly giving statements, even voluntarily talking to the grand jury. Until the grand-jury appearance, Sanders never hired an attorney. "I didn't try to hide," he said.

"Why did you agree to talk to the detectives?" Siegler asked.

"Because I wanted to," he said, describing his treatment by the detectives as "good."

"Mr. Sanders, did you have anything to do with the murder of Belinda Temple?" Siegler asked, after getting in the record that Sanders had come to the trial voluntarily from Arkansas, not under a subpoena.

"No, ma'am," he answered.

For his first question, DeGuerin asked, "Have you been told you wouldn't be prosecuted for your testimony?"

Incensed, Siegler objected to any insinuation that Sanders had immunity on the murder, and an argument broke out at the bench. The judge hurriedly cleared the jury from the courtroom, and the lawyers snapped at each other in the most heated exchange of the long trial, as DeGuerin said that he'd read as much in Sanders's grand-jury testimony.

"Judge, that's about smoking dope [not the murder]," Siegler charged back.

"That's not true," DeGuerin countered. "It doesn't say anything about limiting it to smoking."

As the attorneys waited, Judge Shaver reviewed Sanders's grand-jury testimony, and then peered down at DeGuerin. "Yes, I have read this before, and if you continue reading, Mr. DeGuerin, it goes on where Mr. Wilson explains they are talking about marijuana."

"But it doesn't," DeGuerin protested.

Appearing furious with the defense attorney, Judge Shaver concluded, "Your question is absolutely trying to mislead the jury."

That line of questioning ended, but once the jury returned, DeGuerin shot rapid-fire questions at Sanders. Yet David's old neighbor didn't seem disturbed, instead admitting every offense the defense attorney charged against him. Yes, Sanders smoked pot. He had skipped 131 classes. "It did make me angry," Sanders admitted when Belinda told his parents about his problems at school. The day Belinda died, Sanders was smoking pot with friends, and the week before, he'd been out shooting shotguns. His friends had once knocked down the Temples' Christmas decorations, although Sanders said he'd told the other boys to put them back up.

DeGuerin went at Sanders, but on the stand, the young man never became angry, never argued. Would the jurors believe he was the real killer?

Five weeks after it began, the testimony in David Temple's trial, nine years in the making, came to an end. Closing arguments began the morning of Wednesday, November 14, 2007. Siegler had been up the night before, considering what she would say. Crowds filled every available seat as Craig Goodhart stood to address the jurors.

"That man executed Belinda and his unborn child, a cold-blooded murder," he said, pointing at David at the defense table. "There is no doubt about it."

Goodhart was methodical, contending that although the evidence was circumstantial, there was evidence. Temple had motive and opportunity. The defense, he said, had tried to mislead the jury, telling them that David and Belinda had a perfect marriage, when other witnesses and the jurors' common sense told them it wasn't true.

Goodhart paced through the courtroom, proposing, "Did the sheriff's department make mistakes? They probably did." But that didn't mean that David wasn't guilty. Not one of the shotguns the defense pointed to, including those at the disposal of Joe Sanders, tested positive for glass, blood or brain matter. And there was no evidence against Joe Sanders. "What does your gut tell you?" Goodhart asked. "David Temple is the only human . . . who had motive, opportunity, and the desire to kill his wife."

"There is more circumstantial evidence against Joe Sanders than against David Temple," DeGuerin countered. "Do I think the evidence against Sanders is enough for a conviction? No. But there is stronger evidence against him than against David."

As he proceeded, much of DeGuerin's argument became a prosecution of Sanders for Belinda's murder, as the defense attorney laid out everything from the teenager's potential motives to what DeGuerin saw as evidence against Sanders. When he turned his attention to David, DeGuerin insisted his client couldn't have committed the murder, because David was at the grocery store when the Roberts boys heard the "bang" the defense pegged as the sound of the gunshot that shattered Belinda Temple's skull.

Measured yet impassioned, the defense attorney railed against Sanders, as at the defense table, David, his solid jaw locked firm, watched DeGuerin wage war.

"No one says David had a twelve-gauge shotgun anytime near the murder," DeGuerin insisted. Clint Stockdick hunted with the Temple brothers years earlier, while David was in high school and college. And again, DeGuerin insisted that the affair with Heather was a flirtation, not a motive for murder, and that David loved Belinda.

When it came to the Temple family's denial to the grand jury that they knew David was involved in an affair, DeGuerin asked, "How many of you would remember the exact words you used nine years ago?"

At the end of his time before the jury, DeGuerin again played the 911 tape of David's call for help the afternoon of the murder. "Listen to his words when he describes his beautiful wife and baby, gone," DeGuerin urged.

The courtroom once again filled with David Temple's voice, sounding as if he was crying while he said his wife was dead. But something was different this time around. It was the fourth time the tape had been played, and at each playing, David had appeared less emotional. This time there were few tears. "The man on the tape did not murder his wife," DeGuerin contended. "David Temple is not guilty. The state has not proved their case."

"No matter how much you want to deceive . . . No one can do it perfectly," Siegler then said. When it came to David and the Temple family, she charged, "You know they lied to you and insulted your intelligence.

"The Temple family denied everything, acted like it never happened," she said. "Why? Because that family knows him. Because that family knows what happened."

Throughout her argument, Siegler circled the room, walking toward the defense table, standing behind David Temple as if on cue to point at and accuse him, pointing at the Temple family in the gallery. "They are going to forget about it, and deny that he executed his wife and baby girl."

Siegler, however, said the jurors shouldn't do the same. Of course, she didn't have everything she wanted to show them. "Why don't we have the murder weapon?" she asked, then answered her own question. "Because he got rid of it."

Pointing at Mark Schmidt, Dean Holtke, Tracy Shipley, David Rossi and Chuck Leithner in the courtroom, she said, "For nine years these people right here have been waiting for a courtroom."

Laying out the series of events for the jury, she reminded them that while David was saying he was deeply in love with Belinda, he was making love to Heather and bringing her gifts. Just three days before the murder, David told Heather he loved her. "Do you really think he said that on Friday and a burglar broke into his house, shot Belinda on Monday, and forgot to take anything?"

In the front rows, as in opening arguments, the two families sat directly next to each other, and the tension in the courtroom felt nearly overwhelming. So much was at stake; for the Lucases, the only opportunity for closure for Belinda and Erin; for the Temples, a guilty verdict could put David in prison for most of the rest of his life.

Had David ever attempted to prolong Belinda's life to save Erin? He had no blood on his body or his clothes, nothing to indicate he'd made any attempt to keep his wife breathing long enough to deliver the infant. Why was Belinda executed in the closet? Because David the planner, Siegler said, realized it was the most protected room in the house, without windows and surrounded by clothes to muffle the sound of the gunshot.

"Joe Sanders? You know what you learn from Joe Sanders? He came here from Arkansas without a subpoena and what did he tell you? 'I smoked weed.'

"You know with all your heart that David Temple is guilty," Siegler said.

After deliberating for two hours, the jurors left that evening without a verdict. No one appeared surprised. A decision in such a long and complicated murder case could take days— even weeks. But the next afternoon, November 15, 2007, as reporters and spectators talked in the corridor, Siegler and DeGuerin rushed back into the courtroom, and David Temple and his family were seen hurrying to their seats. In the gallery, Heather appeared frantic, painfully gaunt with black circles under her eyes and surrounded by her friends. She sat behind and not with the Temple family, as the Lucases claimed the right side of the courtroom. Before long the jury was led in.

Behind the defense table, David Temple stood with his attorneys. Later he'd say that he and his family expected a not-guilty verdict, and that they were so confident of it they'd already decided where to go to celebrate. That the verdict was so quick, little more than eight hours, made Kelly Siegler suspect the Temples were about to be disappointed.

As the verdict was read, the word *guilty* hit David harder than a physical blow. His knees buckled, and he threw his head back and looked at the ceiling and cried. Once the jury was removed, Maureen Temple collapsed on the wooden bench, her family rushing to aid her. Her husband and two other sons sobbed into their hands, as deputies moved forward to take David into custody to await sentencing. As he was led away, David Temple looked toward his family and mouthed, "Oh, shit," with a look of utter surprise, as if to say, *This wasn't supposed to happen.*

From that point on, it would seem, there would be little more drama. The attorneys argued the following day over sentencing. A defiant Dick DeGuerin told the jurors that they'd made a terrible mistake and that his client was innocent. All over again, the defense attorney argued that Joe Sanders was the murderer, not David Temple. DeGuerin reached out to those jurors who were uncertain of the verdict, asking them to refuse any sentence but probation. Siegler, on the other hand, told the jurors not to be dissuaded, that they had done the right thing, and that David Temple was indeed guilty of murder.

The decision came quickly, as if the jurors wanted to tell the defense attorney that they had no such qualms. In the end, with the death penalty not on the table, only one sentence fit such a horrendous crime, a husband's murder of his young pregnant wife: life in prison.

On the witness stand, giving his family's elocution, Brian Lucas talked about Belinda, the youngest in the family, professing how much they all missed and loved her, and, looking directly at David said, "Divorce was an option."

When Brian finished, David Temple was led away.

The courtroom slowly cleared, many languishing behind as if stunned by all that had happened. On the courthouse steps, Dick DeGuerin fumed before the cameras and reporters. "Kelly Siegler has finally done it," he snapped. "She's convicted an innocent man."

Moments later, he was replaced by the Lucas family. Tom Lucas hugged his wife, and the Lucases cried. "It's senseless to put a shotgun to my baby's head and blow her brains out," he told reporters. "It's not right. I'm so glad justice has been done."

"We never gave up hope," Carol said.

Later, Kelly Siegler agreed, giving credit to Mark Schmidt and Brian and Tom Lucas for keeping the case alive throughout the investigation's long drought. "Without them, it could have slipped through the cracks," she'd say.

The verdict had taken nine years, and none of those who worked on the case took it lightly. "But we still had a dead woman and child," says Schmidt. "David Temple was going to prison, but we had no reason to celebrate."

Author's Note

This case is stuck in my craw and I will never give up on it. Never," DeGuerin seethed, two months after the verdict. We were in his office in an old brick building with a creaking elevator, not far from the courthouse. The office was cramped and bustling with activity as secretaries and his partners and associates worked on cases, but DeGuerin couldn't forget the one that got away, the case so many thought he'd win. David Temple's conviction filled him with rage. He blamed Kelly Siegler, saying she'd played "dirty tricks," and Tammey and Quinton Harlan for disparaging a man who had once been their friend. "They lied," he insisted. "Absolute lies."

He stared at me and shook his head, as if still in disbelief at the jury's decision. "There's just no evidence," he contended. "Kelly Siegler tried David on emotion, not evidence. He should never have been convicted."

Among those DeGuerin blamed, he blamed himself.

"I've thought about it," the defense attorney said. "I should have rested after Kelly finished. She hadn't proved the case. But I didn't know she was going to ambush all my witnesses."

Weeks earlier, Siegler and I had talked, and she'd agreed, saying DeGuerin's tactics had backfired. "I knew once I heard his opening argument that it was a stroke of luck for our case. The jury wouldn't believe a man having an affair, pledging love to another woman, loved his wife. When we got the Temple family on the stand, I knew the jury would see that they were lying. They're not bad people, but they'd been covering up for David for years."

Saying she often learned from the cases, she maintained the lesson from the Temple case was to trust juries. "We got so caught up thinking it was all circumstantial, we forgot that a jury would be able to piece it all together," said Siegler. "We forgot that the jury would see what we did and be able to figure it out. Maybe it's time to quit thinking we need a perfect case when we're so sure someone is guilty."

After pausing for a moment, Siegler went on: "I bet every day of David Temple's life he thinks to himself, *Why did I do it?* I bet he looks back and wishes he was with Belinda, Evan and Erin, living in that house in Round Valley."

With the case that had haunted him for nearly a decade behind him, many said the old Mark Schmidt was back. "The Temple case was a three-hundred-pound gorilla on his back for all those years, eating away at him," says Tracy Shipley, with a satisfied grin. "The first day he walked in here after the verdict, I said, 'How's it feel to get that monkey off your back?' Mark laughed, something we hadn't seen much of in a very long time."

At Lockwood in the homicide division, I met with Schmidt. "I'll remember this case the rest of my life," he said, explaining that for the first time since 1999 the three binders that made up the Temple murder book weren't sitting on his desk, crying for attention. "I feel as if I've lived it.' "

That first Christmas after his former son-in-law's conviction, Tom Lucas worked as Santa Claus at the Walmart in Nacogdoches. When I went to visit him and Carol, they invited Brenda over, and we spent much of a day talking and looking at photos of Belinda. In the twenty years I'd been writing about murders, the Lucases' daughter was a rarity. All of us are human beings, flawed. We nearly always have enemies, or at least someone we've unintentionally alienated. In more than a year's work on the Temple case, I never heard a bad word about Belinda. The only criticism came from those who said she tried too hard to please David. Along with Erin, Belinda truly was innocent blood.

All Tom and Carol had left of their daughter was their grandson. Nearly a year after his father's conviction, Evan finally met with them. His grandparents were so delighted they took photos of the youngster, by then thirteen, showing a handsome, smiling teenager with Brenda's mop of dark hair and Belinda's eyes. He was a polite, well-mannered boy. Brenda hadn't yet been reintroduced to her nephew, but she hoped that would happen soon. She thought about him often, wondering if he thought about her. She and Belinda had been so close, at times she still felt her twin was with her. One night, in a dream, Brenda saw herself in a car. When she looked over, David sat beside her, but behind the wheel was Belinda. "I didn't know what it meant," Brenda says. "Maybe Belinda was telling me that it was all right now."

Debbie Berger and Cindy O'Brien, too, were waiting to talk to Evan. Debbie still had the "Evan Book" she put together after the murder, filled with tributes to Belinda from coworkers, friends, students and family. "I'll have it when he's ready to look at it," she says. "I'm keeping it safe until that day."

Many saw it as an odd twist that Heather was raising the teenager. "It's hard on Evan," Heather's mother, Sandy, told me. "Everything is hard now with David gone. Thank God that Evan and Heather are so close, like two peas in a pod."

One could only wonder what Evan would think years later, when he was old enough to understand all that happened. Would he believe his father had murdered his mother to be with Heather, the woman he'd grown up calling Mom? Or would he believe David's family and the others who still stood behind David?

For some, it seemed, no amount of evidence would be sufficient. "I don't believe David murdered Belinda," his old college roommate, Reno Moore, told me. "David would have to tell me he did it before I'd believe it."

Along with Belinda and his baby sister, Evan was an innocent victim, his life forever scarred by events over which he
had no control. First he'd lost his mother and sister, then his
father. David wouldn't be eligible for parole until age sixty-
nine, in 2037. By then, Evan would be forty-one.

Nine years after the murder, the house on Round Valley
had changed little. I drove up and parked. I walked up and
down the block, talking to the neighbors who remembered
the Temples, hearing their stories. Some had testified in the
trial, and most believed David was guilty.

Was it possible that someday evidence would materialize
exonerating him? Juries are human beings with the foibles
and limitations that entails, and, of course, they are sometimes wrong. DNA has freed many who have been wrongly
convicted, and it's now impossible to deny that tragic mistakes are made. Yet, as Kelly Siegler said, the bits and pieces
of the Temple case formed a damning picture. Two pieces
of evidence struck me as particularly compelling. On the
surface, they seemed insignificant items: a container of soup
and Belinda's keys.

That day, Ken Temple said Belinda had gone to his house
and picked up a container of Maureen's homemade soup
just before driving home. Belinda left quickly, in a hurry to
check on Evan and to get ready for Bunco that evening. As
she got out of the red Isuzu at the house, she would have carried her car keys and the container of soup into the house. In
the crime scene photos, the soup sits on a kitchen counter.
The keys? Remember, they were found dropped on the seventh step of the staircase.

What mother brings home soup for her family and doesn't
put it in the refrigerator? What mother of a toddler drops
her keys on the stairs instead of putting them where the
child won't pick them up and lose or hide them? Perhaps a
mother who is met at the door by a man with a shotgun, who
marches her upstairs and executes her?

Why do I believe that man was David Temple?

In addition to all the other evidence—including his

motive: the affair with Heather—it boils down to opportunity. From the evidence as we know it, David Temple, by his own admission, was the only one who had opportunity to murder Belinda.

In his statement, he says that Belinda arrived home and then, "while she was resting," he took Evan to the park and the store. "While she was resting" says that he was home when she walked in the door, and that he was still there when she walked upstairs to lie down and rest. If that were the case, wouldn't she have refrigerated the soup? Wouldn't Belinda have put her keys on the plate where she normally kept them? That she didn't have time to do either suggests that the attack was immediate, when she walked in the door, while David was still home.

David could have easily staged the burglary, during the hours he was home alone. Where was Evan? The child was ill and taking Motrin. It's not a stretch to believe he could have been in bed, sleeping, while his father waited for his mother with the shotgun. When Belinda walked in the door, David may have ordered her to put the soup down and then led her upstairs. On the way, she dropped her keys on the stairs. In the closet, she crouched, turned away from him, hoping to protect the baby she carried. It was then that I believe David pulled the trigger.

If more evidence is needed, consider the cordless phone found next to her body. If Belinda had time to grab it and run to the closet, wouldn't she have touched 911? The last call on that telephone was to the Ruggiero household, not the police. We don't even know if Belinda was the one who brought the phone into the closet. It wasn't found in her hand or under her but on the bloody carpet near her body. Perhaps David, staging the burglary, threw the phone into the closet, to make it look as if she were running from an intruder and trying to call for help.

Of course, it's those photos of Belinda inside that closet that few of those involved will ever forget.

One of the hardest things about being a crime writer is

that we see horrific images, terrible crime-scene photos of real murders. There's a vast difference between make-believe violence, like that in the movies and on television, and the real thing. I've spent more than two decades covering real killings, but the murder of Belinda Temple is the most cold-blooded I've ever investigated. I won't forget this case, and I'll always remember the photos of Belinda alive, with her eyes sparkling and her broad engaging smile, and murdered, her face ripped apart by the force of the explosion from that shotgun shell, and her round, firm belly, with little Erin inside, cold and still.

I hope, after so many years, that Belinda and Erin are now finally at peace.

Acknowledgments

For his take on Katy High School football, Dexter Clay, author of *KatyNation*, www.katynation.com.

Jim Loosen at JAL Data services in Washington State for tracking down sources.

Carey Smith for research assistance.

My editor at HarperCollins, Will Hinton, and my agent, Jane Dystel.

For her encouragement, my mother-in-law, Ruth Casey, who passed away while I was working on this book. A great person and a wonderful artist, she's missed.

All my readers, especially those who tell others about my books and spread the word: Thank you! You're the best!